Trials, Tribulations and Triumphs

Trials, Tribulations and Triumphs

Life and Times of a Sociologist

T.K. OOMMEN

Konark Publishers Pvt Ltd
New Delhi · Seattle

Konark Publishers Pvt. Ltd
206, First Floor,
Peacock Lane, Shahpur Jat,
New Delhi-110 049.
Phone: +91-11-41055065, 65254972
e-mail: india@konarkpublishers.com
Website: www.konarkpublishers.com

Konark Publishers International
8615, 13th Ave SW,
Seattle, WA 98106
Phone: (415) 409-9988
e-mail: us@konarkpublishers.com

ISBN: 978-93-220-0888-8

Editor: Dipali Singh

Typeset by Saanvi Graphics, Noida

Printed and bound at Thomson Press (India) Ltd.

To
Rhea, Nisha, Ivan and Shreya,
my grand children

Contents

Appendices

Acknowledgments

This book has been in the making for a few years. But I was keen to publish it as I commence my journey as an octogenarian. This called for an expedient decision to publish the manuscript. I am indeed grateful to K.P.R. Nair, Managing Director, Konark Publishers, for facilitating the speedy publication of the book.

The book was originally conceived partly as a biography and partly as an account of my academic work. The biographical aspect was toned down on the suggestion of Priyanka Sarkar, my editor. I thank her for this valuable advice.

The typing of the manuscript was done at the office of Schumacher Centre for Development, New Delhi. I thank Susan Cherian, Director of SCD for facilitating this. Although several persons were involved in the secretarial work in producing the manuscript, the bulk of it is done by Solly Joseph and Anila James in succession. I thank both of them for their devoted work.

September 2017

Acknowledgements

[illegible]

Preface

Trials, Tribulations and Triumphs is not a biography but narratives about the vicissitudes of an academic; it is conceived as a different literary genre; it is a workography. Born and educated in rural Kerala the author became a sociologist thanks to a natural calamity. He became a full professor at a young age at the Jawaharlal Nehru University, where he faced stigmatization because he was perceived as a non-leftist.

The author was elected as the president of International Sociological Association, the only person to occupy this position so far from Asia and Africa. The narratives regarding this metamorphosis of the author could be inspirational to peers and subsequent generations. Similarly, the account of 'travails of publishing' graphically unfolds the challenges to be faced by emerging as well as veteran authors.

The book provides insights into the functioning of the academic world through the discipline of sociology not only nationally but even globally. A world in which knowledge production and dissemination are becoming increasingly critical, the book holds a mirror to the texture of social milieu in which these activities are undertaken. It also brings out the lack of professionalism among Indian sociologists.

The book unfolds the need for and importance of social scientists in general and sociologists in particular in getting involved in policy-oriented social investigations thus indirectly addresses the question: Knowledge to what end? Finally, the book demonstrates the need for academics discharging their social responsibilities as citizens of their country. It is hoped that the book will motivate other academics to share their experiences.

Part 1
Torments of Sociology

CHAPTER 1

Entering Sociology

After completing my BA, I had to take a break partly due to the health of my parents, both of whom had undergone surgery which required long convalescence, and partly because of financial reasons. My elder brother was in the last year of BSc (Agriculture) Hons and I was required to be at home. But this was also a time to introspect about my future course of action. I had not taken to economics as a subject as I found a gap between what I learnt and the experienced economic reality. I was inclined to pursue political science but its employment potential was rather bleak. After considerable consultations I decided to study social work.

The two prestigious Schools of Social Work at that point in time in India were the Delhi School of Social Work (DSSW) and the Tata Institute of Social Sciences (TISS). While DSSW offered an MA in social work, TISS offered a diploma in social service administration, equivalent to an MA and both were rated as promising where jobs were concerned. I applied to both these institutions. The interview for the Delhi School took place at Ernakulam in May 1958. The interviewers were a faculty member of DSSW, who taught economics there, and a Catholic nun, an alumnus of DSSW, who was then on the faculty of St Theresa's College, Ernakulam. The interviewers appeared to be mighty pleased with my credentials and informed me that I was selected–they also told me that they were recommending a tuition waiver considering my financial situation and academic achievement. But I am still waiting for the letter offering admission from DSSW, although several decades have elapsed! Paradoxically in 1964, six years later, I joined the faculty of DSSW as a lecturer in social sciences.

As I was waiting for the admission offer from Delhi, an interview call letter from TISS came, directing me to go to Bombay (now Mumbai). I left my village to board an overcrowded unreserved railway compartment from Ernakulam situated some hundred kilometres away from my village. This was my second trip out of Kerala, the first being to Madras (now Chennai) after writing the tenth standard examination, to visit my uncle, K.M. Cherian, my father's younger brother who lived in Madras. The train journey to Mumbai stretched to about thirty hours. The year 1958 witnessed huge floods in Kerala, other south Indian states and beyond. When the train reached Poona (now Pune), the station master announced that the train could not proceed to Mumbai because of a flash flood. The passengers were advised to retain their tickets and use them when the train journey was resumed, but it would mean at least seventy-two hours of waiting. I was crestfallen because my interview date at TISS would elapse within twenty-four hours.

I had befriended Panikkar, a co-traveller who lived in Poona (Pune), in the course of the journey. Incidentally, he was doing an MA in sociology from the University of Poona. Sympathizing with my predicament, he offered to put me up at his residence till I could proceed to Bombay. He lived along with two others, bachelors from Kerala. Being in a strange place where Marathi was the local language, one I was unfamiliar with, I had no option but to accept the offer. Panikkar also advised me to try for admission at Poona University as an alternative, because there was no guarantee that I would reach Bombay on time. He also suggested that I try for the MA course in sociology as it was a new subject that was quickly gaining in popularity, particularly in Kerala, and if I did well it would open up opportunities to become a lecturer in one of the community colleges (colleges under the management of a caste or religious group).

I did not have any clue about how to go about the task of getting admitted in Poona University and I had not even filled in an application form, but Panikkar said that the assistant registrar, Venkitakrishnan, called Swami by students who hailed from Kerala, was from Kerala. Swami's influence was far beyond the position he occupied because of what may be called contact-charisma. He was secretary to M.R. Jayakar, the founder of Poona University and he was held in high esteem thanks to his loyalty to Jayakar. On reaching the Poona University campus, a serene place with luxuriant vegetation and old buildings scattered over a vast area, it took some time for me to locate the administrative block, only to learn after I reached the building, that the last date of admission was over a week ago.

Although acutely frustrated, I decided to meet Swami. At his office, the peon asked me to write my name on a piece of paper. I wrote my name and added 'from Kerala'. I was immediately ushered into Swami's room and he beckoned me to sit down, asking the purpose of my visit to Poona in Tamil-laced Malayalam. I narrated my story in Malayalam and how I had landed up in Poona. He asked me to write about it in a letter asking for admission in English and then he marked it for the registrar, W.H. Golay, with the remark, 'May be considered favourably considering the circumstances'. I took it to the registrar, who read the letter and asked me, 'Did you write this?' When I answered in the affirmative, he said 'Good' and wrote 'May be admitted'. I happily went to the fees section, paid the fees and became a student of sociology–which became my vocation for the rest of my life.

I have often reflected on this incident. There are two aspects to it. One is the total absence of the faculty in the admission process which was handled only by the administration, the reason perhaps being less demand for admission to the MA (Sociology) course in those days. If the admission process had been an elaborate process of sticking to the last date of receiving applications by the administration, the faculty shortlisting them, holding an interview for the shortlisted candidates and so on, I could not have been admitted. Secondly, even if all these steps were absent, the favouritism shown to a fellow-Malayalee by Swami and the flexibility adopted by the Poona University administration, allowed my admission. Viewed from the perspective of a distressed young person these are 'positive' factors but seen through the lens of institutional procedures these are 'negative'. That is to say, conflicts between individual interests and institutional norms are perennially present. The dictum that I internalized was that if individuals can benefit without undermining the basic norms of institutions, there is no harm in favouring individuals.

After joining Poona University, I proceeded to Bombay and reported to TISS, which was four days after my date of interview. The delay was caused by a natural disaster and the interviews were still going on. Yet, the authorities at TISS stuck to their position that, 'Once a candidate lost his/her chance of attending the interview, it cannot be restored'. This was indeed a rigid bureaucratic position but TISS had to take this stand because of the severe competition for admission from candidates all over India, instituational exigency sometimes necessitating rigid adherence to rules. Yet it is reasonable to suggest that institutions should understand and accommodate those who are victims of situations beyond their control, such as natural disasters. Ignoring the conflict between individual interests and institutional norms, TISS upheld its 'principles' without understanding and evaluating its consequence for individual aspirants.

The period of two years I spent at Poona University as an MA student of sociology was a turning point in my life. Although I had no previous exposure to sociology, I took to the subject like duck to water. The fact was that Poona was (and is) an important centre of education in Maharashtra with established institutions for social sciences, such as the Gokhale Institute of Economics and Politics, the Deccan College Institute of Postgraduate Studies and the Bhandarkar Oriental Research Institute, with well-stocked libraries. This enabled the enthusiastic learner to read many books in addition to those prescribed. My rough estimate is that I read at least 500 books on sociology and a wide range of cognate disciplines. This academic cosmopolitanism, however, co-existed with socio-cultural parochialism.

Just like the fallow period of one year after my BA, I also had a gap after my MA (1958–60) and could not start work on PhD. Two senior faculty members of the department of sociology and anthropology at the Poona University were not available. Irawati Karve, the distinguished anthropologist, accepted an offer as consultant to the National Planning Commission in Delhi and decided not to enrol any fresh PhD student in that year, while Y.B. Damle who identified himself as a sociologist in the Talcott Parsons and Robert K. Merton mould, had to leave for the USA, to accept a fellowship at the Massachusetts Institute of Technology (MIT). Therefore he also could not enrol any PhD student under him for one year. Under the circumstances, Damle advised me to teach at the H.P.T College, Nashik, till he returned.

Damle recommended me for the appointment at Nashik because I had earned the first position in Poona University in the batch of 1958–60. But finally the position was given to U.B. Bhoite, who stood second, the rationale being that knowledge of Marathi was a pre-requisite to teach at Nashik, a small town. In the meantime Damle talked to his uncle who was the then principal of Wadia College at Poona and I got the offer to teach sociology as a part-time lecturer. My monthly salary was fixed at Rs 125 and I was offered the position of the warden which would entitle me to free accommodation and one meal a day. As this arrangement was about to be clinched a new candidate, Dixit, my classmate, became a competitor. On the day I was to join Wadia College, I came to know that Dixit, a Maharashtrian, had already been appointed. Once again the rationale was based on my incompetence in Marathi because students would want to ask questions and discuss doubts in the language. For the first time in my life I realized that linguistic chauvinism was stronger than academic merit. This was confirmed when I overheard someone ask Damle why he was so bothered about a 'Madrasi' instead of Maharashtrians. That was my experience of the insider–outsider dichotomy so rampant in India–right at the beginning of my academic career.

CHAPTER 2

Tortuous Path to a PhD

My experience of being rejected at two colleges presumably for want of fluency in Marathi, but actually because I was not a Maharashtrian, convinced me that the prospect of getting a lecturer's job in Maharashtra was zero for me. I could go back to Kerala but in those days, sociology was hardly taught there, particularly at the undergraduate level. To teach MA students, one needed a PhD degree. Most Indian universities did not call for applications for a PhD those days, the practice being to admit two or three bright students of the department each year who were inclined to pursue their PhD. The department of sociology in Delhi University headed by M.N. Srinivas was started in 1959 and it had advertised for one PhD fellowship. Since the first MA batch of the department would be out only in 1961, I applied. I was called for an interview but was not selected.

It is necessary to recall here that Indian sociology of the 1960s and 1970s (and it continues till this day although less intense) was torn asunder between British social anthropology and American sociology. M.N. Srinivas was trained first at Bombay

University under G.S. Ghurye, professor of sociology (who did his PhD under noted anthropologist W.H.R. Rivers) and then at the department of anthropology at Oxford University. Those days, Poona University had a combined department of anthropology and sociology. While Irawati Karve, the senior professor, was an anthropologist, Damle, although a student of Ghurye, was pursuing sociology of the American tradition. I was taught by both Karve and Damle, but I was more inclined to follow the sociological tradition advocated by Damle.

The syllabus of the combined department of sociology and anthropology of Poona University drew from both the disciplines. For example, the course on sociological theory taught the theories of Talcot Parsons and Robert K. Merton. On the other hand, there was a paper on the 'Biological Basis of Human Society', a mixture of physical and social anthropology. Yet another paper was devoted to the study of monographs; a dozen monographs mostly by social anthropologists were listed and the student could choose any two for elaborate study. The monographs I chose were *The Gift* by Marcel Mauss and *Social Change in Central Africa* by Wilfred and Monica Wilson. During the interview at the Delhi department of sociology, the discussion was on dowry among Syrian Christians of Kerala, perhaps because of my social background. I was asked to situate the institution of dowry rampant among Syrian Christians in the context of *The Gift*, an arduous task for a fresher in sociology. But since I'd studied the monograph, I could answer the question with considerable ease. This is the reason why I thought that my performance at the interview was excellent.

Why was I not selected? In any interview, there are several factors which contribute to selection, particularly when there is only one position. The person selected for the PhD fellowship in the Delhi department in 1960 was Imtiaz Ahmed who completed his MA in anthropology from Lucknow University and was perhaps planning to do his PhD under D.N. Majumdar, who died abruptly at the age of fifty-nine. My feeling that I had done well in the interview, but yet had not been selected depressed me. To be fair to Srinivas, he tried to rectify the 'mistake'. He perhaps asked Vatsala Rao, who had taught me at Poona University and had joined the Institute of Economic Growth, to advise me to enrol for a PhD from the department of sociology, Delhi University.

Vatsala Rao told me that my interview was assessed to be excellent, which is why I was given this offer. More specifically, it was promised that the fellowship for sociology offered by the University Grants Commission (UGC) for Rs 250 per month (the Delhi University fellowship was for Rs 200 per month) could be arranged for me. Given Srinivas's influence it was indeed a possibility, but not a certainty. To add to the authenticity of the offer, it was suggested that I could work on 'Religion and Society among Syrian Christians of Kerala', a sequel to Srinivas's study of the Coorgs, their religion and society, under the supervision of M.S.A. Rao, who was also on the faculty of the department of sociology. But I was not inclined to accept the offer, telling Vatsala Rao that I was not keen to accept a 'consolation' offer, which indeed was perceived as the arrogance of an immature young man. Vatsala Rao consoled me by commenting, 'Don't worry, Oommen, some day you will be a lecturer in one of the Syrian Christian Colleges in Kerala,' an illustration of how parochial considerations get mixed up with professionalism.

I continued my search for an assignment in teaching or research in Delhi. One of my classmates from S.B. College, George Mathew (not to be mistaken for George Mathew, my student who established the Institute of Social Science) advised me to meet T.K.N. Unnithan, who was at that time on the faculty of School of Planning and Architecture, New Delhi. When I met him, he assigned me the task of assisting him on a project, 'Impact of Social Structure on Accumulation of Wealth in South Asia', on which he was working. No remuneration was offered, but he said I could use part of the material to publish a research paper or two. My first paper entitled 'Impact of Social Structure on Accumulation of Wealth' was published in the *AICC Economic Review* in 1961 based on part of the material I collected for this project. The editor of the journal those days was P.V. John, who did his PhD under the guidance of A.M. Khusru in economics. It was John who advised me to do an MA in anthropology from Lucknow or sociology from Bombay after my BA. In the course of my working on the research project, Unnithan assigned me the task of going to Jaipur and obtaining some crucial information about the newly established Rajasthan University. The university was starting a new department of sociology and had advertised for a few positions.

I visited Jaipur and found out that the vice chancellor was a former diplomat, Ambassador M.S. Mehta. Unnithan hinted at the possibility of my getting appointed as a lecturer in the new department should he join the university as professor and head. Although he applied for a professorship, he was appointed as a reader and head at Jaipur and the two lecturers selected were Yogendra Singh and Indra Deva, both holding PhD degrees and backed by a few years of teaching experience. All three were trained in the department of sociology of Lucknow University, although Unnithan had obtained his DPhil from one of the universities in the Netherlands. The Jaipur department initiated the PhD programme by early 1962 and two PhD scholars were selected: Ravi Dutt Sharma who did his MA in social anthropology from Sagar University, Madhya Pradesh, and I. I joined as a PhD scholar in Rajasthan University in March 1962, with a monthly scholarship of Rs 150 after twenty months of unemployment, despite my first rank in the MA examination in 1960. The university would pay only Rs 125 and the remaining Rs 25 would be released only when the PhD thesis was submitted to the university. Eventually, I could not collect the retained amount because I did not submit my thesis at the Rajasthan University.

The dominant themes of research in Indian sociology and social anthropology those days were family and kinship, caste and religion, and the study of villages, but I was not attracted to those areas. My research guide Unnithan's doctoral thesis was on 'Gandhi and Social Change', which was not based on field study or empirical. He suggested 'Sociology of Non-violence' as a possible theme but I was keen to undertake an empirical study which could be related to the Gandhian movement. When I was spending a year after my BA in my native village (1957–58) Vinoba Bhave, referred to as the greatest living disciple of M.K. Gandhi, passed through a village about twelve kilometres away from mine, as part of his all-India padayatra. I went to see him and listened to him as he said that the future of India lies in bringing about social change in villages by distributing land to those who are working on it. This idea lay frozen in my mind but I did not know how to conceptualize it as a PhD theme. Those were the days of hyphenated sociologies, so falling in line, I formulated my topic as 'Sociology of Gramdan Villages', which smacked of raw empiricism. Since my aspiration was to study an empirical situation to formulate theoretical propositions, I changed the topic to 'Ideology and Social Change'. To get material first-hand, I spent fourteen months in seven Rajasthan villages in the three regions, that is, plains, arid and hilly. Given the importance of land in the context of my study, I thought it was necessary to select villages from all the three regions.

I worked single-mindedly on this theme for over two years (1962–64) and even resisted the temptation of pursuing a PhD in Europe or North America. For example, when Bart Landheer, the research supervisor of Unnithan, was visiting the Jaipur department of sociology, he asked me whether I would like to pursue my PhD work on a scholarship from one of the universities in the Netherlands. I politely declined because it would take another two to three years and I was in a hurry to complete my PhD in order to compensate at least partly for my period of unemployment after my MA. But I did not know that another rude shock was in store for me.

In April 1964, the department of sociology of the Rajasthan University advertised for two posts of lecturers and I applied. I was called for the interview, which went very well. But when the results were announced I found someone called Madhulika Vohra who belonged to the first MA batch of the department, was selected as a lecturer, while I was offered the position of junior lecturer. This, despite the fact that not only had I completed my MA in 1960, but I also had over two years of research experience. Further, I had taught a course on family and kinship to the MA students of the department, so Vohra had actually been my student. I felt deeply humiliated and protested to Unnithan.

However, the rationale of the arrangement communicated to me appeared to be convincing. The junior lecturer's appointment was in the scale of Rs 300-400 so was temporary and as soon as I submitted my PhD thesis, I would be appointed as a lecturer. More importantly, as a junior lecturer I would have to teach only eight periods per week in contrast to the twenty-one periods assigned to lecturers. This arrangement seemed to have been done to facilitate the completion of my thesis at the earliest possible time so I was appeased–but when the time table was announced, I couldn't believe my eyes when I saw that twenty-one periods were assigned to me. I felt cheated. This time I protested not only in words but also in action. I delivered the first eight lectures and then refused to take on the rest. There was a hue and cry about my recalcitrance but I did not relent.

In the light of this bitter experience, I started looking for a job outside Jaipur. My refusal to accept the fellowship offered by Landheer turned out to be a blunder. I responded to an advertisement for the position of a lecturer in social science at the DSSW in August 1964, the institution from which I did not receive the admission offer for an MA in May 1958. There were eight interviewees including two PhDs but this time, I was selected. My advantage was that I had read economics and political science for my BA, sociology for my MA and was a 'near-PhD'. The position was not for sociology but in social science. And so it was that I joined DSSW in November 1964.

After getting my appointment letter from DSSW I went to meet Unnithan. I told him that I made a mistake and that he should pardon me, but he looked puzzled, saying he did not have the ghost of an idea about my 'mistake'. I then told him that I had applied for the position of a lecturer in Delhi University without seeking his permission. He told me that it did not matter and it was good to gain some experience in attending interviews. When I revealed that I'd got the job, he was shell-shocked. I requested for a no objection certificate which ought to have been submitted along with my application. I handed over the letter dated 3 October 1964 seeking a no objection certificate from the Rajasthan University which he had to recommend and forward as the head of the department to the vice chancellor. I had only twenty days to join DSSW till 23 October, and after several reminders Unnithan forwarded my letter of resignation to the registrar. Then I went to meet the vice chancellor, M.S, Mehta, a former diplomat, who knew me tangentially as one of the earliest research scholars of the university.

Mehta Sahib used to walk around the campus at night with his huge Alsatian dogs and spotting lights in the library cubicles he would walk in to instruct the chowkidar to switch off the lights, only to find that some of us were still studying there. If it was a winter night, he would ask whether it was possible to get a cup of black coffee. When we'd remind him that using an electric kettle was against the rules, he would quip, 'Not in the presence of the vice chancellor!' When my case came before him, he summoned the concerned deputy registrar, L.R. Shah. On hearing that my application had been pending for the last three weeks, he reprimanded the deputy registrar and instructed him to issue the relieving certificate immediately. His action enabled me to join DSSW on time, after the delay in obtaining the no objection certificate which caused me considerable anxiety and frustration.

I was keen to continue my PhD with Unnithan and I promised him I'd visit Jaipur every weekend or whenever he desired but he insisted that I should not leave Jaipur before completing it, stating that the departmental tradition did not permit absentee PhD students (incidentally, I was the first PhD student in the department!). He wanted me to reject the job of lecturer in Delhi University and continue as a PhD student at Jaipur and assured me that there would not be any victimization. In his official letter dated 29 January 1965 and in an earlier personal handwritten letter dated 10 December 1964, he made it very clear that he could not continue as my PhD supervisor unless I returned to Jaipur, otherwise he'd cancel my PhD registration. However, his assurances did not give me enough confidence in the light of my experience, particularly being rejected for the position of lecturer against a fresher, Vohra.

Towards the end of 1964, Unnithan organized a conference at Mount Abu on 'Indian Sociology' in which a code of ethics for Indian sociologists was proposed and adopted. One of the proposals was that renegade research scholars from one department should not be admitted for a PhD degree by other departments. He also wrote to several senior sociologists mentioning my name as a research scholar who had left the department without permission. Two of them, I.P. Desai and Y.B. Damle, told me about it. He also wrote to the then principal of DSSW, S.N. Ranade about my 'misconduct'. Under the circumstances I had to register at Poona University under Damle, who would have been my PhD supervisor had he not left for MIT in 1960. I had to wait for two years to submit the thesis to Poona University, the minimum prescribed time after registration. The topic was also reformulated as 'Charismatic Movements and Social Change: An Analysis of Bhoodan-Gramdan Movement in India'. I have tried to demonstrate in the thesis that charisma can be a system-stabilizing force, contrary to what Max Weber argued. Then my thesis was published in 1971 by Thompson Press, a newly established Canadian publisher in India, with the title: *Charisma, Stability and Change.*

I submitted my PhD thesis in 1966 to Poona University. The then rule of the university was that of the two examiners, one should be a foreigner and the other an Indian who would conduct the viva voce. My foreign examiner was reputed sociologist Edward Shils and the Indian examiner, A.R. Desai, known for his Marxist approach to sociology. While both examiners recommended the award of a PhD, Shils thought that the empirical data I had collected and presented were excellent, while Desai opined that I had a good grasp of theory! Shils had two assignments those days, one semester at Chicago in the US and the other at Cambridge, UK. When the thesis arrived at Cambridge by surface mail Shils was at Chicago. Although it was forwarded to Chicago, by the time it reached there Shils was back in Cambridge! Understandably, it took almost two years to receive the report from Shils after it crossed the Atlantic Ocean twice. Indeed I had a tortuous time getting my PhD!

I got the degree a long six years after my MA. Several factors contributed to the avoidable delay. Prominent among them were the absence of proper rules in granting long leave to faculty members who are PhD supervisors; the tendency to recruit PhD students from among the MA students of departments, blocking the entry of outsiders; arbitrary decisions taken by research supervisors to create obstacles in the smooth progress of their research students; vindictive actions taken by departments/supervisors against those research scholars who leave without completing their PhD; and finally, the indifference of academic seniors in the discipline, leaving the hapless research scholars to suffer. The prevailing academic milieu was and is a definite obstacle to creating the much touted 'knowledge society' in India.

Edward Shils was a towering personality in the discipline of sociology. I had a few encounters with him like the one in 1992 when I was attending the Programme Committee meeting of the International Sociological Association (ISA) in Rome as its president. Shils invited me and Salvador Giner, the Spanish sociologist, who was his student, for dinner. When I told Giner about Shils' invitation, he asked me, 'Are you sure that he is hosting the dinner?' I answered, 'Yes' but Giner looked a bit dubious. Later I realized why because after dinner, when the bill was presented, Shils said, 'Let us split it.' Giner was upset because he did not have any money with him, so I paid for both of us!

Shils used to visit Delhi occasionally and also JNU. During one of his visits he told me that he was planning to sell the books in his library and he would be happy if the university would buy them. After getting the details of his personal library and discussing the matter with the vice chancellor and librarian, we arrived at a figure as the price. When I asked Shils about the price he expected, he quoted an astronomical figure. Having heard this, I told him, 'Shils there is a saying in Kerala, my native place, that a good businessman is one who can buy from a Jew and sell to a Syrian Christian. We don't have the required business acumen.' The transaction did not come through.

As my supervisor, Y.B. Damle, lived in Pune and the Indian examiner, A.R. Desai, at Mumbai, I was advised to appear for my viva voce at the department of sociology at Mumbai. G.S. Ghurye, my supervisor's supervisor, was still active and used to visit his office regularly. After the viva voce Damle asked me, 'Would you like to meet the old man?', meaning Ghurye, I answered in the affirmative. When I was ushered into Ghurye's room and was introduced, Ghurye remarked, 'For a Syrian Christian, you are dark'. Thinking that Syrian Christians cannot be identified on the basis of their pigmentation, since they are not a racial category, I told myself, 'This illustrious scholar can formulate generalizations without any empirical basis.' We conversed for twenty minutes about the state of sociology in India and his proclivity to make assertions without verifiable evidence was clear all along, a tendency evident in his writings too.

CHAPTER 3

The Academic and Political Milieu of Jawaharlal Nehru University

I joined DSSW in 1964 November and taught there till July 1971. Although I enjoyed teaching there, as a sociologist I experienced several academic disadvantages. I was the only faculty member in social science and had no academic peers. The course I had to teach was 'Man and Society' which covered social, political and economic institutions with a slant towards India. Earlier the course was not integrated in this vein and was taught by scholars drawn from three different disciplines: sociology, political science and economics, usually as visiting faculty. Teaching the entire course was a challenging task but as I have studied economics and politics for BA and sociology at the MA level, I could cope with it. My students at DSSW were not trained as sociologists so I could not continue my academic links with them, and further, there was no chance of supervising PhD scholars as the topics were social work-oriented. Understandably, I was at the academic margin of sociology and was very keen to enter the mainstream. An opportunity for this unfolded when the Jawaharlal Nehru University (JNU) launched teaching programmes in July 1971 and I joined the faculty.

At first, I occupied two types of positions at JNU: As warden of boy's hostel, provost of the Dakshinapuram Halls of Residence, and the dean of Student's Welfare. There are several myths about JNU. One is that it was conceived as an institution different from other universities in India. However, when the JNU Bill was piloted and introduced by M.C. Chagla on 2 December 1964 in the Rajya Sabha, the then education minister of the Indian Republic said JNU was thought of as a university that would meet the growing pressure on Delhi University, thanks to the increase in numbers of students because of the influx of refugees following partition in 1947. In fact, the affiliation of the existing colleges to JNU based on a territorial division of Delhi between Delhi University and JNU was the original plan. Further, the integration of Jamia Millia Islamia University situated in South Delhi and the affiliation of three professional institutions–the All India Institute of Medical Sciences, the Indian Institute of Technology and the Indian Agricultural Research Institute, too, was visualized. Mercifully, this did not happen.

Similarly, Chagla proposed the introduction of seven new institutes, none of which materialized. Three institutes for Indian, Asian and African languages conjointly gave birth to the School of Languages of JNU and the already existing Institute of Russian Languages was absorbed into it. The Institute of Russian Studies became the Centre for Soviet Studies in the School of International Studies, which was in existence as an independent entity known as the Indian School of International Studies (ISIS). The Institute of International

Affairs and the Institute of International Law and Diplomacy proposed by Chagla also did not fructify. Curiously, the School of Social Sciences, which became the cynosure of JNU, was not even proposed by Chagla.

From the JNU Bill to the JNU Act, the legislation which gave birth to the institution, there have been substantial differences. Many objected to the very name: Nehru-baiters were ill at ease. Quite a few were afraid that JNU would put into operation the Nehruvian vision, particularly socialism and secularism. Paradoxically, JNU later came to be identified with Marxian socialism, far more radical than Nehru's 'socialistic pattern of society'. The uniqueness of JNU lies in its relative academic autonomy conceded to teachers; its national (read all-India) character visualized and achieved through the admission policy of students and recruitment procedure of faculty; and a high degree of interdisciplinarity, became the birth marks of JNU.

JNU's cosmopolitanism is loudly heralded and much of this is true thanks to the admission policy. The admission tests are conducted in nearly two dozen cities and towns dispersed all over India, which provides instant accessibility to aspiring candidates. Apart from spatial dispersal, thanks to the allocation of twenty points to caste/tribe, economic and regional deprivations, students were drawn from a wide variety of backgrounds. But this cosmopolitanism did not apply to karamcharis (workers) particularly those who placed at the lower level.

Let me recall two instances. Once there was no sweeping done in a particular hostel for a couple of days. When the matter was brought to my notice in my capacity as hostel administrator, I made enquiries and discovered that almost all the workers were consanguinal or affinal relatives and had gone for a wedding to their native place in a nearby district.

The other discovery was in relation to the dietary needs of the student population, which was all-India in composition. The demand was that the cuisine served in the hostels should reflect that, but there was a lack of cooks who could prepare south, east, or west Indian cuisine. It turned out that an overwhelming majority of cooks and other kitchen staff were from the hills; they were Pahadis recruited by a deputy registrar with the same background. Subsequently, it was decided that there should be at least one warden in the Interview Board when these members of staff were recruited so that a wider social base was ensured.

JNU also earned notoriety for its licentiousness, which was largely misplaced. But since there were interactions between men and women students, molestation or sexual harassment did occur. While in a few cases such interactions would eventuate in marriages there were instances when dating created problems because of class backgrounds. The girls with upper middle class background had a different perspective on pre-marital interactions as compared to lower middle class boys, particularly from rural India. This culture difference did create frustrations for boys from rural background because in their perception visiting the canteen or going for a film together was a sure indicator of their female companion's interest in them and willingness to marry. I had to handle a few cases of mental breakdowns of boys but only one case of pre-marital pregnancy when the progenitor backed out. The girl was quickly repatriated to Tamil Nadu before she reached an advanced stage of pregnancy.

JNU evolved as an innovative institution in Indian higher education, both structurally and in its mode of functioning. There are no departments of particular disciplines or science and arts faculties. Instead there are Centres and Schools. While each Centre is a collective of academics drawn from different disciplines, several Centres constitute a School. However, those who conceive and launch new institutions, often forget that the gap between the old and new institutions have to be kept within acceptable limits. For example, when the MA course was introduced in the School of Social Science in JNU it was *not* in particular disciplines but in 'Social Science'. The transcript would indicate the courses taken by students and grades obtained. But these graduates were not eligible for applying to most universities in India because university applicants must have a master's degree in specific disciplines like economics, history, political science and sociology. Those with a master's degree in 'Social Science' were not even called for interviews. Confronted with such a reality, JNU quickly responded by awarding degrees in particular disciplines.

JNU had introduced the letter grade system from A plus to C minus as against the then existing numerical system of grading and had to work out the equivalents of letter grades in numericals. Several universities were sceptical about the equivalents worked out by JNU because they thought the numerical value allotted to letter grades were exaggerated. For example, B+ was assigned 6 per cent marks. The argument here is not against innovation but about its acceptability. If the acceptability is weak or low, the sufferers will be students and not educational innovators.

The initially contemplated fanciful idea of appointing faculty members for a tenure of five years could have been disastrous for JNU. Those who were working in other established institutions–universities, institutes and laboratories–in permanent positions would not have accepted the offer and those institutions would not have sanctioned such long leave. Consequently, JNU would have attracted only those who were unemployed, if not unemployable. But in the initial crop of the faculty who joined JNU, most were enthused by the promised autonomy to faculty and innovative orientation of the new university.

JNU follows the semester system wherein only 50 per cent of evaluation is done through end-semester examinations, while the other 50 per cent evaluation is done as the teaching progresses. The evaluation is entirely internal, often creating conflict situations as students allege partiality on the part of the faculty. The attributed partiality of teachers is based on political ideology, regional-linguistic or religious or caste backgrounds, and even gender. As students and faculty are drawn from all over India with widely varying backgrounds the social milieu is complex and consequently, often tension-prone.

The residential pattern of JNU, too, was different from other universities. Each residential area consists of a cluster of faculty houses of three types meant for professors, associate professors and assistant professors as well as a set of hostels, each accommodating roughly 200 students. A hostel has four wardens, each looking after fifty students and provisions exist for wardens to reside in the hostel. The first residential area to be launched was Dakshinapuram with seventy-two faculty houses and three hostels named after south Indian rivers: Godavari for women and Periyar and Kaveri for men. The pattern is replicated in the Uttarakhand residences where the names of hostels are derived from rivers of north India and Poorvanchal where the hostels are named after rivers of east India. The physical structure is conceived in a way that promotes close interaction between faculty and students. I was the first warden of the boys' hostel along with Suvira Jaiswal, who was the warden of the girls' hostel. The karamcharis have a separate residential enclave.

The purpose behind providing this skeletal description of JNU is to indicate that the teacher–student relationship was expected to be nurtured in a harmonious vein. While this was achieved to a large extent, the unintended consequence was to develop a patron–client relationship between teachers and students, particularly those who professed the same political ideology.

Given the fact that elected representatives of students are given an opportunity to participate in the decision-making process, student–faculty relationships often take unexpected turns. The student members of the student faculty committee (SFC) in each Centre, which discusses the lists of students to be admitted, often insists on a lower cut-off point to accommodate some of their 'candidates'. Students also have representation at all levels, except the Executive Council. Often, the politically active students protested against the university administration and even faculty. While most of these mobilizations were non-violent, in 1983 there was a particularly violent protest on the JNU campus when the houses of some key administrators and faculty members perceived as 'class enemies' were attacked and vehicles of several faculty members were also damaged. I was among the few privileged enough to be targeted. I wrote a piece published in the *Times of India* (29 July 1983) entitled 'Patron–client Ties: Bane of JNU' in which I argued that it is the patronage extended by politically attached faculty members to their student clients which results in such violent attacks. Understandably, neither the students nor the faculty implicated in the analysis approved of my position. Nothing more was required to caricature me as an arch-reactionary and a confirmed 'class enemy'.

Given the ideological polarization in JNU's School of Social Science, there was hardly any possibility of reading, let alone objectively evaluating, the publications of those faculty who were dubbed as non- or anti-Marxists. In a book by a former student and a present JNU faculty member entitled *JNU: The Making of a University*, 'leftist' scholars are favourably commented on, 'non-leftists' are accommodated but those who are labelled as 'anti-leftists' are subjected to a cognitive blackout. When the Naxalbari revolt occurred in the 1960s, the CPI(ML) hailed it as a revolutionary stirring but both CPI(M) and CPI(R) viewed it as the failure of capitalist path of development pursued in India. 'The leftist factions in JNU endorsed these views'.

More concretely, India's Green Revolution increased rural disparity and hence the revolt, went the argument. Leftist academics of JNU put forward their arguments adjusting with those of their political masters.

The formula was Development → Disparity → Conflict: the greater the development, steeper the disparity and hence, more intense the conflict. After making a comparative study of the rice-growing Alleppey district in Kerala and Ludhiana district, a wheat growing area in the Punjab, I have exposed the un-sustainability of the argument. Disparity in Ludhiana was much steeper as compared with Alleppey and yet conflicts in Alleppey were much more intense and frequent as compared with Ludhiana. I argued that it was the level of politicisation which caused conflicts and not increased disparity. But the leftist faculty dismissed it as a bourgeoisie argument and their students echoed them.

Before joining JNU I was in three other campuses–Poona University, Rajasthan University (Jaipur) and the DSSW–where the level of politicization was rather low. The JNU campus was a contrast; the students were organized into unions which functioned as front organizations of political parties. The strong unions those days were the Student Federation of India (SFI) affiliated to the Communist Party of India (Marxist), the All India Student Federation (AISF) affiliated to the

Communist Party of India, and the National Students Union of India (NSUI) affiliated to the Indian National Congress–but the most popular and strongest union was the SFI. I often heard people remarking those days that the CPM was powerful in four places in India–West Bengal, Kerala, Tripura–and JNU. Subsequently, two other student unions affiliated to the CPI (ML) and the BJP, emerged. Teaching and doing research were largely unencumbered by politicization, but university administration, was not smooth as most matters were viewed through the lens of political groups. Unfortunately, I was the warden, provost and dean of student welfare, successively, and I was constantly targeted by student politicians. Retrospectively viewed, accepting those administrative responsibilities was a great blunder, earning many enemies for me but hardly any appreciation.

In the beginning when JNU was located in the 'Old Campus', as it was known, there were only two hostels, one for boys and another for girls. G. Parthasarathi, the first vice chancellor (VC), wanted either Yogendra Singh (also professor of sociology), or me to be the warden of the boys' hostel. Yogendra Singh wriggled out of it but I accepted it, albeit reluctantly. Students came from all over India and admission to hostels was more difficult (as hostel seats were fewer) than admission to the university which also meant that one had to follow rules and regulations strictly. If these rules were violated there would be instant protests which the hostel administrators had to face.

There was the case of a student from Kerala whose family was associated with the CPI. Both Moonis Raza, who was the first adviser for student affairs and N.V.K. Murthy, the registrar, who were said to be CPI sympathizers, wanted me to admit him to the hostel without the required initial deposits.

I insisted that the student should get this in writing from those who recommended his case, but he did not pay the dues for the whole semester. When this matter was brought to my notice, I asked the university office to put the list of defaulters on the notice board. When the students got to know about the Kerala boy's default and his political background, there was an instant agitation. When the VC enquired about the reason for the agitation, he was told about the Kerala boy's huge arrears. The VC promptly asked me for an explanation. I reached his office with the hostel admission card of the student in which the recommendations of Moonis Raza and N.V.K. Murthy were recorded. The VC was taken aback and understood the insinuation implied in the communication that the student was from Kerala, suggesting that the trouble arose because of the favouritism I had shown to a fellow Malayali.

Yet another instance of confronting the influential authorities was when M.S. Venkataramani, the dean of the School of International Studies recommended that a PhD student from Nepal, who was also a senior government official, be allotted a double room for single occupancy and be charged double the rent. I did not accept the recommendation and the matter was reported to the VC. When the VC asked me about it, I remarked that although it was possible for a rich industrialist's son to pay the rent for the entire hostel, it was untenable to allot the entire hostel to him. The VC smiled and said, 'No action to be taken.' It may have been a victory for me, but in the process I antagonized a senior professor.

Parthasarathi was a great diplomat who could change his stance swiftly. Once he remarked that he had to negotiate both with Sheikh Abdullah (the legendary leader of Kashmir) as the nominee of Gandhi, the Prime Minister, and V.C. Koshy (the president of the JNU student union) in the course of the same day. He said this in the context of the first convocation of JNU when the university authorities persisted with inviting the great film actor Balraj Sahni to deliver the Convocation Address although the Trotskyite faction of the leftist students vehemently disapproved of it. (I remember Balraj Sahni delivering a disarming speech, even saying that if he were asked to sweep the floor of the university, he would deem it a privilege). The JNUSU demand was that its president should also be allowed to address the convocation. After a lot of negotiations, the VC agreed, provided Koshy's speech was approved by the VC's nominee and I was entrusted with that task. But to my chagrin, the version of the speech I'd approved and the version read out by Koshy were poles apart, embarrassing the university authorities terribly since he said that events such as convocation were a sheer wastage of taxpayers' money–they should be dispensed with and the money diverted for the students' welfare. The union hailed the speech as a revolutionary act but it was a total breach of faith on the part of the JNUSU president. That day I realized that trusting those who attest the dictum 'the end justifies the means' is dangerous and foolish. And, all the diplomatic skill of Parthasarathi was of no avail when he was negotiating with those who threw ethical principles to the wind.

Another instance occurred when K.R. Narayanan became the VC. The then rule was that a PhD student should vacate the hostel six months after the submission of his/her thesis, but one student did not do so in spite of repeated communications sent to him. In the meantime several applicants for rooms in the hostel were constantly reminding me of the illegal occupation of the room by the student. Finally, as the dean (DSW), I was constrained to order locking of the room. Within a few hours, I was asked to meet the VC who told me that there was a communication from the FM's (the then foreign minister was Atal Bihari Vajpayee) office that the student may be allowed to continue in the hostel. My reply was that if the student stayed, I would resign. The VC at once retracted and insisted that I should continue as DSW and the student would be made to leave the hostel.

These instances illustrate that to occupy administrative positions, even in a university, one should be pliable, if not an accomplice of the higher authorities. If one sticks to a principled stand one is labelled 'bureaucratic'. To be 'non-bureaucratic' one should favour a particular political group, as illustrated by the following instance. There was a violent confrontation between four SFI supporters and three NSUI supporters, leading to physical injuries to the NSUI students. As the DSW, I ordered an enquiry and suspended all the seven students till the enquiry report was submitted. But several faculty members, including senior professors, suggested that I should withdraw the suspension order, reminding me that one of the suspended students (P. Sainath, who later became an ace journalist) was politically connected as he was the grandson of the then President of India, V.V. Giri.

Out of the three JNU VCs–Parthasarathi, Nag Chaudhary and Narayanan–I worked with as a hostel administrator, I had the most pleasant experience in working with VC Nag Chaudhary. Whenever students or faculty members went to him to complain against any of my actions, the first question he asked was, 'Did you talk to Oommen?' If the answer was in the affirmative, he would say that he could hardly do anything in the matter. If the answer were in the negative, the advice would be, 'Go and talk to him'. This made it easy for me to work as a hostel administrator, the principle being that any superior authority who takes decisions without consulting his juniors in administration unleashes administrative anomie. Let me mention in passing that Nag Chaudhary wanted me to work as the registrar of the university with him and when I told him that his offer was an insult to my academic standing, he was bewildered and said, 'But in Calcutta renowned professors often work as registrars,' However, I was not pressurized to accept the VC's offer.

The general impression conveyed through tracts published on JNU is that Nag Chaudhary was authoritarian, particularly because of the 'excesses during the emergency' when he was the VC, but I saw him as quite fair. For instance, when the student organizations opposed to the emergency, particularly the SFI (the AISF supported the emergency following the line taken by the CPI) had stocked anti-emergency pamphlets in hostels, the security officer of JNU raided the hostels and seized the 'anti-government' material. When this was brought to my notice, I went to the VC and told him that the security officer's high-handedness was unacceptable to me. He promptly spoke to the officer and told him that entry into and administrative actions in the hostels should not take place without the prior permission of the DSW. This fairness made hostel administration less cumbersome for me during those days.

I found a sense of humour often came to my rescue when handling tense situations. Let me recall one incident. It was usual for the activist students to march to the residence of the DSW or even the provost to present their 'grievances', for the flimsiest of reasons. The time chosen was invariably post-dinner because it was not possible to gather enough protesters during the day time as the students were not free. The understanding the JNU authority (read Moonis Raza) had with the student union was that the monthly mess bill would not exceed Rs 100, but when it did it was a sure invitation for an agitation. And so it happened that when the monthly mess bill was Rs 105, a group of protesters reached my house at 11 p.m. on a cold winter night of December shouting, 'DSW Murdabad!' I woke up, came out and told them, 'Whatever may be the urgency, I cannot go to Muradabad now. I can do it only tomorrow morning.' Some of them burst into laughter and the crowd dispersed. Maybe it was a small dividend for being a 'Madrasi' perceived to be an illiterate in the 'rashtra bhasha'!

As an academic, most of my triumphs occurred while at JNU but there were a few tribulations too. The fact that I was perceived not only as 'anti-left' but as an 'arch-reactionary' was a major problem I faced. When I joined JNU as an associate professor in July 1971, I was thirty-four years old and when I became a professor in 1976, I was less than forty. Quite a few obstacles were created to prevent my elevation as professor, political misinformation and sexual allegations being the prominent ones. When one of the colleagues in Centre for the Study of Regional Development asked Moonis Raza, 'Why are you against Oommen becoming a professor?' pat came the reply, 'If he becomes a professor at this young age, nobody can stop him from becoming the VC of JNU.' Well, the irony is that his wish was fulfilled.

Once Nurul Hasan, the well-known historian, who became minister of education in the Union cabinet asked S.C. Dube, an eminent sociologist, 'Is Oommen an arch-reactionary?' Dube replied, 'If I am a reactionary, so is Oommen.' This was recounted to me by Dube himself who asked why such misinformation had spread. I could not answer his question but I told him what I thought could have created this antagonism. At the initial stage, there was no organized political group among the JNU faculty although the majority were perceived to have left leanings. I was told that Nurul Hasan, while visiting

Paris for a conference, on being asked whether there was any leftist university in India as in France, had answered, 'Yes, the Jawaharlal Nehru University in New Delhi.' In fact, in the 1970s, articulations were often made in the media and questions were asked in the Parliament whether JNU was packed with left-oriented faculty. I remember that when Prime Minister Morarji Desai visited JNU in his capacity as chancellor of JNU, he asked the awkward question, 'Is it true that all of you are communists?' There was deadly silence for a while, but I was constrained to break it. I said, 'Respected Prime Minister, your question is wrongly phrased. You should be asking: "Is it true that all of you are academically incompetent?" What matters is academic competence and not political affiliations of the faculty.' An animated discussion followed and I believe the PM left the campus with some clarity about the political leaning in JNU although he persisted with the idea of conducting an enquiry about JNU.

In spite of the ethos which prevailed in JNU there was no elections to the faculty association in the first few years. An effort was made to instal Moonis Raza as the first president of Jawaharlal Nehru University Teachers Association (JNUTA) through a signature campaign. While the authority structure of JNU was yet to fully evolve, the trio that governed JNU those days were the VC, the registrar and Moonis Raza, whose designation was officer on special duty (OSD). To propose his name as the president of JNUTA was tantamount to suggesting a person in the establishment as 'the leader of the opposition', the perceived role of the JNUTA president. When the signature campaigners reached me, up to fifteen faculty members had already signed, but I said I thought the proposal was odd and suggested that the faculty members should not proceed with it. As a result, another senior faculty member, a non-

Marxist–Yogendra Singh–became the first JNUTA president, with Parimal Das as the first secretary of JNUTA. But my position was interpreted as arising from my attributed anti-left orientation. Incidentally, there were only three attributed identities those days in JNU: Marxist, non-Marxist and anti-Marxist. I belonged to the last category and this perception was reinforced because I was part of the hostel administration, which rendered me an instant enemy of students also.

The impression that everybody looked at issues only through the political lens was internalized by the student union of JNU. An amusing instance confirmed this. The faculty of the Centre for Historical Studies (CHS) of the School of Social Sciences was widely believed to be of a leftist inclination. In 1973–74, there was a dispute between the student union lead by SFI–AISF and the CHS faculty regarding the students selected for the MA course, alleging irregularities and favouritism. The VC set up a two-member faculty committee for an enquiry; I was one, the other being Urmila Phadnis. On being asked about why they had agreed to my name as a committee member, the union leaders' rationale was that, 'Since Oommen is anti-left and the CHS faculty is pro-left, he would provide an adverse report.' Bipin Chandra of CHS told me about this much later in an informal conversation. It was a pity that the student union leadership forgot about my class solidarity with the CHS faculty!

The following incident is more telling in its illustration of the attitude of 'leftists' towards me. A few days before the interview which was slated to take place in September 1976 for the professorship in the Centre for the Study of Social Systems (CSSS), which I was applying for, a rumour spread like wild fire on the campus. It was that I had 'molested' a visiting Japanese scholar in her twenties. She was not a JNU student but had come to Delhi to do research on Dalits and I had allotted her a room in the Godavari hostel. I don't know what really transpired but the Japanese student was sent to my home to complain about me to my wife. The same day Moonis Raza telephoned and told me that 'such things' could happen on university campuses, which mystified me as I had no clue about 'such things', but when I reached home I found my wife utterly upset and she told me what the Japanese girl had accused me of. The amusing thing was that the Japanese scholar wanted to consult me even after the day I 'molested' her, but of course, I refused to meet her.

The adverse impact of such character assassination was long-lasting. As reported to me, in a conversation between M.N. Srinivas and S. Gopal, Gopal had said, 'Don't you know Oommen's reputation as a womanizer?' But the most damaging instance of character assassination was when my son's mother-in-law told one of her colleagues in the Reserve Bank of India, an ex-student of JNU, that her daughter was getting married to my son, she met with the comment, 'Oh, that womanizer's son?' My son shared this with me and I roared with laughter. Although I tried to camouflage my embarrassment with laughter, such vilification was the price I had to pay for my perceived 'anti-left' orientation. Incidentally, the durability of rumours is incredible. In September 2015, Mahabir Singh, one of my walking companions at the National Media Centre told me that one of his friends, D.V. Singh of JNU, had told him that I was implicated in a molestation case. The date of manufacture of the rumour was September 1976 and its expiry date had not arrived even in 2015, thirty-nine years later! Mercifully, the popularity of social media was yet to emerge in the Indian media firmament in 1976, otherwise my 'reputation' would have spread far and wide.

I learnt later that the same group misguided the VC about a scholar who came to JNU from a West Bengal university for a professorship interview in the School of International Studies. The story circulated about him was that he was indulging in incest with his sister. The reason for this malice? The scholar in question dared to be anti-CPM, that too, in West Bengal. I have known about political parties embroiling their opponents in stories of financial embezzlements and sexual harassment so as to discredit them, but that such political maligning could be enacted on a university campus was beyond my imagination. However based on my experience in the JNU campus, I can confirm it.

I am referred to as a teacher in the tracts published on JNU but they are totally silent about me as an administrator, perhaps because silence was preferred to negative comments. Hostel life is ignored, but a disproportionate importance given to the Ganga Dhaba and this or that person's canteen. The comments about hostel administration, even if they were negative, would have helped to improve the prevailing pattern of governance. Similarly, observations about my 'authoritarian and tyrannical' style as hostel administrator would have helped my successors to tread a more acceptable path.

CHAPTER 4

The Social and Academic Formation of the Centre for the Study of Social Systems

As hinted earlier, my PhD topic was an unconventional one in Indian sociology and social anthropology at the time. When I appeared for an interview in the Centre for the Study of Developing Societies, Delhi, in 1964, Srinivas, who was a member of the Interview Board, asked with ample sarcasm, 'Is the Bhoodan–Gramdhan movement a relevant topic for research in sociology?' (remember, he wanted me to work on 'Religion and Society among Syrian Christians'). This attitude was a handicap for me when I tried to join conventional departments of sociology in India. As JNU was conceived differently and was established to fight 'the crisis of irrelevance in Indian higher education', I did not have a problem there.

The CSSS was not a conventional department of sociology. It consisted mainly of sociologists and social anthropologists, with no sharp differentiation between these disciplines. The appointment of a social psychologist was on the cards too but the CSSS did not succeed in recruiting one, until recently. In the beginning an attempt was made to recruit Sudhir Kakkar, the accomplished social psychologist and psychoanalyst, but the post available was only that of an associate professor and Kakkar was inclined to join only as a professor. The post lay vacant till 2008, that is, for thirty-seven years, when Bimol Akoijam, a social psychologist joined the Centre. The huge time-lag between the initial envisioning and its eventual realization is indeed telling.

The courses offered at CSSS belong to three broad areas: theory, methodology and structure, and process. Theory courses include both social thought and social theory. Similarly, methodology courses consisted of the philosophy of social science and techniques of collection and analysis of data. The two-year MA course is offered in four semesters and the student has to take four courses in each semester. Of the sixteen courses, six are theory and two methodology courses, while the remaining eight courses deal with substantive themes relating to Indian society. While the theory and methodology courses are compulsory, nearly 50 per cent of the courses in the structure and process rubric are optional. Of the six courses in theory, one is in social anthropology and another in social psychology designated as 'Society, Culture and Personality'. For the two-year MPhil course there are only four papers one each in theory and methodology and two substantive courses followed by a dissertation, one third of the credits being allotted to it.

At the initial stage there were two courses on sociological thinkers; one on Karl Marx and Max Weber and another on Emile Durkheim, Alexis de Tocqueville and Vilfredo Pareto for the MA programme. I taught the latter course initially but later, the course on Marx and Weber too. I used to carry the original texts to read out relevant parts, along with notes, to the lecture hall. There was no roll-call, so some students would try to enter the lecture hall late, but I insisted that if anyone wanted to attend my lecture s/he should be seated before I start lecturing. Unfortunately, often mine was the first lecture, starting at 9 a.m. A student called Susan Paul remembers: 'I would have run at great speed by the shrubs and weeds and rocks and glistening streamlets to be in time for T.K. O's first class. He was very aloof, very detached, very severe and very military-like. Sometimes he smiled, particularly when he taught Emile Durkheim and Tocqueville.'

I might have smiled even when I taught Marx and Weber but I may not have taught that course to her class. In a system, where attendance is not compulsory, the teacher is often compelled to maintain a stern demeanour to keep up a semblance of order, given the tendency of students to consider lecture halls as places of entertainment.

The academic autonomy of a JNU teacher was to be discerned in terms of his/her freedom to formulate and teach courses unencumbered by bureaucratic restraints. At CSSS, we introduced a course on 'Philosophy of Social Sciences' rarely taught in conventional departments. At the MPhil level, I introduced courses on 'social movements' and 'modern professions', areas I had researched initially. This combination of teaching and research was possible in JNU because of the academic autonomy available to teachers.

Students interrogated teachers both inside and outside classrooms although sometimes they were misinformed. Once in the course my teaching Marx, a sympathizer of the SFI thought that I was misrepresenting Marx. The text in question was *Economic and Philosophic Manuscripts of 1844*. I retorted by observing that, 'You must distinguish between "Pavement

Marxism" and "Original Marxism".' It was a joy for me to teach although those who perceived me as a 'class enemy' might not have enjoyed my teaching. What I am pointing to is the human proclivity to mix up content, ignoring contexts.

A few documents published by the Alumni Association of JNU contain reminiscences of students of the CSSS. While quite a few comments on my lectures are positive, those who are politically aligned are usually silent. It is indeed a risk to appreciate a 'class enemy' publicly. But the fact that I was strict was commented on: 'He was the guru of punctuality in JNU', goes one remark. On the other hand, my sense of humour was appreciated. However I got a sense of gratification when Paromita Sanyal who joined Harvard University said: 'Sir, I learnt nothing new through my course on sociological thinkers'. I taught the course to her batch. But what intrigues me is why some teachers are popular–they are not necessarily those who cultivate academic rigour but those who are 'friendly', 'compassionate' and interact informally.

Following the innovative trail of JNU, an Advisory Committee was constituted which created working groups for each of the Centres. The working group for CSSS consisted of six persons: three sociologists, two political scientists and one educationist, which augured well for the interdisciplinary thrust of the Centre. The three sociologists were M.N. Srinivas, Ramakrishna Mukherjee and M.S. Gore, which indicated the blurring of distinctions between sociology and social anthropology.

The first three faculty members who joined the CSSS were Yogendra Singh, C.N. Venugopal and I. C.N.Venugopal and I being the first two faculty members recruited through the routine procedure as Assistant and Associate professors respectively. I remember S.C. Dube and M.S. Gore as experts on the Selection Committee, both of whom knew me as a junior colleague due to my publications and participation in seminars and conferences.

G.Parthasarathi, the VC who chaired the Committee, was keen to know why I wanted to leave Delhi University, where I was already a reader. I explained to him that since I was at the DSSW as a sociologist, I was at the academic margin and wanted to be in the mainstream of the discipline. The fact that M.S. Gore, a former principal of DSSW, was present as a member of the Committee was a little embarrassing, yet I did not mince words.

In his characteristic pomp and style, Dube started the academic part of the interview after the administrative queries by the VC, and began by saying that he was familiar with my work, yet had to to ask a few questions as a formality. This initiation relieved my tension and I felt comfortable, so the interview was a smooth affair. As far as I remember, P.N. Mukherjee was a serious contender. It seems that the selection committee was quite impressed with him and was willing to support the selection of two associate professors instead of one, but the VC's position was that it would create administrative hurdles. Later, I came to know, quite accidentally, that considerable political pressure was exerted on the VC to select Mukherjee, when A.P. Sinha, a peasant leader and MP from Bihar came to my home to make a telephone call. He was staying at Mukherjee's home where the telephone was not working He started talking and confided that he had made several MPs to talk to the VC to appoint Partha and commented, 'Yet you were selected. There must be something extraordinary about you.'

In 1972–73, three more faculty members joined CSSS–Partha Mukherjee, K.L. Sharma and M.N. Panini, the former as associate and the latter two as assistant professors. This time also, Mukherji had a formidable competitor, Ratna Naidu who had a PhD from the US and a couple of books to her credit, but Mukherji was selected. K.L. Sharma had all the required qualifications, but Parthasarthi's rationale was quite different. He told me cryptically, 'It is good to have somebody with a rural background also on the faculty.' Perhaps he did not take cognisance of the fact that both Yogendra Singh and myself too had rural backgrounds!

M.N. Panini, who was teaching at the Department of Humanities and Social Sciences at the Indian Institute of Technology, Delhi did his MA in Economics and M.Litt in Sociology from Delhi School of Economics (DSE). Given the interdisciplinary thrust at CSSS it was prudent to have a person who could teach and research in economic sociology. But the general perception was that what mattered in his selection was his 'kin capital': being the nephew of M.N. Srinivas, who was closely associated with JNU in general and a member of the Working Group of CSSS. It is not uncommon in India that people relegate to the background a person's achievements if she/he has the requisite connections. Viewed thus I was fortunate not to have any political or academic patrons/ connections. The appointment of Nandu Ram as Assistant Professor in 1978 brought about a radical shift in the social composition of the Centre and in fact of the School of Social Science in JNU. He was the first Dalit (Scheduled Caste) faculty member and the policy of reservation (By 2015 the Centre had several members from the SC/ST category) had not been introduced in JNU at that time. Nandu had completed his masters from Banaras Hindu University and PhD from IIT (Kanpur). His competitor, among others, was Ehsanul Haq, the first PhD of the Centre, and I was his PhD supervisor. Incidentally this happened when I was the Chairperson, and Haq told me that he was given the impression that his non-selection was the resultant of the Chairperson's 'wrong strategy'. And, he became my permanent enemy.

As is well known, Selection Committees in Indian Universities, certainly in Central Universities, have a complex composition. In the case of JNU it was more complicated. The Committee under reference had to select a professor in social anthropology, in addition to an assistant professor in sociology. Therefore, it had three experts who were all very distinguished sociologists/social anthropologists. As usual, the Vice-Chancellor chaired the meeting and the mandatory presence of Visitor's nominee was ensured. In JNU those days, the norm was that a senior professor from the Centre too was nominated to the Selection Committee which was Yogendra Singh. Thus, there were six persons on the Committee, in addition to me, the mere Chairperson of the Centre, who was the junior most member of the Committee. To attribute the selection or rejection of a candidate to the junior most, and hence the least significant, member of the Committee is the most ludicrous. And yet, human beings tend to believe what is convenient to them and I don't fault Haq for endorsing what was told to him. From Haq's point of view it was very legitimate to expect that he would be selected because he was a PhD of the Centre and the Chairperson of the Centre was also his PhD Supervisor. While we all assert that human beings are rational, the fact is that we are rationalisers rather than rational.

There was indeed a paradigm shift in 1986 in the composition of the Centre's faculty with the entry of Patricia Oberoi and Tiplut Nongbri, two women faculty members. For fifteen long years from 1971 to 1986, the Centre was staffed exclusively by men, and no concerted efforts were made to recruit women. It is necessary to note here that recruiting faculty members of particular socio-cultural backgrounds is also a compulsion of the academic milieu. By the 1970s, the importance of researching on 'women in society' surfaced in Indian social science. By the mid-1980s, the need to view issues through the gender lens came to be widely recognized and CSSS was one of the earliest academic centres in India to introduce 'Gender and Society' courses for master's and post-master's courses. The initial deficit with regard to gender also stands rectified; at least one third of the faculty were women by 2015.

What was true of gender studies was equally true of subaltern and minority studies. Although Nandu Ram joined the Centre just seven years after it was established, and also in spite of the fact that several optional courses on these themes were listed, most of these courses were not taught. Nongbri was the first Scheduled Tribe faculty member to join the Centre. A large number of M.Phil and PhD students researched on Scheduled Castes and Scheduled Tribe and a handful even on religious minorities. But with the subaltern turbulence in India by 1980s, not only that a substantial number of faculty members of these backgrounds were recruited to the faculty but courses on the theme/themes relating to these categories also came to be taught as MA and M.Phil courses. I have often felt that there is a close link between the biographical background of knowledge producers and disseminators and the themes they researched/taught. An examination of this hypothesis seems to be an enterprise worth attempting.

The social composition of the CSSS faculty largely reflects the stupendous socio-cultural diversity in India. They are drawn from all the regions of India, but the western region is somewhat under-represented. The CSSS faculty members are also drawn from the different religious groups, but there was no deliberate effort to create this impressive diversity, except in the case of SCs and STs for which policy prescription exists. Further, unlike in some Centres, the CSSS faculty do not belong to any committed political or ideological group.

However, this does not mean that no effort was made to induct left-leaning faculty members to CSSS. I remember that a Centre-wise list of faculty members based on their ideological orientations–leftists and non-leftists–were made in the late 1970s and the CSSS had a huge deficit in this context. Informal discussions and consultations were held to bring in scholars like A.R. Desai and P.C. Joshi (the economic sociologist) who were known as Marxists. But the first recruitment of a leftist to CSSS was that of Nirmal Singh, who was teaching at the Rajasthan University for a long time. He was senior in age even to Yogendra Singh who was professor and chair of the Centre and came to JNU as the deputy director of the Northern Regional Centre of ICSSR at JNU. He was a former member of the CPI and his joining the Centre added a new dimension, that of political-ideological diversity.

The point which needs to be underlined in achieving this socio-cultural and ideological diversity is that CSSS followed an open policy in recruiting its faculty. Indeed equity can be achieved through transparency. This point is also reinforced by the fact that over 50 per cent of the faculty are not trained at the Centre, academic incest being a widespread pathology which prevails in most departments which boast of a high academic quality.

I spent three decades at the CSSS and it is but natural that I experienced moments of joy as well as sheer desperation, conditioned by the organizational structure. I was the chairperson of the CSSS for five years in two instalments; the first term for three years and by the time I became eligible for the second term, it was reduced to two years in the university.

The administrative responsibilities associated with the chairperson's position is arduous, particularly his role in the recruitment of students and faculty. To give a flavour of this, I'll narrate a few instances.

JNU's admission process was/is an admirable one, involving elected student representatives on the Student Faculty Committee (SFC). The idea is laudable but it presupposes great integrity both on the part of the faculty and students. The divisive factors are one, the high socio-cultural diversity of both students and faculty based on religion, caste and language and two, their ideological polarization based on political affiliation. The intensity of this divide varies from Centre to Centre but no Centre is entirely exempt from it. At the CSSS, there was no sharp ideological–political polarization of the faculty during my time, but students were clearly divided into political camps–leftists and free thinkers. The admission process ended with the meetings of the SFC, consisting of an equal number (five each) of students and faculty members who were nominated. The contentious issues were the number of students to be admitted and their background, the students always wanting the maximum number to be accommodated.

The numbers to be admitted is complicated by the points allotted to written and oral (interviews) tests as well as the deprivation points. Out of 100, twenty points were allotted for deprivation, taking into account the district in which applicant was born, parental income and the caste/tribe background. While the caste/tribe certificate can be occasionally false, the district data was the most reliable, as the information was based on the Indian census data. But the most manipulated aspect was the income certificate. I remember two distinct cases: in one case both the father and mother of the applicant were MPs and in the other, the applicant's father owned a stud farm–but both produced the required low income certificates. I used to say, 'Income certificates do not reflect the material condition of the certified but the moral condition of the certifier.'

The issue of the huge gap in scores between the written and oral tests was also a source of tension. Some students who scored very high marks in written tests scored rather poor marks in the interview and vice versa, students often alleging that this gap was due to the elite bias of faculty members traced to competence in the English language. Often this gap between written and oral tests metamorphoses into rural versus urban and more uncomfortably, into Hindi versus English tensions. Unfortunately, this perception was not always confined to students but also infected faculty members which created a lot of bad blood among them. The target of attack both of students and their faculty sympathizers would be the hapless chairpersons. If the chairperson was perceived to be urban, English-medium educated and from a non-Hindi region, she/he would be an easy target.

Merit versus deprivation scores often got the SFC into ugly situations which affected the admission process adversely. For example, if an applicant with zero scores in deprivation got say fifty-six marks out of eighty and another applicant got fifty marks out of eighty but had seven marks out of the twenty earmarked for deprivation, thus scoring fifty-seven marks, and if the cut off was fixed at fifty-seven, the former with a higher score based on merit would not get admitted. Further, fixing the cut-off point was often tricky because increasing or decreasing the cut-off by one point could make a substantial difference, increasing the total number of admissions.

Since the required scores for SCs and STs were slightly less and their quota being, 15 per cent for SCs and 8 per cent for STs, it meant a strenuous tightrope walk while finalizing the admission list. In the case of the MPhil courses, it was still more complex, because the top six rankers were eligible for fellowships and while these were based on merit, ranking could not be so because of deprivation points. In negotiating and settling these cases, the chairpersons of the Centres had a tension-prone and conflict-ridden role because of the tendency of some members in SFC to ignore norms and principles.

The recruitment of faculty was especially tricky if the competitors were from within the specific Centre, the competition between an insider and outsiders being less problematic. Thus when I was appearing for my professorship interview in 1976, my formidable competitor was D.N. Dhangare who was teaching at IIT Kanpur those days. On seeing me sitting among the interviewees he commented, 'Had I known that you were a candidate I would not have come.' I learnt from informal sources that a concerted effort was made to induct Dhangare into the CSSS, partly to rectify the deficit of not having an acknowledged 'Marxist' on the Centre's faculty. But his non-selection did not create any friction within the Centre.

When Associate M.N. Panini appeared for his professorship, there were three aspirants from within: Venugopal who became an associate professor after Panini, J.S. Gandhi and Dipankar Gupta. Venugopal did not apply but both Gandhi and Dipankar did. I was the chairperson when the selection committee selected Panini although the committee commended on the competence of Dipankar and suggested that he should be appointed professor as soon as a vacancy arose. I was told that a pamphlet in circulation soon after the results of the selection and complained about the 'injustice' done and Dipankar Gupta came to my office at the Centre and shouted, 'You always talk about the need for promoting merit, but what you did is contrary to that.' Once again, the chairperson, the junior-most in the selection committee, was held responsible for what happened in the selection committee meeting! Panini's selection was also attributed to my pro-south Indian orientation–an example of the price one paid for holding office.

One of the joys of working at the CSSS was the intermeshing of teaching and research. Thus faculty members could introduce courses on themes they researched, most optional courses being formulated on that basis. Similarly, the supervisor's research interests could also be pursued and reinforced through those students who worked with him/her for MPhil dissertations and PhD theses. However, this in no way circumscribed the students' choice of topics. Thirty-eight students completed their PhD under my supervision on a wide variety of topics.

The relationship between the research supervisor and research scholars is one of 'intimate tension'. In the case of classroom teaching, the teacher–taught relationship is that of an individual and group, but the research supervisor and research student have a one-to-one relationship for a long time, usually for a minimum of three to four years, sometimes even up to a decade. As in all human relationships there would be ups and downs in this context also. Most students acknowledge their indebtedness to the research supervisors, but not all of them.

Out of the thirty-eight PhD theses completed under my supervision, quite a few were published and most of them acknowledge the fact that they worked with me. However, some would evade even mentioning the research supervisor's name or camouflage it. One student listed a dozen persons to whom he was indebted, including me, without specifying that I was his supervisor. Another wrote in the book he published based on his thesis: 'I gratefully acknowledge Oommen's comments and suggestions on the preliminary draft of the book', but I had gone through at least three drafts of his PhD thesis! A third student expressed her gratitude for the constructive criticism offered without revealing that I was her PhD supervisor. Yet another mentioned that the book was based on the doctoral thesis he did at CSSS, again omitting my name. It is quite possible that PhD students might not have benefited from their research supervisors' guidance, but the fact that they completed their thesis under that guidance ought to be made explicit. Not doing this is like denying one's maternity.

In India, the teacher–student relationship, particularly the relationship between the research supervisor and the supervised, is patterned after the traditional guru–sishya (disciple) relationship. If one fancies that it is a professional relationship, one is grossly mistaken. It is common that felicitation volumes are published honouring teachers and colleagues. But in spite of the fact that thirty-eight students had completed their PhD theses and many more their MPhil dissertations, no felicitation volume was published to honour me. I know of two unsuccessful attempts. One was initiated by Tanveer Fazal, R. Tirunavukkarasu and Nabanipa Bhattacharjee, who wanted to publish a book entitled *Conversations with T.K. Oommen* and another by professors G.K. Karanth, Rajendra Singh and N. Rajaram who completed their PhD during 1985–86 and were to jointly edit a volume in my honour, but no progress made. The latest is a project launched by Susan Viswanathan and Vineeta Menon, whom I taught for their MA, to edit a felicitation volume. The project is yet to fructify.

There are also instances of research scholars not being accepted by supervisors. At CSSS the usual practice, particularly at the initial stages, was that research scholars could discuss their topics with prospective research guides after which there would be a mutual agreement to work as research supervisor and research student. There were also instances of 'stealing' brighter students. I was appointed as professor of 'sociology of social movements', perhaps the first of its kind in an Indian university, so those who wanted to work in this area would discuss their topic with me. Thus Dipankar Gupta who was very keen to work on the Shiv Sena movement in Maharashtra discussed the topic with me. When in the course of our conversation he characterized the Shiv Sena as a fascist movement, I told him, 'Dipankar, you don't have to do any research on the movement because you have already arrived at your conclusion.' Eventually, he did work on the same movement but with Yogendra Singh. Similarly, Anjan Ghosh wanted to work with me on the 'Political Mobilization of Coalmine Workers' invoking the Marxian framework. When I told him that preliminary empirical work was needed before finalizing the theoretical framework, he shifted to M.N. Panini as his supervisor. These instances show that if potential supervisors do not endorse the students' predetermined ideas, the arrangement does not work out.

Institutions and organizations give birth to their own folklore, which is also about personality clashes. If these do not exist, they are manufactured and gossiped about. As far as I know, I had no supporters within the CSSS who would stand by me irrespective of contexts, while Yogendra Singh did command a set of loyalists over which he had no control. Some of them would go out of the way to spread misinformation that I, Oommen, led a faction that constantly endangered the harmony of the Centre by challenging Singh's authority.

Maitrayee Chaudhari made a fleeting reference to this in her article on CSSS published in 2011. It is extremely difficult to verify who says what about whom but the victims cannot escape the brunt of backbiting. Let me recall an instance. I was visiting Baroda sometime in the 1980s where I met I.P. Desai, the most transparent and affable Indian sociologist I have known. As I was leaving, he said amiably, 'Oommen, give my namaste to Yogendra–that is, if you are on talking terms with him.' I don't recall any breakdown of communication between me and Singh in our three-decade long collegiality but Desai, who lived in far away Gujarat knew about it!

The deanship of schools in JNU are usually offered to the senior-most professors in rotation for two years. I became professor in 1976 and by 1990 my turn for a deanship arrived. However, it was a very inopportune moment to accept the position for two reasons. I was elected as president of the International Sociological Association (ISA) in July 1990 and was also invited to be a visiting professor in the department of sociology, University of California at Berkeley beginning August 1990 for one semester. Under the circumstances I decided to opt out of the deanship. But both VC M.S. Agwani and Registrar P.N. Sharma persuaded me not to reject the important position and taking their suggestion, I requested Yogendra Singh and he was good enough to accept the deanship for one semester, when I would be away to California. Thus my tenure as the dean of the School of Social Sciences was only for three semesters, January 1991 to June 1992.

Generally speaking, the dean's role was less problematic than the chairperson's, but since the School of Social Science had a number of academic luminaries, the dean had to be the adjudicator when issues cropped up between students and faculty members. I recall an instance in the Centre for the Study of Regional Development (CSRD) relating to the appointment of examiners for a PhD thesis, which illustrates the kind of issues the dean had to handle. The research supervisor was a geologist and the rest of the faculty were economists, geographers and demographers. The usual practice in all Centres was that the supervisors provided a list of four to five names in the order of preference for the Centre to approve. But it had to be approved by the dean also through the Committee for Advanced Studies and Research (CASR). There was a disagreement on the order of preference indicated and the formidable faculty of CSRD wanted their position to be upheld. I took the position that as it was a thesis in the area of geology, the supervisor was more knowledgeable and hence the Centre should go by his suggestion. There was much debate suffused with acrimony in the CASR, which ended only when some members of the CASR observed that the dean's position was a principled one and accepted the supervisor's position, much to the chagrin of the CSRD faculty.

I was also the Co-ordinator of Special Assistance Programme (SAP) of UGC at CSSS. I succeeded Yogendra Singh, the first co-ordinator. As my five-year tenure as co-ordinator of SAP was about to finish, I wrote to the Vice Chancellor that the next senior-most professor was Ravindra K. Jain who may be appointed to the position. To my utter surprise a couple of faculty members informed the V.C that Jain was an anthropologist and hence was not eligible for the position. When I wrote and spoke about the distinction between Sociology and Social Anthropology these faculty members disapproved it. But they discovered the distinction between the two cognate disciplines when they thought that it was necessary to grab a position. I often found that taking inconsistent positions was an asset to achieve one's objectives.

As individuals, most faculty members of CSSS were conscientious teachers and competent researchers, but as a team the performance of the faculty was rather poor. The

Centre had initiated three research projects at the initial stage and none of them fructified as collective enterprises. In the early 1970s, sociology in India was under the shadow of British social anthropology, the dominant approach in research being collection and analysis of qualitative data through participant observation. In fact, quantitative data relating to the macro level was associated with economists and at the micro level with psychologists. Political scientists also collected and analysed quantitative data with reference to analysis of electoral behaviour. But most sociologists in India shunned collection and analyses of quantitative data at that time. CSSS too did not have had the resources–funds and personnel–or the inclination to undertake large-scale surveys. In spite of these limitations, the Centre decided to launch a project on 'Social Indicators' to identify and operationalize indicators to measure and understand phenomena such as development, social change, social conflict based on secondary data, most of which had been generated by official agencies. In fact, the Centre appointed a statistical assistant who worked on the project for several years, but nothing came out of this project.

The second project initiated by CSSS was on social movements. Five faculty members were involved in the project, analysing movements of their choice and writing substantial research papers of roughly fifty printed pages on each movement. Yogendra Singh opted to study the neo-Buddhist movement in Uttar Pradesh in collaboration with Ramsagar Singh who was a research assistant at CSSS. As far as I know nothing was published based on this study. I had initiated the study of agrarian movement in Kerala but since the project did not fructify, my book *From Mobilization to Institutionalization; The Dynamics of Agrarian Movement in 20th Century Kerala*, emerged out of the project. P.N. Mukherjee analysed the

Naxalbari movement with special reference to West Bengal in a monograph and a few papers, while C.N. Venugopal's study of the Lingayat movement in Karnataka and K.L. Sharma's study of the Jharkhand movement in Bihar also led to the publication of several papers. Thus a project which started as a collective endeavour of five faculty members resulted in publications by four of them–but as a team effort, it was a failure.

The third project initiated by the Centre was called 'Craft of Social Research in India' and three faculty members were frontally involved: Yogendra Singh, P.N. Mukherjee and myself. There were two volumes on doing field work in India, one edited by Andre Beteille and T.N. Madan published in 1975 and the second by Srinivas and others published in 1979, which presented a very limited perspective on sociological research in India, reducing it to doing field work through 'participant observation'. In contrast, 'Craft of Social Research' wanted to capture the wider and indeed the whole picture of social research pursued in India by social scientists, particularly sociologists and political scientists. Studies which collected and analysed data from documents, respondents, informants and through observation–participant and non-participant–were taken into account. Contributors included I.P. Desai, Ramakrishna Mukherjee, Rajini Kothari, Y.B, Damle, the three editors and several others. We did receive many papers and spent numerous hours editing them, but the volume remained stillborn. I remember I.P. Desai once asking, 'Will you people bring out the volume before my death?' Disgusted with the delay he published his paper in the *Economic and Political Weekly*.

All the three projects CSSS launched at the initial stages were not simply innovative but pioneering. The publications emerging out of these projects could have provided a distinct academic flavour to CSSS. But alas, this did not happen. Thus the Centre remained an aggregation of academics without an organic unity. This diversity without unity was both an asset and a liability, an asset in that it provided the required autonomy to individual faculty members to flourish academically, but a liability because the Centre could not leave a stamp on Indian sociology. Viewed retrospectively, it was due to inadequate academic leadership and I plead partially guilty to that.

I spent thirty-one years in JNU–from 1971 to 2002–and after retirement I was appointed as Emeritus Professor, although some of my former students who joined the faculty opposed it vehemently. Faced with such an impasse the then VC, Bhattacharya, an economist, sought the opinion of the then chairperson of the Indian Council of Social Science Research, Andre Beteille, but he played it safe by observing that the VC should go by the opinion of faculty. Perceiving it as factionalism in sociology, the VC sought the view of P.C. Joshi who was both an economist and a sociologist, his senior colleague at the Institute of Economic Growth. When a surprised Joshi asked the VC, 'How come Oommen is not an Emeritus yet?', the VC then took the decision and I became Emeritus Professor a few years after my retirement.

Let me close this account with the farewell that my colleagues at CSSS organized in October 2002 (see Appendix 1). Attended by a large number of sociologists from all over India, it was inaugurated by President K.R. Narayanan, a former VC of JNU with whom I had the privilege of working closely. When he joined JNU, I was the dean of Students Welfare–satirically referred to as the dean of Student Warfare. Since the DSW was to be appointed by the VC, I had submitted my resignation. The new VC requested me to continue but I resigned within six months as our styles of functioning vastly varied. He used to change decisions instantly because of pressure from student activists and I once had to tell him, 'Vice Chancellor, a good administrator should take decisions after due deliberations. But once the decision is taken s/he should stick to it at least for some time.' VC Narayanan got easily upset and perturbed about the style of functioning of the JNUSU and once he asked me in Malayalam, our common mother tongue, 'Will it help if we go and meet Swami (that is, communist leader and twice chief minister of Kerala, E.M.S Namboodiripad)?' I said, 'It may, but you will get numerous requests at the time of admission to accommodate budding comrades.' He dropped the idea instantly! In spite of our not so cordial relationship, President Narayanan was gracious enough to inaugurate my felicitation seminar.

M.N. Panini, my colleague, was the key figure in the seminar as the chairperson of the organizing committee. Several scholars from India and abroad presented papers in the three-day event on themes I had focused on–social movements, modern professions, citizenship and nation-building. But it went to financial and academic waste as the seminar papers are not published, the reason remaining a mystery.

Quite a few scholars wrote to me as I was preparing to leave JNU, but one letter, which was from Satish Sabarwal, a fellow sociologist who worked at the Centre for Historical Studies, JNU wrote on 19 October 2002, moved me. He wrote:

Dear T.K., I gather you will soon be completing your JNU innings! Surely you can look back on a fulfilling career, making significant contributions to the shaping of the discipline as well as your department, not least through the long lines of your students. You will no doubt continue to play several other innings simultaneously in the years to come, much to the joy of your countless admirers, among them me.

For the first time in my life I discovered that I, too, have admirers in this world!

My teacher, Y.B Damle, who lived in Pune, could not attend as Rekha Damle, his wife passed away a few days before the event. But Damle wrote an 'ode' which I am reproducing below as compliments from one's teacher yields great gratification.

An Ode to Professor T.K. Oommen

I have had the privilege and pleasure of being associated with Professor Oommen for over forty years and I have been closely watching and of course enjoying his phenomenal professional growth. I had congratulated myself for being able to participate in the major event of his Felicitation Seminar. However, heaven decreed otherwise! Right from the inception of his career Prof. Oommen has thought it fit to question the Western formulations regarding Rural-Urban continuum and later on the entire Western sociological theory or for that matter social theory in general, be it of Marxian variant or the so called liberal type. At the same time he has also been a critical student of the so called tradition bound explanation and inspirations of social change by using traditional idioms and values. His concern for the analysis of 'Protest and Social Change' evinces his emphasis on the processual aspect of social change.

Prof. Oommen has taken upon himself the task of critically examining the favourite not to say naive concepts like 'Nation and Ethnicity' in view of the diversities, some of which according to him cannot be wished away and hence even at the risk of courting unpopularity he has continuously challenged the idea of a nation and instead suggested that India is composed of different nationalities. Likewise Prof. Oommen has suggested important amendments for the study of social movement. Situational analysis has been his forte. He does not shy away from critically examining not to say rejecting 'pet formulations' which stem from western experience. I would not hesitate to call him 'Charvak of Indian Sociology'. He has been one of the most prolific, prodigious and productive scholars perhaps next only to Prof. G.S. Ghurye. I would end by wishing him 'all the best and continuance of sustained, prolific and productive work'.

(Y.B. Damle)
Pune, 18 October 2002

CHAPTER 5

The XI World Congress of Sociology: Global Acclaim and Local Vilification

Forming associations is a well-known trend among all professional groups, including academics, and the International Sociological Association (ISA) was founded in 1949 under the auspices of UNESCO. At its inception only twenty-one countries were represented in the ISA. The World Congress of Sociology (WCS) is a quadrennial event of the International Sociological Association (ISA). The first WCS was held in Zurich, Switzerland in 1950 with 124 participants drawn from thirty countries. From 1950 to 1962, the WCS met at an interval of three years and after that it became a once-in-four years event. Of the first ten Congresses, six were held in West Europe, two in North America, one in East Europe (Bulgaria) and one in Latin America (Mexico). That is, in the then tripartite division of the world, the First World had eight out of ten Congresses, while the Second World and the Third World had only one Congress each. But Asia and Africa did not have had a single WCS till the mid-1980s and it is against this background that the significance of the XI WCS is to be discerned. Even the theme of the XI WCS had the stamp of a developing country committed to planned economic development, such as India. It was: 'Social Change–Problems and Perspectives'.

Attended by 2600 delegates from eighty-one countries, the WCS was massive in its scale. The Indian delegates to the WCS varied between five and fifty till then but 1050 Indian delegates attended the XI WCS as it was held in New Delhi. Some 100 sociologists of Indian origin living and working outside India also attended it. Nearly 200 resident Indian sociologists enrolled as members of the ISA after the XI WCS and became active participants of the ISA Research Committees (RCs). The Indian Sociological Society (1SS), the official association of Indian sociologists, was established in 1951.

RCs of the ISA are research groups of fifty to 200 specialists drawn from a wide variety of countries. Subsequently, several practices of the ISA were adopted by the ISS, the two notable ones being establishing RCs and conducting workshops for young sociologists at the venue of ISS conferences to facilitate close interactions between established professional elders and budding bright sociologists. It is no exaggeration to suggest that the XI WCS put India on the world map of sociology.

The ISA Congress had a three-tier structure in addition to the inaugural session. The presidential session was the opening plenary meeting and the valedictory session was the plenary chaired by the vice president (Programmes). The six symposia sessions were held as parallel sessions in the forenoon. The nearly forty RCs attended by fifty to 250 delegates were also held as parallel sessions in the afternoon, needing as many rooms. Each RC held up to six to ten sessions, some stretching up to midnight. This means the Congress had to be held in buildings with huge halls (for the two plenary sessions) which could accommodate 2000 to 3000 persons, six rooms seating 500 to 800 persons for symposia and forty rooms which could fit in fifty to 250 delegates. Since all this accommodation could not be found under one roof, the Congress proceedings were held in three nearby places with continuous transportation facilities. The Indian National Organizing Committee (INOC) formed by the ISS also provided lunches and beverages within the Congress premises.

To hold a WCS was and is perceived as a great achievement by national associations and the ISS should be justly proud of the XI WCS. However, the task of making the ISA agree to hold its Congress in one of the Third World countries was indeed tortuous in those days of the pre-liberalization era. Given the prevailing scepticism of ISA decision-makers, predominantly drawn from the First World, it was indeed difficult to break the ice. The ISA decided to send a three-person delegation to New Delhi, an unprecedented step, to evaluate the available infrastructure. Most of the previous World Congresses were held in universities but the XI WCS was to be held mainly in hotels–the Ashok and Taj–in New Delhi in addition to a few smaller sites such as the Vishwa Yuvak Kendra, situated very close to Hotel Ashok. The delegation was impressed with the proposed arrangements and consented to the ISS proposal. The idea of holding the XI WCS in Delhi was mooted by the Dubes (S.C. Dube and Leela Dube) who participated in the X WCS held in Mexico in 1982 and was vigorously pursued by M.S. Gore and Y.B. Damle, ISS presidents during 1981–82 and 1983–84 respectively. V.S. D'Souza succeeded Damle and was the ISS president during 1985–86. My name as secretary general of the WCS was initially proposed by Damle and approved in 1985 by D'Souza.

My first task as secretary general of the WCS was to create an organizational structure acceptable to most Indian sociologists. I proposed a three tier structure–the Indian National Organizing Committee (INOC), an INOC Working Committee and seven sub-committees. The INOC consisted of thirty-nine members–social scientists, technocrats and bureaucrats–of which nineteen were located in Delhi/New Delhi. Of the thirty-nine INOC members, only seventeen were sociologists or social anthropologists. But the real challenge was to identify a chairperson and several names were floated by different groups/factions. At that juncture I suggested that the senior-most living president of the ISS should be the chairperson of the INOC, because the Congress was hosted by the ISS. The principle was unanimously endorsed and M.N. Srinivas became the chair.

The Congress was inaugurated on 18 August. An INOC working committee was constituted to manage the Congress, the ex-officio chairperson being the then president of the ISS, Victor S. D'souza. I was the secretary general and P.N. Mukherji, was the treasurer. Each of the seven sub-committees had a convenor engaged in national promotion, press and media, social events, accommodation, transportation, documentation and resource mobilization. The Congress bankers were the American Express and the State Bank of India, the official carriers were Air India and Indian Airlines and the official Congress organizer was the Travel Corporation of India. In spite of such an elaborate organizational structure almost all tasks had to be handled by me as the secretary general. Some of the committee members rarely responded to communications and a handful even spread misinformation which adversely affected the management of the Congress.

One of the formidable tasks I had to handle was ensuring the issue of visas for foreign citizens and non-resident Indians, the most excruciating of my experiences being related to delegates from Israel and South Africa, with whom India had hardly any diplomatic relations those days. Matters got complicated because the ISS had to sign a memorandum of understanding (MoU) with the ISA which explicitly stated that all bonafide delegates intending to attend the Congress would get visas. The INOC had to pay a high 'political price' for insisting on this. When the Congress preparations started, we approached Indira Gandhi, the then prime minister who agreed to inaugurate it on 18 August 1986, but she was assassinated in October 1984. When we approached Rajiv Gandhi, her son and successor, two conditions were put forward: no delegate from Israel would be permitted to attend the Congress and two, only those delegates from South Africa cleared by the African National Congress (ANC) would be given visas by the Government of India. Both these conditions went against the letter and spirit of the MoU signed between ISA and INOC. After several negotiations with the representatives of the Government of India I decided to forgo the political advantage of getting the XI WCS inaugurated by the prime minister of India and stood by the commitment given to the ISA by the INOC.

The South African case was easier of the two to handle. All delegates from South Africa had to produce a letter from the resident representative of the African National Congress (ANC) at New Delhi, certifying that they were not supporters of the apartheid regime, to be endorsed by the Secretary General of INOC. Handling the Israeli delegates was more cumbersome because the bona fide delegates were to be certified by the ISA office which functioned from Amsterdam those days. Communication was not easy at that time, emails almost absent and telegrams as sluggish as ever. The most efficient and speedy mode of communication was a telex which had to be very brief. If one wanted elaborate information about a particular delegate it was not easy to obtain. To complicate matters there was only one telex in JNU those days, in the VC's office. My familiarity with Israeli delegates was limited and a lot of time was spent finding out about the background of the Israeli delegates to the XI WCS. Mercifully their number was limited to only around a dozen.

The point to be underlined here is the undesirable mixing of professional/academic matters with political/diplomatic relations. Delegates to academic conferences being professionals should not be viewed through the political lens, but this is precisely what happens most of the time, which thwarts the free flow of knowledge producers and disseminators.

The most arduous task was resource mobilization and to complicate matters while seeking permission from the Government of India to hold the Congress in Delhi, Damle was asked to give a written undertaking that no financial help would be sought from the government for the Congress. The rent-free WCS office was located at JNU and the first institutional contribution of Rs 10,000 also came from the then VC P.N Srivastava. My workload was heavy, the organizing WCS stretching upto eighteen months on an average of twelve hours a day. I had to attend numerous meetings and interact with many persons, and used my own car without charging the INOC or ISS. When all accounts of the Congress were settled, there was a surplus of rupees ten lakhs which within six years became 35 lakhs.

It is worth re-calling the experience of raising funds for the XI WCS. I wrote to more than a hundred universities and research institutes requesting financial contributions, but only ten contributed; the donations ranging from Rs 5000 to 10,000. Government funding was the only hope, so I met Gopi Arora, an IAS officer with an extremely positive attitude towards higher education, who occupied a crucial position in the PMO. After hearing that the XI WCS was the first ever social science Congress in India with a global reach, Arora was surprised that my request was for only Rs 10 lakhs–finally he sanctioned Rs 18 lakhs! This was indeed a pleasant surprise and in contrast to my experience with others who occupied top positions in the field of higher education. For example, the then secretary of the Ministry of Education told me that he had received complaints about the misuse of funds collected for the WCS from a Member of Parliament, who was a sociologist. When the secretary remarked sarcastically, 'Oommen, you have lost your virginity,' I retorted, 'All of us need not hold virginity as a great virtue in all contexts.'

Although the nodal ministry for the WCS was the Ministry of Education (now the Ministry of Human Resource Development), the organization through which it functioned for our purpose was the Indian Council of Social Science Research (ICSSR) and G. Parthasarathi, the then chair of the ICSSR, and the first VC of JNU was a tower of strength in organizing the XI WCS. I telephoned C. Rangarajan, the then governor of the RBI with whom I had a nodding acquaintance at Jaipur where he was a reader in economics when I was a research scholar. He agreed to pay Rs 3.5 lakhs, which was the upper limit of his financial discretionary power. My meeting with K.R. Narayanan, the then Minister of External Affairs, also a former VC of JNU, brought in another Rs 3 lakhs.

The most interesting meeting in this connection was with Manmohan Singh, the then deputy chairman of the Planning Commission. After hearing me out, Manmohan Singh, who was extremely polite in receiving and communicating with the three-member delegation, offered one lakh and added, 'The Commission has no precedent in giving more than this amount for such a purpose.' The senior colleagues who accompanied me did not utter a word, but I broke the silence and said, 'Singh, men and women are often remembered for breaking old precedents and creating new ones.' Singh then graciously agreed to give three lakhs. I learnt later that he broke this new precedent by offering Rs 15 lakhs for the World Congress of Economics which was held in December 1986 in New Delhi.

The XI WCS was widely praised as a thumping success: remarks from delegates of the First World including 'A Congress which appeared to attract nothing but positive comments,' 'The New Delhi year will be remembered by a great many sociologists', 'The organization of the Congress was perfect', 'This is one of the best ever'.

In contrast, my 'rewards' and 'recognition' from fellow sociologists in India are indeed painful. Let me recount just two instances. As the WCS was drawing to a close, the ISA Executive Committee for the next four years (1986–90) was to be elected; the ISA practice was to elect at least one member to the ISA Executive Committee from the country which hosted the World Congress. The process of nomination was informal and the consent of the candidates was not even sought. On the last but one day (that is, 22 August) the *Congress Bulletin* broke the news that I was one of the members of the new EC and had polled the largest number of votes. This news must have been unpalatable to many but a couple of my colleagues at JNU took the initiative to vilify me in print through one Mahajan, a legal correspondent of *Hindustan Times* who had nothing to do with sociology or the WCS. His attack was vicious and vitriolic, his main point being that I was not distinguished enough to be a member of ISA EC. But it was more upsetting that none of the 1050 Indian delegates who attended the XI WCS rebutted Mahajan's attack. However, I was happy that Martin Albrow, the founding editor of *International Sociology* in a letter to the editor of the *Hindustan Times*, roundly condemned Mahajan's comments. The most unsavoury part of this despicable incident was that it was inspired by a former student of mine who became a faculty of the Centre for the Study of Social Systems.

The other instance which pained me deeply was the accusation of financial corruption. After the XI WCS was held in Delhi, the ISS annual conference was held in December 1986 at Shillong where I was present as a delegate. A fellow sociologist there told me, 'Doctor sahib, the rumour doing the rounds is that you made at least 7 lakhs of rupees in the process of organizing the World Congress,' to which I retorted, 'Dr…, you people have always underestimated me, the actual amount I made was 12 lakhs!' As mentioned earlier, at the initial stage of organizing the WCS, I had spent money from my own pocket to fill petrol in my car to attend meetings. This incident illustrates the persisting paradox of Indian public life that those who handle public funds are perennial suspects.

The XI WCS started in a precarious financial position but it ended with a substantial surplus of Rs 10 lakhs. If the surplus money were not invested within five years some 30 per cent of it would be taxed by the government, so a standing committee was constituted to decide how to utilize the funds judiciously.

Fortunately, we located a flat near the then ISS office at Nelson Mandela Road that belonged to an income tax commissioner. He was willing to accept the entire amount in 'white' money as against the prevailing norm of paying at least half in 'black' and half in 'white'. Thus the XI WCS became an asset-creating device for the ISS.

CHAPTER 6

The Presidency at the International Sociological Association: The Crowning Glory

My acquaintance with the International Sociological Association (ISA) started only in 1985 when I was designated as the secretary general of the XI World Congress of Sociology. Then I was elected as the president of the ISA in 1990 at Madrid and this meteoric rise was a great triumph in my professional career–and calls for some elaboration.

The XI World Congress was a resounding success notwithstanding some negativities. I was elected as a member of the ISA Executive Committee in 1986 for a period of four years, but my first official exposure to the ISA EC was in 1985, exactly a year before the 1986 WCS. It was conventional to invite the key functionary to the last annual EC meeting to make a presentation about the state of preparedness regarding the forthcoming Congress. The last meeting of the outgoing EC (1982–86) was held in Lisbon, and I went there on behalf of the INOC. My presentation covering all aspects of the forthcoming 1986 Congress took an hour and the response was a thunderous applause.

During the four years (1986–90) of my ISA EC membership, I attended all the EC annual meetings as well as the meetings of the Membership and Finance Committee, one of the sub-committees of the EC, of which I was a nominated member, the other sub-committees being the Research Co-ordinating Committee, the Publications Committee and the Programme Committee. My membership was a great learning experience, the only constraint being finance for travel. The ISA norm in those days was that members had to raise the required travel funds, although local hospitality was provided by the host institution of the country in which the meeting took place. This norm continued during my presidency (1990–94) of the ISA during which I had to attend numerous meetings, including those of sub-committees. The usual practice I followed was to write to one or two well-known departments or institutes of sociology in the country or a neighbouring country about my visit so that they would ask me to deliver a couple of lectures for which I was paid. This was not always a smooth process and occasionally, tension-prone, because there was no guarantee of a financial flow. However, the gossip in circulation among some of my Indian colleagues was that I had amassed at least a crore of rupees through my foreign travels during my ISA presidency!

The venue of the XII World Congress of Sociology was Madrid, Spain. Nobody in the ISA circle thought that I was a likely presidential contestant. Two probable candidates were Neil Smelser, the well-known American sociologist, and Salvador Giner, president of the Spanish National Congress Organizing Committee (CECOM), the host organization of the XII World Congress. In fact Giner and his wife visited

New Delhi in June 1990 and told me that I should not contest because Smelser was a formidable candidate. Giner did offer support to me as one of the vice presidents if I withdrew from the presidential contest. Let me recall a hilarious incident in this connection.

When the Giners visited New Delhi and were staying with the Spanish ambassador, we invited them for a dinner at our residence. My wife prepared a dish with cauliflower in which finely chopped green chillies were added liberally. Giner found it unbearably hot, so much so that he thought he was going to die. He asked me to call a doctor immediately as I roared with laughter. At this point he may have imagined that it was an attempt to kill him so that I would have a smooth path to the ISA presidency!

The news about my probable candidature got around because I addressed a letter to all the presidents of national associations affiliated to the ISA, announcing my intention to contest. I was in two minds about contesting, but when I talked to Fernando H. Cardoso, the first ISA president (1982–86) from the Third World, he told me: 'T.K., if you contest, you will win.' This remark emboldened me and I decided to go for it.

One of the ISA rules regarding election to the EC was that if a contestant for the presidential polls got at least 10 per cent votes, s/he was then eligible to contest as a vice president. The inner circle of the ISA (read those from North America and West Europe) were convinced that Neil Smelser was invincible but I would poll enough votes to make me eligible to contest as one of the three vice presidents to take charge of Finance and Membership, a position devoid of any academic content. The election procedure of the ISA had to take place in three stages in succession: the presidential election, election of the three vice presidents and then members of the EC because those defeated in the 'higher' category can contest for the 'lower' one. When the result of the presidential election was announced almost everybody–including me–was stunned. Not only had I won but I had received 72 per cent of the total votes polled!

Although I won with an overwhelming majority I was not very happy, let alone excited, for two reasons: one was that I had defeated Smelser. He was like a mentor to me and when I had completed my PhD thesis in 1968, I wrote to him as I was very influenced by his classic *Theory of Collective Behaviour.* He replied promptly and asked for a copy of my manuscript on which he made copious comments that enabled me to revise the manuscript. The second reason was that the nomination committee did not approve Giner's candidature and he had to withdraw: It was Giner who first told me after listening to my vote of thanks in 1986: 'T.K. you should be our president'. (See Appendix-2)

When Neil Smelser congratulated me, I pleaded with him to be one of the vice presidents. He agreed to contest if I assigned him the position of vice president of the Programme Committee. I readily consented and he became vice president (Programmes), who automatically becomes the chair of the next World Congress on behalf of the ISA. The other two vice presidents were Daniel Bertaux (Research Council) from France and Vladimir Yadov (Membership and Finance) from the USSR. Of the thirteen EC members, one was from Latin America (Brazil), one from Asia (Singapore), two from East Europe (Hungary, Yugoslavia), seven from West Europe and one from North America.

For the first time in the history of the ISA, a president from the Afro-Asian World had been elected. Some Europeans and North Americans thought that I had been elected because I was a 'black' and some Indians pronounced that I was elected because I was a Christian. Denigrating achievements of a person who is not 'one of us' is a universal phenomenon. Although comparisons are odious let me recall a famous instance. Albert Einstein in an address at Sorbonne said, 'If my theory of relativity is proven successful, Germany will claim me as a German and France will declare that I am a citizen of the world. Should my theory be proven untrue, France will say I am German and Germany will declare that I am a Jew.'

The news about my election as president of the ISA was out on 11 May 1990. The European newspapers, particularly the Spanish papers, covered it prominently. The highlight of the reporting was that an Asian/Indian had became the president of the ISA for the first time. Most of the Indian delegates present at Madrid congratulated me and an impromptu informal congratulatory meeting was held.

Indian newspapers, both English and Hindi, reported the news, but parsimoniously, on 17 May and the Malayalam newspaper *Mangalam* interviewed me and published a full-page write-up after my return to India. I returned to Delhi on 18 May and several of my colleagues in JNU congratulated me. I received about 104 congratulatory letters, but the most laudatory one was from D. Narain, head, department of sociology, Bombay University which read:

> What glorious news that you have been elected president of [the] International Sociological Association, defeating Neil Smelser! Heartiest congratulations to you, from all my colleagues in the department and myself. On this unique honour to you and vicariously to all of us in India and indeed, Asia, we send you our warmest felicitations and good wishes.

Since it was vacation time no felicitation meeting could be held. However, students of the Centre for the Study of Social

Systems organized a felicitation meeting on 1 August which was chaired by Yogendra Singh. Those who spoke were Ravindra Jain, P.N. Mukherji, Nirmal Singh, Anand Kumar, Ashwini Ray, a political scientist, who was the then president of the JNU Teachers Association and several students. Strangely, the JNUTA did not hold any felicitation meeting although a sociologist, Dipankar Gupta, was the secretary at that time. It was conventional for JNUTA to hold felicitation meetings even when a colleague got appointed to high technocratic/bureaucratic positions, but mine was a professional achievement. However, several fellow social scientists in India were awestruck. One asked in disbelief, 'How did it happen?' Another wrote, 'It is equivalent to four vice chancellorships bundled into one.'

The attitude and response of the government of India was disappointing. Margaret Archer of the UK, my immediate predecessor, wrote a letter to the then prime minister, V.P. Singh, in July 1990 highlighting the importance of the ISA presidency and its relevance for India, but there was no response. I was amused to read four years later (in 1994) in the Indian newspapers that the then PM met and had congratulated Miss Universe of the year, an Indian. Perhaps a beauty queen is more relevant in building a knowledge society than an academic!

The ISA had 3000 individual members from eighty countries; in 1990 it was a federation of over fifty national sociological associations and also forty-four Research Committees. Admittedly the scale of the task the ISA president had to undertake was enormous. Margaret Archer had written, 'To assume this position is always a source of honour for one's own country and I am sure India will take great pride in Oommen's achievement, especially as this is the first time that a president of the ISA comes from the Afro-Asian region.' But the response to the communication was one of disturbing indifference.

An Indian became the ISA president only in its fortieth year; for eight years (1962–70) there was no representation from India. While there was a vice president from India during 1959–62, another Indian, Sujata Patel, became the ISA vice president during 1994–98.

Table 6.1 Indian Presence in International Sociological Association (ISA)

Period	Position in the I.S.A Executive	Person
1950-52*	Member	G.S. Ghurye
1953-56	Member	G.S. Ghurye
1956-59	Member	D.P. Mukerji
1959-62	Vice President	D.P. Mukerji
1962-66	Nil	––
1966-70	Nil	––
1970-74	Member	M.N Srinivas
1974-78	Member	Ramakrishna Mukherjee
1978-82	Member	Leela Dube
1982-86	Member	S.C. Dube
1986-90	Member	T.K. Oommen
1990-94	President	T.K. Oommen

* In the first four Executive Committees of ISA from 1950 to 1962, the tenure of the EC was three years and after that four years.

I cannot claim that my achievements as ISA president were spectacular but they were substantial. Till 1990, ISA stood on two unequal pillars: the ISA Council consisting of the presidents of national associations who elected the ISA president and the Research Council consisting of the forty-odd RCs who elected the vice president. While the Research Council had at least one inter-Congress meeting, in addition to the specific meetings of RCs, the ISA Council met only once in four years at the venue of the World Congress. Thus the ISA Council was an inactive body, so I initiated the practice of an interim meeting of the ISA Council in 1993 for the first time in the history of the ISA.

Although a world organization, the ISA functioned informally without clear-cut rules and regulations in several contexts. For example, when I was put up as a candidate for the position of the ISA EC membership in 1986, nobody took my consent. Given this background I thought that it was absolutely necessary to appoint a sub-committee to revise ISA statutes and bye-laws. The ISA Council met during August 10–11 1993, at Gavle (Sweden) to finalize the new statutes and bye-laws which came into effect on 1 January1994. According to the new procedure the names of candidates 'should be proposed and seconded by ISA members, the candidate should consent to contest and if elected, serve the ISA in the specified post for the required time-period.' This procedure was adapted from the Indian Sociological Society (ISS).

The new statutes also created the position of a fourth vice president (Publications) since publication activities of the ISA were substantial and no one was in charge. In 1994–98, a post for a fifth vice president (National Associations) was created. The two official languages of the ISA were English and French, but the new statutes recommended the adoption of Spanish as the third language. I also made an effort to create an ISA fund to tide over financial difficulties and an appeal was issued through the ISA *Bulletin* to all members to make a one-time contribution of one day's salary to be collected by the national associations and sent to the ISA office at Madrid to create a Corpus Fund (Appendix-3). But the appeal not only fell on deaf ears but met with opposition from some First World countries so this initiative was a dismal failure. My effort as the ISA president was to enhance the participation of all sociologists irrespective of gender and geography, to ensure a global presence in an association which was global only in form (Appendix-3).

After the amendment of statutes, the ISA Council, consisting of presidents of national associations affiliated to the ISA, started meeting once in two years, like the Research Council. The president and vice presidents came to be elected by the Joint Council consisting of the ISA Council and Research Council thereby augmenting their legitimacy for the entirety of ISA membership, both associational and individual.

The amendments brought about the increased democratization of the ISA's organizational structure and at least partly loosened the earlier stranglehold of a few countries. The efforts made by some members to transform the ISA into an individual membership association, which would have increased the entrenchment of countries with substantial individual membership, was scuttled. With the ISA Council and Research Council being put on an even keel both the associational interests (through the ISA Council) and individual interests (through the Research Council) are kept in balance.

The story of my ISA presidency would remain incomplete unless I narrate some of the difficulties encountered. That Salvador Giner, the eminent sociologist of Spain, was an aspirant to the ISA presidency has already been alluded to. But as the nomination committee did not shortlist him as a candidate for technical reasons (as he has already served two terms in the ISA Executive Committee), there was widespread discontent among the Spanish sociological community. In spite of that, the Spanish Sociological Federation (FES) had offered to hold the first ISA Council consisting of all presidents of national sociological associations affiliated to the ISA in Spain in 1992. But a communication from the executive secretary of the ISA to the FES infuriated the office-holders of the FES. To understand this, one needs to take into account two points.

Till 1990, the executive secretary of the ISA was a sociologist who functioned from his/her country with the office located in his university/institute. Thus the ISA office moved from place to place. But with the appointment of a non-sociologist as the executive secretary, the ISA office had to be at one place on a long-term or permanent basis. From 1986–90, the ISA office was at Amsterdam (the Netherlands) when Felix Geyer, a sociologist, was the executive secretary; in 1990 it was shifted to Madrid (Spain), and started functioning with Isabella Barlinska, a non-sociologist, as the executive secretary. This was a sea change in the administrative arrangement.

The other point relates to the structure of the ISA Council consisting of presidents of national associations. There was a likelihood of more than one national association from the same country claiming membership in the ISA Council and thereby claiming eligibility for more than one vote in the Council. Since the ISA follows the principle of one-country, one-vote, the problem of national associations from the same country claiming eligibility for more than one vote in the Council had to be solved by categorizing the national associations into A and B, allowing only category A to vote. Some countries solved the problem by assuming voting rights in alternate years of successive councils. For example, Canada with two national associations, one for English- and the other for French-speaking sociologists, voted alternately in the ISA Council. There are other national associations: one for 'academic' sociologists and the other for 'professional' or 'applied' sociologists. While this issue was discussed in a meeting at Tampere (Finaland) meeting no decision could be taken because it called for an amendment of ISA statutes. But the executive secretary informed the FES in a letter dated 19 June 1992 that the ISA EC had decided to elevate the status of the National College of Doctors and Bachelors of political science and sociology to the 'A' category. Understandably, the FES was upset about this decision, which meant amending the ISA statutes.

Francisco J. Llera, the president of the FES in his letter dated 10 July 1992 objected to the 'decision' and withdrew the invitation to hold the ISA Council meeting in Madrid in September 1992. While I reprimanded the executive secretary for writing the letter to the FES even before the minutes of the Tampere meeting had been approved by the chair, a few members of the EC supported her action. In the meantime an invitation to hold the ISA Council meeting in Madrid was received from the other national association of Spain (Professional Sociologists) who thought that they were an 'A' category member. But given the conflict between the two associations, academic and professional, I decided to postpone the council meeting. Thus the first ever ISA Council meeting took place in Gavle (Sweden) in August 1993 thanks to the initiative of Goran Therborn, an eminent sociologist of Sweden.

When the expectation that a Spanish sociologist would become the ISA president did not come through in 1990, the FES withdrew their offer to locate and finance the ISA secretariat at Madrid. In fact Llera wrote to me as early as 4 November 1991 that the FES would provide a rent-free office for the ISA only till December 1991 and the Spanish government would also withdraw its subsidy to ISA. I wrote to the king, the prime minister and the minister of education of Spain to let the status quo continue till the end of 1994 when the XIII World Congress was slated to take place, but the deep uncertainty regarding the ISA office in Madrid persisted. An attempt was then made to shift the ISA office to Paris, but a new obstacle arose because Isabella Barlinska, the executive secretary, refused to leave Madrid for Paris and expressed her desire to resign. Because it was not easy to locate an executive secretary with adequate knowledge of English in Paris, shifting the ISA office from Madrid to Paris was aborted. Isabella Barlinska continued to be the executive secretary and the ISA office remained in Madrid, bringing some continuity and efficiency but with the iron law of bureaucracy at play.

As a spin-off to my association with the ISA, I was drawn into a few other international academic associations such as the International Society for the Sociology of Religion (SISR), the International Conference for the Sociology of Religion (CISR) and the International Institute of Sociology (IIS). The SISR functions through an elected council, the tenure of the council being two years. I was a member of SISR Council for two terms: 1989–91 and 1993–95 and attended two of their conferences; one in Budapest and the other in Ireland. The organization publishes a well-regarded journal, *Social Compass* and I published two papers in it, one an invited comment on the paper 'The Sociology of Religion: 1945–1989' presented by the well-known sociologist of religion, James Beckford, in an SISR conference; the other a paper entitled 'Religion and Development in Hindu Society', presented by me in one of the plenaries of the SISR Conference held at Ireland.

I was a member of the CISR during the early 1990s and published a few research papers such as 'State and Religion in Multi-regions Nation-States: The Case of South Asia', in *The Journal of Oriental Studies* (in Japanese) and the *South Asian Journal* (in English); 'The Shifting Saliency of Religion in the Construction of Nationalism: The Indian Experience', in *Journal of Peace Studies* and 'Religious Nationalism and Democratic Polity: The Indian Case in *Sociology of Religion.* I am not a sociologist of religion and yet my association with the SISR and CISR prompted me to publish several papers in this area and facilitated my interaction with several specialists in the field such as James Beckford, K Dobbelare, L. Voye, R. Cipriani, B. Wilson, H. Ralston, J. Zylberberg, R. Campiche, E. Pace, G. Davie, W.H. Swatos to list a few. Thus, associational activities became my stimulants both for academic work and interpersonal interactions.

The SISR and CISR are not competitors of the ISA but rather, specialist associations focusing on a particular field. In contrast, International Institute of Sociology (IIS) is a parallel academic association; while the ISA is massive with a global reach and spread, the IIS is somewhat elitist and mainly confined to West Europe and North America. The IIS holds its conference once in two years. I have participated in two World Congresses of the IIS and in one of them was a co-organizer of a plenary session along with M. Sassaki of Japan, which had participants drawn from Belgium (E.H. Roosens), Bulgaria (N. Genov), the USA (S. Sassen) and France (Mattei Dogan), apart from the organizers. Ours was one of the five plenary sessions and its theme was 'Ethnicity, the Nation-State and Globalization'. I had introduced the plenary session with the poser: 'Citizenship, Nationality and Ethnicity in the Context of Globalization'.

I also participated in the thirty-sixth World Congress of IIS in 2004 held at Beijing, the first IIS Congress to be held in Asia. The theme of the Congress was 'Social Change in the Age of Globalization'. I was a speaker in the inaugural session and my presentation was titled: 'On the Historicity of Globalization: Construction and De-construction of "Others"'. This incidentally, is the opening paper in the book edited by Jing Tiankni, Masamichi Sassaki and Li Peilin consisting of eighteen select papers presented in the six plenaries, published by Brill (the Netherlands). I was also a member of IIS Executive Council during 2001–05 when Eliezer Ben-Rafael of Israel was its president. My first visit to China gave me an opportunity to observe the spectacular achievements of both ancient and contemporary China first-hand. Scaling the Great Wall of China right to the top and visiting the Oriental Pearl TV Tower, which resembles the Eiffel Tower of Paris, are experiences which I have always cherished.

The IIS, the first international association of social scientists, was established in Paris in 1893 by Rene Worms. The IIS used to publish Annals consisting of papers presented in its Congresses in addition to the *International Review of Sociology*, the first international journal of sociology. The Annals published my paper entitled: 'Social Movements and Social Policies: A Misplaced Polarity in Social Research' in 1992–93. When the *Review* celebrated its centenary in 1992 at Rome I was among the invitees. Among the well-known scholars associated with the IIS were Franz Boas, George Le Bon, Karl Mannheim, W.F Ogburn, P.A Sorokin, Georg Simmel, Werner Sombart, Gabriel Tarde, Ferdinand Tonnies, Thorstein Veblen, L.F Ward, Sidney Webb, Max Weber and Florain Znaniecki.

I got invitations from far and wide to attend seminars and conferences. For instance, when the 'Nordic Conference on

Social Movements in the Third World–Economy, Politics and Culture' was held at the University of Lund, Sweden in August 1993, I was invited to deliver the key-note address. Then a major conference on 'Nationalism, Identity and Minority Rights' was organized by the University of Bristol (UK) in September 1999 and attended by outstanding social scientists such as Jan Nederveen Pieterse, Rogers Brubaker, T.H. Eriksen, Will Kymlicka, Iris Marion Young, Bhikhu Parekh, Nira Juval-Davis and Craig Calhoun. I presented a paper: 'New Nationalisms and Collective Rights: The Case of South Asia', in the conference. My paper presented at the conference on 'Ethnic Diversity and Citizenship Education in Multi-Cultural Nation-States', held at Rockefeller Foundation's Study and Conference Centre in Bellagio, Italy in June 2002 was entitled: 'Crisis of Citizenship Education in the Indian Republic: Contestation between Cultural Monists and Pluralists'.

I suspect that familiarity with some of my papers might have prompted the editors of *The Sage Handbook on Nations and Nationalism,* Gerald Delanty and Krishna Kumar, to invite me to be a contributor, so I wrote on 'Nation and Nationalism in South Asia'. The forty-five chapters in the *Handbook* represented a variety of themes and regions and the contributors included such authorities on the subject as John A. Hall, Michael Hechtar, Ruth Wodak, Sylvia Walby, Liah Greenfield, Anthony D. Smith, Mark Juergensmeyer, Steve Fenton, Charles Turner, Bryan S. Turner, Anthony King, Gerald Delanty, among others.

Once a scholar is in circulation s/he gets noticed internationally. Thus when the Beijing Forum held a global convention in 2007 on the theme: 'The Harmony of Civilizations and Prosperity for All--Diversity in the Development of Human Civilization', I was invited to present a paper. One of the sub-themes of this global meet was 'Ethnic Relations and Religious

Co-existence' in which my paper on 'The State, Majority Religions Community and Co-existence of Religions: Situating Indian Republic' was presented.

In all these conferences and seminars my mission was to contest Western theories and concepts with the help of empirical reality from South Asia. I don't know whether I succeeded in my mission but it is for my South Asian colleagues to judge. I believe that invitations to these seminars and conferences occurred because of the global visibility I secured through the ISA.

CHAPTER 7

The XIII World Congress of Sociology

The first World Congress of Sociology was held in 1950 in Switzerland with a mere 124 delegates, not one of them Indian. If in the first four Congresses the delegates were in hundreds, from the fifth onwards the participation was in thousands. The highest attendance was in the XII Congress at Madrid when I was elected as president. I presided over the XIII Congress at Bielefeld. In the sixth Congress at Evian there was a substantial increase of Third World delegates, but only six Indian delegates. The number of Indian delegates increased to fourteen at the VII Congress at Varna and jumped to forty-eight at Toronto. The XI Congress at New Delhi witnessed what may be designated as the 'Indianization of the World Congress of Sociology', with nearly 50 per cent of the delegates drawn from India.

Table 7.1 World Congress of Sociology: 1950 - 1994

S. No.	Venue	Year	No. of delegates	Presidents
1	Zurich (Switzerland)	1950	124	Louis Worth (USA)
2	Liege (Belgium)	1953	281	Louis Worth (USA)
3	Amsterdam (Netherlands)	1956	524	Robert C Angell (USA)
4	Stresa (Italy)	1959	980	George Friedmann (France)
5	Washington (USA)	1962	1000	T.H Marshall (UK)
6	Evian (France)	1966	2076	Rene Konig (FRG)
7	Varna (Bulgaria)	1970	4000	Jan Szczepanski (Poland)
8	Toronto (Canada)	1974	3000	Reuben Hill (USA)
9	Uppsala (Sweden)	1978	4000	T.B Bottomore (UK)
10	Mexico City (Mexico)	1982	4500	Ulf Himmelstrand (Sweden)
11	New Delhi (India)	1986	2500	Fernando Cardoso (Brazil)
12	Madrid (Spain)	1990	4730	Margret S Archer (UK)
13	Bielefeld (Germany)	1994	3678	T.K. Oommen (India)

As soon as a new executive committee is in place, the necessary steps to identify the site for the next World Congress starts. Given the numbers and spatial spread of the Congress delegates, four years is not much time for preparation. A Congress Site Selection Committee was already in place, with the vice president (Programmes) Neil Smelser as its chair, with Rudolf Andorka (Hungary), Alberto Martineli (Italy) and Gyorgy Szell (Federal Republic of Germany) its members. The Committee, after taking into account all factors, decided to hold the XIII World Congress of Sociology at Bielefeld.

The University of Bielefeld is situated in the Westphalia region of Germany. Although not located in a big city, it is well-connected by air, rail and road and the university has a sprawling campus, an excellent infrastructure, including a huge auditorium which can seat 4000 persons, and a dining hall which can serve 6000 persons at a time. Not many luxury hotels were available but delegates could easily commute from a distance of 40 to 50 kilometres. Also, Bielefeld University had the biggest department of sociology in Europe at that point in time.

The Memorandum of Agreement was signed on 25 November 1992 by three representatives of the ISA: the president, vice president (Programmes) and the chair (Finance Committee), and three representatives of the organizing committee drawn from Deutsche Gesellschaft Soziologie (DGS), the Gesellschaft Internationale Soziologie (GIS) and the University of Bielefeld. The MoU clearly specified the organizational division of labour between the ISA and the GIS, which was specifically created for managing the World Congress. Academic associations such as the ISA depend on revenue generated by their Congresses accrued through registration fees, which is shared between them and the local organizers, but the responsibility of mobilizing finance other than registration fees mainly devolves on the local organizers. The funds are raised from governments, foundations and international organizations, such as UNESCO, to meet the travel expenses of principal speakers from 'Third World' and 'Soft Currency' countries. Also the funds for a Worldwide Competition of Young Sociologists and a one-week work-shop preceding the Congress need to be raised by the local organizers. While financing of *Sociological Abstracts* was the responsibility of the ISA, the funds required for the Programme Book of the Congress need to be provided by the local organizers. I am indicating these details just to provide a flavour to the reader regarding the mammoth organizational tasks.

The inaugural session of the ISA World Congress starts with a welcome speech by the president of the ISA followed by an address by the chief guest, who at Bielefeld was Rita Susmuth, the president of the German Parliament. This is followed by several short speeches and important announcements. As the inaugural session was about to start and I was about to deliver my welcome speech, there was a 'non-violent' interruption. A lunatic person who was known in the Bielefeld University and roamed around naked on the campus entered the hall, climbed the podium took his erect penis in hand and shook it for a few times. As the hall had a circular shape he had to repeat this exercise facing all the four directions for the benefit of all present. Then he departed with a smile. There was no commotion in the hall although some 4000 delegates and guests from eighty-five countries were watching the 'performance'! If such an incident were to take place in India a posse of security men would have suddenly surfaced and taken away the man forcefully not to speak of some among the audience too volunteering to help the security force. In the event, we would have lost at least thirty minutes, if not more. But the time loss caused by this 'performance' at Bielefeld was barely ten minutes.

The theme of the XIII World Congress of the ISA was 'Contested Boundaries and Shifting Solidarities', but after the incident, the delegates and guests in the auditorium were in a state of unease, if not shock, so I had to partly improvise my speech. I began by saying, 'What we have witnessed just now is an example of boundaries being contested and broken but I am not sure whether it is leading to the crystallization of any solidarity.' There were peals of laughter and the delegates relaxed. I then delivered my written welcome speech (Appendix-4).

The commitment of the GIS was to raise a sum of DM 750,000 which it hoped to receive from the government of the Federal Republic of Germany. But thanks to the fall of the Berlin Wall and the unification of Germany which followed, the new German government reneged on the promise because of political developments. Some GIS representatives argued that the ISA should contribute DM 450,000, but this was never in the tradition of the ISA World Congress MoUs. While appreciating the financial consequences of political changes, the ISA insisted that it was the moral responsibility of the GIS to secure the amount promised by the government of the Federal Republic of Germany. What needs to be underlined here is how the political unification of Germany adversely affected an event such as the XIII World Congress of Sociology at Bielefeld. The unanticipated consequences of changes in macro structures on micro events could be distressing.

The academic agenda of the World Congress started with the first plenary, the presidential session chaired by the president. At Bielefeld there were four speakers in this session, including the chair. The other three speakers were: N. Luhman (Germany),

A. Touraine (France) and W.J. Wilson (USA). Luhman was rated as one of the top German sociologists and coincidentally, was working at Bielefeld's department of sociology at that time. It was an appropriate symbolic gesture to have him on the presidential plenary. Given the proverbial contestations between German and French sociological traditions, we needed to have a French sociologist also in the session. During one of my visits to France I asked a bright middle-level sociologist who the top living sociologists of France were. He answered, 'We have three and a half of them.' Touraine was one among them and I was already familiar with his works on social movements. The real challenge was to identify a speaker from the USA and after considerable consultations, I decided to request W.J. Wilson, the most distinguished 'black sociologist' of the USA and he agreed. Since I advocated the need for representation of gender and geography in the affairs of the ISA, I wanted to have a woman sociologist in the presidential session but gave up the idea because of constraints of time and the difficulty in locating anyone outside Europe, North America or Asia, regions already represented in the presidential session.

The other plenary meeting was the valedictory session to be chaired by Neil Smelser, Vice-President (Programme). There were five speakers including the chair selected on the basis of broad regional representation including S.N. Eisenstadt (Israel) and Saad Ibrahim (Egypt). The idea of publishing a volume based on papers presented at the two plenary sessions was proposed by me and Smelser agreed. But when these papers, after the required editing, were submitted for publication, the publishers (two of them considered the manuscript in succession) observed that the nine papers did not make a coherent volume in spite of the editors' efforts to provide it through an introduction. When eminent scholars are approached for their contributions they rarely stick to the suggested theme. They write on their pet themes. Consequently the expected coherence of a volume can be scarcely achieved in such volumes. I recollect what a distinguished social scientist told me when I suggested a topic for his talk at JNU: 'T.K. whatever is the topic that you suggest my talk will be the same.'

The six symposia sessions of the XIII World Congress were on the Global and the Local; Markets and States; Old and New Forms of Solidarity and Identity; The Polity and Dynamics of Civil Society; The Environment; Technology and Power; and Challenges to Sociological Knowledge. Each symposium had two co-ordinators and there were four sessions in each symposium with two co-convenors each. The principles followed in identifying the co-ordinators, convenors and speakers were based on gender and geography to make the academic deliberations truly global.

From all accounts the XIII World Congress was a great success. Although I am not entitled to lay any claim for its success, I am proud of having presided over it.

CHAPTER 8

Academic Accolades

As in all vocations, academics too are recognized through two types of rewards–instrumental and symbolic. Instrumental rewards entail recognition through positions of power, such as those of the vice chancellor and chairperson or membership of organizations such as the UGC, ICSSR or commissions. In contrast, symbolic rewards come in the form of awards, the material component being negligible. In India and perhaps elsewhere too, to get instrumental rewards the aspirant needs to cultivate those who matter in politics and administration. But to obtain symbolic rewards one has to cultivate one's intellect. I have not been recognized through appropriate instrumental rewards but was fortunate enough to get symbolic rewards from academic peers and seniors.

Sociologists of India are eligible for four Indian awards: the V.K.R.V Prize in Sociology, the G.S. Ghurye Award in Sociology and Social Anthropology, the Swami Pranavananda Award in Sociology and the Life Time Achievement Award of the Indian Sociological Society. As far as I know I am the only sociologist who has received all these awards and I must thank my professional peers and seniors who select these awardees.

The first award I received was the V.K.R.V. Rao Prize in Sociology for 1981. My name was proposed by T.N. Madan, a distinguished social scientist and a former member-secretary of the ICSSR. The prize was instituted by the Institute for Social and Economic Change, Bangalore and administered by the Indian Council of Social Science Research (ICSSR), New Delhi, and is 'awarded to persons who have made significant original contributions to human knowledge and progress, applied or fundamental, who are citizens of India, below the age of forty-five years...'

The Board of Governors of the Institute for Social and Economic Change at its meeting held on 19 January 1977 approved the regulations governing the V.K.R.V. Rao prizes for economics, political science, public administration, demography and sociology. I was the first sociologist to receive the prize. The award function was held at the Institute for Social and Economic Change, Bangalore and the awards were given away by K.N. Raj. Part of the citation for my prize read:

> Professor T.K. Oommen has made significant contributions to the studies of social movements, agrarian relations, political sociology, sociology of professions, research methodology and the sociology of youth... His works transcend the conventional concerns of sociology and social anthropology to put forward new perspectives on comprehending Indian social reality... He rejects the traditional dichotomy between the rural and the urban; he advocates the identification of the 'Core Institutional Order' specific to each social system in order to understand meaningfully social change.

The awards were widely reported in the print media (the electronic media hardly existed those days) partly because it was for the first time they were awarded and partly because Rao was not only an outstanding economist but a great institution-builder as well as the minister of education in the Government of India.

I received many congratulatory messages from all over India, mainly from non-sociologists. But I was particularly happy to receive messages from the then VC of JNU, P.N. Srivastava and G. Thomas who taught me at the Mar Thoma High School at Venmony, my ancestral village. I was proud to receive a letter from the legendary Justice V.R Krishna Iyer. He wrote: 'It fills me with some pride that you, a good friend of mine, have been awarded the VKRV Rao Award. Let me congratulate you'. But the letter which moved me most came from Savithri Devanesan, the widow of Chandran Devanesan, who was principal of the Madras Christian College and the first VC of the North Eastern Hill University (NEHU), Shillong. I did not know Chandran well but participated in a seminar which he organized at Madras on: 'Religious Pluralism in India'. Later when he became the NEHU VC he invited me along with V.M. Sirsikar, political scientist, of Poona University to conduct a workshop on research methodology for the social science faculty of NEHU. I was an associate professor at JNU those days and Chandran invited me to join as professor and dean of the School of Social Sciences at NEHU. I politely declined the offer, saying that I was too young to be a dean. Actually I was not keen to leave JNU for NEHU.

Savithri Devanesen wrote:

> I know that if Chandran had been alive he would have promptly written to say how happy and proud he was that this well deserved honour has been given to you. I do join with him in expressing the same sentiments and send you our congratulations and good wishes ... I remember the very interesting paper you read at the colloquium (which Chandran organized) which has left a mark on many of our minds. The

complexity of social structures and our religious differences was really brought to light in your paper.

This was indeed a symbolic gratification for me.

On 13 August 1987, I received a letter from the registrar of Bombay University on behalf of the executive council informing me that the G.S. Ghurye Award was going to be given to me for my book entitled *From Mobilization to Institutionalization: The Dynamics of Agrarian Movement in 20th Century Kerala*, which has been 'considered deserving of the award as the best published work of the calendar year 1985.' I was instructed to fill in a bill to claim the amount of the award. The letter also stated the following regulation: 'All prizes not claimed within twelve months from the date of publication of the award shall lapse to the University'. I was not only annoyed but intrigued by the content and tone of the letter. At any rate, I expected a letter from the department of sociology, informing me about the award function and at the very least, I thought the department would send me a citation saying why the book was selected for the Award. Instituted in 1970 at the time of the Golden Jubilee celebrations of the department of sociology, Bombay University, the award was 'in honour of the distinguished sociologist G.S. Ghurye who built and nurtured the department'. Earlier Ghurye awardees were M.N. Srinivas, Veena Das and Ratna Naidu, but the award for 1993 was given after a gap of seven years to M.S. Gore, while the 1994 award was given to K.S. Singh. This lackadaisical style of administering the award is an insult not only to the recipients but also the scholar in whose name it is instituted. Understandably, the Ghurye award for 1985 for me was scarcely reported in the press and I received just eleven congratulatory messages.

The third award I received was the Swami Pranavananda Award (SPA) administered by the University Grants

Commission (UGC). The awards are given from the endowment created out of the funds provided by Swami Pranavananda Saraswati, director, Yoga Societies, America. It is envisioned as a distinguished career award and usually given to those who have completed their career as university teachers irrespective of their subjects, from physics to philosophy. The UGC sends a circular to all universities for recommendations and shortlists them. When the UGC circular was discussed at the CSSS and my name recommended and forwarded, some senior faculty members were not very happy, one of them remarking: 'I don't need that award money.'

I received the SPA for the year 1997 (but in 1999) from the then minister of Human Resource Development, Murali Manohar Joshi, the chief guest at a grand function organized by the UGC at Delhi. The citations were printed and circulated but not read out. The Minister delivered an eloquent speech on his pet theme: 'Science in Ancient India'. There were letters of congratulations but nothing comparable to the applause which followed after I received the V.K.R.V. Rao Prize. The award ceremony was held in the Indian National Science Academy (INSA) in an officious and bureaucratic manner. As soon as the awards were distributed the chief guest and the host, the UGC chairperson, disappeared from the scene leaving the 'distinguished award-winning academics' high and dry. The redeeming feature was that I received a letter dated 7 May 1999 from Armaity Desai, the then UGC chair which is quoted below: (I hope that other awardees too received similar letters)

> Thank you ever so much for being present in person to receive the Hari Om Ashram and Swami Pranavananda Award. I am sorry that I could not meet you at the tea. By the time I could do so, you had already left. Generally, the chief guest has tea with the awardees and the invitees. It appears that for security

> reasons, tea was arranged in a room near the auditorium with the result that I found myself in a difficult position to play host at two locations at the same time. I was caught unawares as it appears that this arrangement was made by the security staff of the minister, with the authorities at INSA, unbeknown to us. I deeply apologize for the same. It was my personal loss that I did not have an opportunity to interact with you.

The awardees were outstanding scholars but were not treated with the respect they deserved. By the turn of the twentieth century, India started building a 'knowledge society', but this enterprise will never succeed unless the country respects those who produce and communicate knowledge. Sadly, I can certify without any hesitation that those who produce and disseminate knowledge in India are held in low esteem, compared with politicians and bureaucrats. This at least partly explains why this ancient land of knowledge lags far behind many countries in producing 'modern' knowledge.

The last academic award I received was the Life Time Achievement Award in the year 2010 instituted by the Indian Sociological Society (ISS). I am tempted to reproduce below parts of the glowing tribute in the citation of the ISS.

> Professor Tharaileth Koshy Oommen is an eminent sociologist who has put Indian sociology on the world map. He was the secretary general of the XI World Congress of Sociology of the International Sociological Association, which met in New Delhi in 1986, and is the only scholar from Asia and Africa to be elected president of the International Sociological Association (1990–94). He is also a former president of the Indian Sociological Society (1998–99). ...While at the Jawaharlal Nehru University for thirty-one years, sixty students completed their MPhil dissertations and forty students their PhD theses under his supervision.

> Professor Oommen has served as Governing Council/ Executive Committee member of several professional associations and institutions such as the International Sociological Association, International Association for the Scientific Study of Religion, and International Institute of Sociology (Rome). He was Chair, Programme Advisory Committee of Gujarat Harmony Project (2002-04). In recognition of his contributions to the field of higher education Professor Oommen was conferred Padma Bhushan by the Government of India, in 2008.

There is yet another genre of academic honour–the invitations to participate in academic associations' meetings. The American Sociological Association's meetings are huge, attended by a few thousand delegates from the USA. I was invited twice for ASA annual meetings, the first at the 1987 ASA annual meeting held at Chicago. The theme of the meeting was Cross-national Research and the ASA president was Melvin L. Kohn. I read a paper entitled 'Ethnicity, Immigration and Cultural Pluralism: India and the United States of America', which constitutes a chapter in the book, 'Cross-National Research in Sociology', edited by Kohn and published by Sage in 1989. The second invitation to the ASA annual meeting was extended by James S. Coleman (1926–95), then the ASA president to organize a thematic session on 'Citizenship and National Identity', at Pittsburg in 1992. I edited a book entitled *Citizenship and National Identity: from Colonialism to Globalism*, published by Sage in 1997, based on the papers submitted in the thematic session.

There are several other such instances. For example, the multi-national Nordic Sociological Association invited me to deliver a keynote address in 1992 in their annual conference. The latest in this series was indeed an ex-office invitation to address the XVIII ISA Congress at Yokohama, Japan in 2014. All the ex-presidents of the ISA were invited to address a session entitled: 'ISA at Sixty-five, Looking Backward and Looking Ahead'.

The reader may think that I do not consider invitations from institutions in India as important. Quite the contrary, I have had the privilege of delivering talks and reading papers in scores of Indian institutions. I consider their invitations as a great recognition for me, especially that from the UGC, which had instituted a scheme of National Lectures to make 'the services of outstanding teachers available on a wider basis to the students and staff of universities', and nominated me as the National Lecturer in Sociology for the year 1985–86. This was not a particularly convenient time for me as I was immersed in the preparations for the XI World Congress of Sociology, but the redeeming feature was that I was required to visit only four institutions in a year. Then the Indian Council of Social Science Research, which had established the North Eastern Regional Centre (NERC), attached to the North East Hill University, to encourage the development of social science in the region invited a distinguished social scientist every year to deliver three lectures. I was invited to do so for the year 2004. My lectures were published with the title 'Development Discourse: Issues and Concerns'. I was very pleased to note that Mrinal Miri, a distinguished philosopher, the then VC of NEHU, wrote in his foreword: 'I cannot think of a better introduction to the development discourse of recent times than Oommen's three lectures', observation by a philosopher on the 'wisdom' of a sociologist.

From 1994–2015, I delivered twenty-three distinguished lectures in addition to the numerous keynote addresses and inaugural speeches at seminars, workshops, conferences and congresses in social science. But the first of these was the ISA presidential address, which seems to have produced a domino effect.

Finally, I was privileged to contribute to books published in honour of public figures such as M.K. Gandhi, Jawaharlal Nehru, Indira Gandhi and B.R. Ambedkar as well as Indian social scientists, including V.K.R.V. Rao, M.N. Srinivas, S.C. Dube, Ramakrishna Mukherji, Yogendra Singh and foreign sociologists such as Erving Goffman, Alain Touraine and S.N. Eisenstadt. I consider invitations to contribute to books published to honour such persons an academic recognition for me.

As I noted at the beginning of this chapter, appointments to important positions are offered mostly to those who are on the right side of the political parties in power. In independent India, the Indian National Congress was in power for most of the time so the academic/intellectual pool was drawn from those directly or indirectly connected to the party. When the National Democratic Alliance (NDA) come to power, several scholars who were aligned to this new political formation or were patronized by persons who belonged to it found favour. The second NDA government from 2014 is one in which the Bharatiya Janata Party has a clear hegemony, and one understands from the media that those appointed to important positions are those approved by the Rashtriya Swayam Sevak Sangh (RSS). Some of these appointments have been severely criticised in the media since attachment or affiliation to the parties in power, rather than academic or professional competence, are deciding factors. If this is the major consideration, it is an invitation for the decay of crucial institutions. In turn this would undermine the health of the polity itself. I have often wondered if one drains out the political affiliations of these 'academics' what will be left of them?

I referred to my not being offered any instrumental rewards. But it is not entirely correct and I must put the record straight. I have been sounded for three such positions which I did not accept, either because I thought they would impair my academic career or because I thought they were not of the level I was aspiring for. In the 1970s, when the ICSSR was established J.P. Naik, the well known educationalist was the member-secretary, offered me the position of director vacated by Yogesh Atal who had left for an assignment in UNESCO in 1974. I declined the offer because accepting an administrative position at that point in time would have adversely affected my academic progress.

Malcolm Adiseshiah who was the chairperson of Madras Institute of Development Studies (MIDS) sent a message to me enquiring whether I would like to take up the assignment of MIDS director, but I politely declined. Similarly, M.N. Srinivas was keen that I should join the Institute of Social and Economic Change (ISEC) as director which he had co-founded along with V.K.R.V. Rao. I did not find that too attractive so did not take it up.

The ICSSR offer came when I was an associate professor and my singular aspiration then was to become a professor. In 1976, I became a professor and was eager to consolidate my position so did not consider any offers. But by the time I was ready to accept appropriate administrative positions in the early 1980s, they eluded me. And in the mid-1980s I was sucked into the ISA. Additionally, my disinclination to cultivate influential people in politics and administration stood in the way of my getting positions of power. And, by the time I realized that was the way to go, it was too late to mend my ways.

CHAPTER 9

Getting Elected as the President of the Indian Sociological Society: An Agonizing Experience

When the Indian Sociological Society (ISS) was established in December 1951, G.S. Ghurye of the department of sociology, Bombay University, became its president and he continued for a tenure that stretched for fifteen years (1951–66). The All Indian Sociological Conference (AISC) which functioned mainly from the department of sociology, Lucknow University, merged into it in 1966. The first president of this combined association was M.N. Srinivas (1967–69). The tenure of the three office-bearers, president, secretary and treasurer is two years, the president and the secretary being elected positions while the treasurer is nominated by the president.

The ISS has two types of members, apart from foundation members, life members and annual members, the overwhelming majority being life members. In 2011, when the ISS celebrated its Diamond Jubilee it had around 3000 life members but only a handful of annual members. I became a life member of the ISS only in 1973 and I was nominated as treasurer first by S.C. Dube, the ISS president during 1975–76, and for a second term by I.P. Desai, the ISS president during 1977–78. Yogendra Singh was the secretary during 1975–78 and the office of ISS was located at the CSSS so the physical location of secretary and treasurer in the same university ensured the smooth functioning of the ISS.

When I became the president of the ISA, my holding any position in the ISS was almost ruled out. The convention of the ISS was to persuade well-known senior sociologists to accept the position of president and a middle-level sociologist to be the secretary. This consensual approach to identify the president and secretary facilitated the smooth functioning of ISS in a cordial atmosphere although not in consonance with the western notion of democracy.

As far as I know, a contest for ISS presidency occurred for the first time for the 1985–86 term, a crucial time because the ISS was hosting the World Congress of Sociology. To be the president of the ISS at this juncture was to gain global visibility. Victor D'Souza was elected as president, Suma Chitnis, located at Tata Institute of Social Sciences, Bombay, was elected as the secretary. The treasurer, Neera Desai, too was from Bombay. Generally speaking, caste and communal factors never figured in ISS elections but in the 1985–86 election of the ISS presidency it did. I was told that two Christians, Victor D'Souza as president of the ISS and T.K. Oommen as secretary general of the World Congress of Sociology, would impart a distorted picture about India as a predominantly Hindu country and therefore, D'Souza should be defeated. There were three candidates for ISS presidency for the 1985-86 term. But the fact that D'Souza was elected with an overwhelming majority conclusively proved the professional credentials of ISS voters who were unaffected by primordial considerations such as religion.

Brijraj Chouhan succeeded Victor D'Souza as president of the ISS during 1987–88 without a contest, thus the convention of persuading a senior active sociologist to become the president was resurrected. It was for this reason that Parthanath Mukherjee and I went to the Institute of Economic Growth (IEC) to request P.C. Joshi, both an economist as well as a sociologist, to be the next president of the ISS (1990–91). As an economist he had a tremendous reputation as one who worked in the area of land reforms. Once he told me that some people would call him L.R.–that is, land reforms–Joshi!

Joshi agreed to be the president of ISS on one condition, that I should be the secretary. This put me in an extremely awkward position because I was already the president of the ISA. To insist that the president of an international association should accept the position of secretary of a national association was indeed amusing, but since Joshi insisted, I accepted it with considerable embarrassment. So I was simultaneously the secretary of the ISS and the president of the ISA. Had I refused to be the secretary of the ISS, it could have been interpreted as an instance of my arrogance.

As secretary of the ISS I could not do much as I was immersed in the activities of the ISA. As far as I know this was the only time (1990–91) that the ISS conference did not take place. By the year 2000, holding an annual conference became the norm for ISS; prior to that there used to be only one conference during the two-year tenure of a president. But even that did not happen during the ISS presidency of P.C. Joshi because during 1990–91 India was departing from the path of planned economic development and was passionately pursuing the structural adjustment programme (SAP) popularly referred to as globalization. With the liberalization of the economy, the government became rather stingy about financing professional activities, so since neither the UGC nor the ICSSR was forthcoming during 1990–91 with the usual financial help the conference did not take place. Consequently, P.C. Joshi remains the only person who did not deliver his ISS presidential address.

However, I look back with some satisfaction regarding the institutionalization of the post of managing editor of the *Sociological Bulletin* during my tenure as the secretary of the ISS. Earlier, the editorial responsibility was given to office-bearers and during my four years as treasurer (1975–78), I did assist Yogendra Singh, the then secretary, in this matter. But I always felt editorship required considerable time and high competence in the English language, which I lacked. An earlier effort was made in this direction, perhaps by M.N. Srinivas, and Andre Beteille was named as the managing editor. However, he did not accept the assignment. It was M.N. Panini who became the first managing editor for a period of five years, which was a boon for ISS, and I consider the appointment of a managing editor as an important institutional innovation. He edited the *Bulletin* for a decade, ensuring its regularity of publication and improvement of its academic content.

Having been a treasurer for four years and a secretary for two years of the ISS, the only position I could have aspired for in ISS was that of the president. Since I knew that contesting for the ISS presidency was not the norm, I was willing to wait for my turn to be sounded by others. When the time for the election of the 1994–95 ISS president approached, M.S. Gore wrote a letter to Yogendra Singh suggesting that I should be the next president of ISS, his rationale being that when I addressed the World Congress of Sociology in 1994 as the ISA

President, I should be doing so as the president of the ISS. However, before Yogendra Singh shared Gore's letter with me, I had already initiated steps to float Singh's name as the next president of the ISS, given his academic standing. Gore's letter would have been a little unsettling for Singh but I made it clear to him that I had no intention to contest

On the last day of submitting the nominations for the 1996–97 term I telephoned the ISS office to find out who the candidates were. I was told that no nomination was submitted for the post of president. To avoid a crisis situation of the election process being delayed/repeated, I filed my nomination for the ISS presidency. It was not an easy task because there should have been a proposer and a seconder. Having done that I discovered that Indra Deva also filed his nomination at the last moment, facilitated by K.L. Sharma and Dipankar Gupta, at the CSSS, JNU. In all probability Yogendra Singh too knew about it but I was not sure. I was deeply pained and disturbed because they knew of my interest and involvement with the ISS but still did not tell me about Indra Deva's candidature.

A few days before the last date for withdrawal Indra Deva and Yogendra Singh came to my house to persuade me to withdraw from the contest. Both of them were my seniors at the department of sociology, University of Rajasthan, while I was a research scholar so no effort was required on their part to persuade me to withdraw from the contest since I respected them–and Indra Deva became the president of ISS (1996–97), uncontested. However, it was intriguing that the filing of Indra Deva's nomination for the presidency of the ISS was kept as a well-guarded secret from me. I could have been asked to propose or second Indra Deva's name as I did in the case of Yogendra Singh. But then, one cannot thrust one's integrity on others and there is no treatment for a trust deficit.

Feeling that it was legitimate for me to aspire to the presidency of the ISS, I filed my nomination for the 1998–99 tenure, the last in the twentieth century. I fervently hoped that I would be elected unopposed but it was not to be. When during 1985–86 the ISS presidency was contested for the first time, all the three contestants were sociologists of high standing. But the person who contested against me was one Sudhir Rangan, not known as a sociologist. I only knew about him because he wrote a letter dated 5 August 1990 congratulating me on my being elected as the president of the ISA and introduced himself as a person doing research (I assume PhD) at the department of sociology, Maharshi Dayanand University, Rohtak. In the letter he indicated that he was happy that a person from Asia and Africa was elected as the ISA president for the first time and hoped that in the future also I would break such records for India. Between 1990 when he was a research scholar and 1998, the year in which he filed his nomination, he could not have scaled the high peak of sociology. Even if he did, nobody seemed aware of it. For example, Leela Dube thought he was a JNU sociology student I'd given a B minus grade to!

Sudhir Rangan filed his nomination for three positions–president, secretary and member of managing committee. Two faculty members from M.D. University proposed and seconded his name, but it was a most irresponsible and unprofessional act because elections to academic/professional bodies ought to be based on competence and experience in the discipline. It was more appalling that Sudhir Rangan polled ninety votes. One life member of the ISS rightly remarked, 'These are not pro-Sudhir but anti-Oommen votes.' It was an extremely horrendous omen for sociology in India; a clear indication of the utter lack of professionalism among a segment of the ISS members. Some sociologists wanted to pacify me by saying that

I had secured most of the of the votes polled, but I told them that I was really worried about those ISS members who had gone astray, and stigmatized me by voting for Sudhir Rangan.

I have known of instances in politics when weak or incompetent candidates were put up to insult invincible candidates. But I never imagined that this was ever possible in an academic association. This is the reason why I consider the election to ISS presidency an agonizing experience. And, some of those who encouraged and misguided this young man were my own colleagues at the CSSS–as Yogendra Singh told me, 'Our own people did it.'

When the candidates' names were announced for the 1998–99 elections, some colleagues advised me to negotiate with Sudhir Rangan so that he would withdraw. Even if he had wanted an assurance of support from me for the managing committee membership, I could not have done it because even that position was not meant for an unemployed sociologist. However, what was most unsettling and indeed intriguing for me was the imperviousness of Yogendra Singh who knew that 'our own people' were behind the murky incident. He knew pretty well that I did not jump into the ISS presidential election fray in 1994 in spite of M.S. Gore's suggestion. He also knew that I readily withdrew from the contest in 1996 at his suggestion. Probably he wanted me to request him to intervene but I thought it would be unethical on my part to do so. Reciprocity should not emanate out of pressure tactics, not even requests, but ought to flow out of introspection and professional responsibility.

I cannot claim any spectacular achievement as the ISS president. Aneeta Minocha who was elected as secretary and Mohini Anjum whom I nominated as treasurer were from Delhi University and Jamia Millia Islamia respectively, and both were helpful and co-operative. The All-India Sociological Conference during my presidency took place at Aligarh Muslim University in 1999 and I worked on identifying and chiselling the theme of the conference, 'Nation and National Identity in South Asia', so far a preserve of historians and political scientists. In the combined issue of volume 48 of the *Sociological Bulletin* ten select papers presented at the All India Sociological Conference held at Aligarh were published. Although the *Bulletin* was published regularly since 1952, the ISS had never published a book under its auspices. But the papers contained in volume 48 were published with an introduction by S.L. Sharma, the then managing editor of the journal, as a book by Orient Longman. B.S. Baviskar who succeeded me as president of the ISS, rightly observed in his foreword to the book, 'With this publication, the Indian Sociological Society has opened a new chapter in its history'. It is a matter of gratification that following the trend I initiated, several volumes were published by the ISS based on papers culled from the *Bulletin*.

In my presidential address to the ISS, I identified the different and confusing ways in which a nation is defined in the subcontinent. I argued that India cannot be a nation-state of the West European type because it consists of several nations and most of these are state-renouncing ones in that they do not even aspire for their exclusive sovereign states. Given India's socio-cultural complexity it is more appropriate to designate India as a national state. Understandably, this unconventional vein of thinking is an anathema to many, and my position came to be perceived as 'anti-national'.

When I filed my nomination paper for the ISS presidency in 1998 I had been a full professor at JNU for twenty-two years, received three awards, published fourteen books and more than a hundred research papers in academic journals apart from serving the profession both nationally and internationally. And yet some of my colleagues misguided a person who had not even started his academic career to contest against me. In this context, I wrote a paper entitled 'Professionals without Professionalism: Situating Sociology' in a special number of *Seminar* on 'A Symposium on Knowledge, Institutions and Practices in a Discipline' in 2000. Some colleagues told me that my judgement was harsh but let me confess that I am incapable of self-deception. It was my experience as a sociologist which prompted me to write that piece. Therefore it is reproduced in this book as an 'epilogue'. We all know that production of knowledge in social science cannot be completely divorced from one's biography. It seems to me that in India there are gurus and disciples, patrons and clients but not professionals and colleagues. And unless this transformation takes place, our efforts to create a knowledge society will remain aborted.

CHAPTER 10

Foreign Visiting Assignments

In the first decades of independent India, the colonial hangover continued in almost all fields. In the academic context this meant coveting a degree, preferably a research degree, from a foreign university. Further, foreign degrees were overvalued in that one could get a direct appointment as a full professor in social science if one had a PhD from one of the prestigious universities in the UK or the USA. I was trained only in India. When I was an associate professor, some of my well-wishers suggested that I should spend at least a year as a post-PhD researcher in a foreign country to facilitate my elevation as a professor, but I was not persuaded. I became a full professor in 1976 at the young age of thirty-nine, not so common in sociology in India.

I have visited over fifty countries for seminars and conferences but no university or research institute had risked inviting me for a teaching or research assignment. I was invited as a visiting professor at the department of sociology, University of California (Berkeley), USA in 1990, the year I was elected as president of the ISA. The invitation was initiated by Neil Smelser and Arlie Hochshild; the first I knew for quite some time, the second I met only in late 1980s when we were participants at a seminar organized in memory of Erving Goffman, who was their colleague at the department. The Berkeley department had a large faculty in sociology, quite a few of whom had a global visibility.

I was assigned two courses: a lecture course on 'Indian Society' and a seminar course on 'National Identity'. Berkeley students were drawn from a wide variety of national and ethnic backgrounds. The strategy I followed in the seminar course was giving each student an assignment based on his/her national/ethnic background and asking them to present it in the class. This approach proved to be a great success because the students were happy to do their academic exercise on a theme which was emotionally satisfying too. The lecture class was so large that I had to use a microphone while lecturing. Teaching in US universities is a strenuous enterprise because the teacher is responsible for formulating the course, undertaking the interim and final evaluations and submitting the grades on time. An established senior professor could hire a few teaching assistants, but a short-term visiting professor did not have this facility so it was pretty hard work. On the whole, my stay was enjoyable and I learnt from the then head of the department, Mike Hout, that the students rated me highly.

What intrigued me was the near absence of interaction among faculty members. Most of them came to the department, taught their courses and vanished. I remember having tea with one faculty member to whom I said in the course of our conversation, 'I met Kornhauser today.' She was surprised, and said, 'I've been here for six years but have never met him.' Indeed, I had sought out William Kornhauser, the author of the fascinating book, *Politics of Mass Society* and was amazed that very few faculty members had met him. There were others like the lead author of *Habits of Heart*, Robert N. Bellah, and Reinhard Bendix who wrote on Max Weber among other things. Of course I did not meet several others, for example the prominent young sociologist, Michael Burawoy who became the president of the ISA, (2010–14). My stay at Berkeley was revealing in that I had read or knew about published works of several faculty members but hardly anybody had any idea of my published works even though several of my research papers were published in international journals and books by global publishers. Indeed, academic colonialism persisted.

Most of my foreign assignments were short and research-oriented and entailed no teaching. I met Daniel Bertaux, a French sociologist, through the ISA. He was vice president, research (1990–94) when I was president of the ISA but before that both of us were executive committee members during 1986–90. I learnt from him that Pierre Bourdieu, Raymond Budon and Alain Touraine were the leading living sociologists of France. I hardly knew of Budon but had certainly read Bourdieu's works including *Reproduction in Education, Society and Culture,* from which I learnt the notion of symbolic violence and thought it eminently captured a terrain of violence not covered by physical and structural violence. But Touraine I had read extensively partly because of his seminal contributions in the area of social movements.

In September 1990, I received a letter from Maurice Aymard, the administrator of Maison des Sciences de l'Homme inviting me to spend a month as a visiting professor and I suspect that the invitation was extended to me at the instance of Alain Touraine. But I could spend a month only in June–July 1992, given my prior commitments. Coincidentally I was invited to contribute a paper to the centenary seminar of the *International*

Review of Sociology, the first sociology journal. The founder of the journal was Rene Worms, the French sociologist, who was believed to have migrated from Paris to Rome, to escape from the 'persecution' of Emile Durkheim. The theme of the seminar was 'Advanced Societies at the Threshold of the Third Millennium: Status and Perspectives' and was held at Rome. The participants included Anthony Giddens, Jean Bethlae Elshtain, Sidney Verba, Joachim Israel, Daniel Bertaux, among others. My Paris sojourn provided me an opportunity to write the paper, 'Reconciling Pluralism and Equality: the Dilemma of "Advanced" societies', which I presented at the seminar; it was included in Vol. I (1) of the new series of the journal started in 1992. I could not have easily accessed the material I used for the paper if I were in Delhi.

I spent two summers, May–July 1993 and June 1994 at Wissenshaftszentrum, Berlin since my presence was required in West Germany. The XIII World Congress of Sociology was slated to take place in Bielefeld and I had to attend several meetings there. As the universities were closed for the summer vacation it was a convenient time for all the members to meet. During my stay at Berlin, I formulated two papers entitled: 'Race, Ethnicity and Class: An Analysis in Interrelations' written at the instance of UNESCO and published in the *International Social Science Journal.* This paper was incorporated into a text book entitled *Sociology*, edited by N.J. Smelser and published by UNESCO, in the Blackwell series in contemporary social science.

At Wissenshaftszentrum, I was required to present at least one paper to the monthly seminar of the institute. The debate about 'the other' was very much in the air those days and I attempted a comparative analysis of the contents and processes involved in the construction of the other in West Europe and

South Asia. It was presented in the weekly seminar of the Centrum, included in the institutes' occasional papers series and subsequently published in the *Sociological Bulletin*.

My West German sojourn occurred at a politically exciting time which followed the fall of the Berlin Wall. While the artificial division of Germany into East and West hardly altered its culture and society, the economic and political realities varied vastly. When I occasionally visited Humbolt University to meet Arthur Meir, my friend and a former ISA vice president, I travelled by bus but had to carry my Indian passport. More amusing was the fact that I could purchase bus tickets in East Berlin at half the prize I had to pay at West Berlin. In one of my earlier visits to East Berlin before the fall of the Wall, Arthur wanted me to help him by expediting his visa for India. I talked to the visa officer at the Indian Embassy in East Berlin. When I introduced myself, he assured me that the visa would be issued within seventy-two hours. The officer was a JNU student, who had done his MA from the School of International Studies but offered my course on Sociological Thinkers. Indeed a small gratification for being a JNU teacher! But Arthur was mightily impressed by my 'great influence' in India's vast bureaucracy.

I was invited to spend one month as a visiting fellow at the Research School of Social Science of the Australia National University (ANU), Canberra. I opted to be there in December 1993 because JNU's winter vacation was from 5 December to 5 January so I did not have to take any leave. I do not remember how the invitation came about but the person who corresponded with me was Frank Jones, a sociologist working at ANU.

During the month I spent at ANU I collected materials on multiculturalism in Australia with special reference to the aboriginal people. But the opportunity to use the material surfaced only in 1998 when I was invited to contribute a paper to the seminar on 'Individual, Community, Nation: Fifty Years of Australian Citizenship' organized by Kim Rubenstein of the Law School of Melbourne University. The papers read at the seminar were published by Australian Scholarly Publishing edited by Rubenstein. The title of my paper was 'Citizenship, Nationality and Ethnicity in the Context of Globalization: Situating Australia'. I was curious to know how she zeroed on me and pat came the reply, 'Your book on *Citizenship, Nationality and Ethnicity*.' As my conceptual frame was already distilled, I needed only to organize the Australian material which I had collected at ANU a few years ago. Only two scholars from outside Australia were invited for the seminar, myself and Peter H. Schuck of Yale University Law School.

A few years later in 2003, I read another paper 'Multiculturalism in Australia and India', in a seminar on 'India and Australia: History, Culture and Society'. The seminar was organized in Delhi and its proceedings were published by the India International Centre. The seminar was an Indo-Australian venture in which equal number of scholars from India and Australia participated. While most presentations focused either on India or on Australia, only a few attempted comparative analyses of the two countries, and mine was one.

My longest stay outside India was as senior visiting fellow at the Institute of Advanced Studies, Budapest (Hungary). I received a letter dated 23 August 1994 from Lajos Vekas, rector of Collegium Budapest, Institute for Advanced Study, stating, 'Upon the recommendation of the Academic Advisory Board I am pleased to offer you a fellowship at the Collegium Budapest for the academic year 1994–95 (October through June).' Rudolf Andorka, who was the rector of the Budapest

University of Economic Sciences was closely associated with the ISA and was on the Academic Advisory Board of Collegium Budapest. Andorka was impressed not only with my sociological knowledge but also English. He used to tell me, 'T.K., your BBC English is a great advantage,' without realizing my predicament with English. I had just completed the strenuous ISA presidency and this stint was a welcome relief.

However, my likely absence from Delhi posed problems both professional and familial. The professional problem was that I was very keen to accept the offer of the National Fellowship by the ICSSR. I requested the ICSSR to keep the fellowship in abeyance but did not get any response. The family problem was that to be away for an year from the JNU campus posed a big challenge. I had never stayed away from my family for such a long time and was a highly domesticated householder. Then my wife, Josephine, was the principal of a school in Delhi and could not get leave easily. To complicate matters my sons, Koshy and Johnny, were in their early twenties and both were students. Although the Collegium would finance their travel to Budapest, the trip could jeopardise their studies. To leave them alone had its attendant risks, our main worriy being their exposure to the drug- and liquor-consuming hostel boys. But I took courage in both hands and took the decision to go to Budapest with Josephine.

We left Delhi for Budapest via Amsterdam in early October 1994. When we arrived at Budapest, a suitcase in which the choicest saris of Josephine were packed was missing (we are yet to get it back from KLM). Apart from the material worth of the missing clothes, the symbolic value and sentimental attachment to them was irreplaceable. Like most Indian women, Josephine could not resist buying saris from Kancheevarams to Pochampallis and Banarasis to Kotas, all bought on special occasions, be it on a birthday or wedding anniversary or while visiting particular places. I don't think Josephine has recovered from the shock even today, two decades later. I did tell her that Indian saris are not the most appropriate in Europe, particularly in winter, and kurta-pyjama makes for a better dress. However, that advice fell on deaf ears. Our immediate challenge was to get adequate and appropriate clothes for the nine-month-long stay in Europe. I tried to ease the situation by suggesting that she write a series entitled: 'Indian Lady in Hungary without Clothes', but she did not appreciate my advice.

The stay at Collegium Budapest was academically productive. The idea of writing a book on the intersections between citizenship, nationality and ethnicity had almost crystallized in my thought process and Polity Press was willing to publish it. I only had to attend a weekly seminar and present a paper or two during my stay but the rest of the time I could devote entirely to my research. The Collegium's library had a rich collection and the library staff could get books on inter-library loans from prominent libraries in Vienna or London. I finished writing the manuscript of the planned book during my stay at Budapest, with the help of my wife. Both of us left our flat, which was within a distance of ten to fifteen minutes' walk from the Collegium, after breakfast and returned only in the evening. The walk was not easy as the temperature was minus 20 to 30 degrees Celsius in the winter months. We would have lunch at the Collegium so we spent the whole day there with Josephine using the available computer to key in the bits and pieces of the manuscript as I produced them. The book is dedicated to Josephine for her 'grudging' co-operation in its making!

While at Budapest, we travelled to many places both within Hungary and outside. My friend, Rudolf Andorka, and his wife

Judith drove us around in Hungary, Andorka driving most of the time so that Rudolf and I could chat. We spent most of the time in rural areas of Hungary, breaking the journey at night. In one of the Hungarian villages, we saw a huge mansion and Rudolf told us that it belonged to the village tanner. This was the most pleasant shock of my life; imagine a leather worker owning the biggest house in the village situated right at the entry point! I couldn't help comparing the pitiable predicament of leather workers particularly in north Indian villages (traditionally referred to as 'chamars' and treated as 'untouchables') who are not only steeped in poverty but forced to live at the outskirts of the village. I also recalled my pleasant surprise when I discovered that the next-door neighbour of Erwin Scheuch, professor of sociology, in the University of Koln, in Germany was a barber and lived in an upper middle class residential colony. Erwin told me casually that some barbers are better off economically than most professors. The travails of India's caste system vividly unfolded before me through such experiences.

The other memorable but bitter experience related to our trip to the Czech Republic. Czechoslovakia was bifurcated into Slovakia and Czech Republic and the first ISA EC meeting of the new president, Immanuel Wallerstein (1994–98), was held in the exquisite city of Prague, the capital of the new state. I was invited to attend it as the immediate past president. Ordinarily I would not have travelled all the way from Delhi to Prague but being in the vicinity, I decided to attend the meeting. Josephine and I went to the embassies of the Czech Republic as well as Slovakia and were assured that there was no need to take a visa for Slovakia. We travelled by train from Budapest to Prague, and as soon as the train entered Slovakia, the visa inspectors appeared and found that we were travelling without visas! We were detained and taken to the border post. All our pleadings that our destination was Prague and I, a former president of the ISA, was going to attend the ISA EC meeting were of no avail. However, after a couple of hours, a person who spoke English appeared, and fortunately, understood our plight so we were allowed to travel by the next available train to Prague. But as a precaution, the train inspector took away our passports with the promise that we would get them back on arrival. Perhaps it was to prevent our escaping from the train on the way and joining the force of illegal Asian workers in Slovakia! We were very tense until we got our passports back.

The exit from the Czech Republic was more complicated. The Slovakian embassy at Prague was not willing to issue an exit visa via Slovakia as we had no entry visa to Slovakia. Therefore, the return journey to Budapest had to be by road. There were a couple of checkposts on the way back, the first at the Czech–Slovakia border and the second at the Slovakia–Hungary border. We actually had to hide in the bus while the clearance for the vehicle was obtained on the basis of our co-passengers' documents. This tortuous experience occurred because of differential interpretations of rules by the bureaucracy of the government of Slovakia. The officials at Budapest were of the view that since our destination was the Czech Republic we did not need any visa for Slovakia, while the officials posted at the Hungary–Slovakia border insisted that we did. Our journey was in 1994 when we were already in a borderless world! Paradoxically, I was at that time working on a book with the subtitle 'Reconciling Competing Identities', the identities to be reconciled being citizenship, nationality and ethnicity. I became convinced that the crucial identity in such contexts was that of citizenship which can be changed overnight. The citizens of Czechoslovakia were bifurcated into citizens of Slovakia and Czech Republic even as some of them had retained their shared nationality and ethnicity. But the borders between the two new states were brittle and for two innocent Indian citizens crossing them, it was a brutal experience.

My last foreign sojourn was as fellow of the Swedish Collegium for Advanced Studies in Social Sciences (SCASSS) at Uppsala, January–June 1998. When I arrived in early January at Uppsala it was severe winter which continued till April and difficult to cope with. My flat was some twenty minutes walking distance from the Collegium and convenient public transport was not available. Walking the distance through thick snow was not easy but my shoes purchased at Budapest came handy. While at Budapest thanks to Josephine, life was enjoyable, Uppsala was desolate. As in other advanced institutes of Europe, fellows had the freedom to do what they chose to do although each Fellow was expected to hold one seminar at the SCASSS during the fellowship period.

At the time, the SCASSS was a small community of scholars numbering about dozen drawn from a wide variety of disciplines, mainly from Europe and North America. The administrative director of the SCASSS was Bjorn Wittrock, a political scientist and the permanent fellow was Goran Therborn, a sociologist of repute who helped me in hosting the ISA Council in Sweden in 1993.

I worked on two papers entitled 'Changing Modes of Conceptualizing the World: Implications for Social Research' and 'Religion as a Source of Violence: A Sociological Perspective'. The first of these was published in a volume edited by P.N. Mukherji in honour of Ramkrishna Mukherjee, the distinguished sociologist. I argue in this paper that during colonialism the major tendency in social science in general and sociology/social anthropology in particular was to construct a series of binaries–traditional–modern, rural–urban, sacred–secular, community–society. The assumption which informed these dichotomous constructions was that the attributes found in the first set were absent in the second set. But I suggested in the light of empirical evidence these elements could co-exist. Further, instead of viewing them as dichotomies it was more appropriate to conceptualize them as falling on a continuum.

With the advent of the Cold War the series of postulated dichotomies disappeared and in their place a trichotomy was implanted–the First, Second and Third Worlds. The First World consisted of capitalist democracies and were economically, politically, culturally and socially 'modern'. The Second World was partially modern in that it was economically and technologically advanced but politically backward because of the absence of multi-party democracy and autonomy of civil society. The Third World was backward in all respects. I have suggested that the Cold War was all about annexing the Third World into one of these modernities.

However, the disappearance of the Cold War witnessed the crystallization of One World from which the deficits of the Third and Second Worlds vanished. The defining features of the global age are 'multi-party' democracy, 'free' market and an 'autonomous' civil society. In my seminar presentation at the SCASSS, I argued that these shifting conceptualizations are simplistic and at variance with empirical realities.

The other paper which I wrote while at SCASSS was an invited paper to be included in the official journal of the World Council of Churches, the *Ecumenical Review*. It was a special number on religion and violence. I argued that all religions while preaching about peace are prone to indulge in violence which are of three types–physical, structural and symbolic. While some religions did not indulge in physical violence they were apt to commit structural and symbolic violence. Secondly, religions differed in their proclivity to commit violence during different historical periods, a retreat into the present by ignoring the past was highly misleading to situate religions in terms of their violent character and potential. Finally, linking religion with the state was a sure invitation to unfold the violence potential of religions.

Apart from these long-term teaching and research assignments, I was a visiting faculty member for May–June 1971 at the Asian Leadership Development Centre (ALDC), Tokyo. Young leaders from different Asian countries come to the ALDC for training. I was also a member of faculty at the Bishop's Institute for Social Action (BISA) in November 1975, at Kuala Lumpur, Malaysia. BISA participants were Catholic bishops drawn from Asian countries, large numbers of them being from India and the Philippines.

Two other foreign assignments are worth recalling. In 1973 I had an opportunity to visit the Soviet Union for three weeks as a member of Social Science Cultural Exchange Team consisting of five scholars. It was a multi-disciplinary team sent by the UGC to understand Soviet higher education. We travelled all over Soviet Union touching Moscow, Leningrad, Tashkent and Samarkand.

As I was making preparations to leave for the Soviet Union, my friend Jaisekhar who taught at the Centre for Soviet Studies of the School of International Studies and who had spent several years in the Soviet Union gave me a small packet and said, 'Somebody will come and ask for it so please give to him.' Out of curiosity and fear that I may be carrying something not quite right, I asked him what the packet contained and he revealed reluctantly that it contained toothbrushes. When

I laughed loudly, he said with a smile, 'You will understand when you visit the country.'

The visit to the Soviet Union was a revelation in many ways. On my return, a journalist asked me to describe the country in one sentence and I said, 'The Soviet Union was Lenin writ large.' Viewed in terms of high technology and precision instruments, the advancement of USSR was mindboggling but there were long queues for foreign consumer goods and not infrequently, young men would ask me for a foreign cigarette. I often experienced the gratitude of people I helped out with Western currency to buy things in 'foreign' shops. I also noticed that party membership was the bases of privileges, be it single rooms in the university hostels or access to state-run highly subsidized canteens.

The other foreign assignment was at the Review Commission, Human Sciences Research Council (HSRC) of South Africa in 1977. Nelson Mandela constituted the Review Commission as he was winding up his political-administrative career. It drew its membership from all over the world and I represented the South Asian region. The over-representation of whites and negligent participation of blacks in knowledge production and the consequent bias in knowledge was the central issue which faced the HSRC, like most other institutions of South Africa at that time. The Review Commission recommended equity and redress in the representation of blacks and whites in the HSRC. The Indian experience of the reservation policy came in handy for me while participating in the lively discussions of the Review Commission and in drafting a chapter on equity and redress.

My only visit to Israel was a memorable one. I travelled with Josephine, because it was an opportunity to see the 'Holy Land'. We travelled from Mumbai to the Tel Aviv as there was no direct flight from Delhi. We were subjected to the most gruelling interrogations at the Mumbai airport to find out all possible reasons and motivations for our visit, including the sources of finance and the purpose of visit.

The purpose of my visit was to participate in a seminar in honour of Shmuel N. Eisenstadt the illustrious Israeli sociologist, when he turned an octogenarian in 2003. The theme of the seminar was 'Comparing Modernities: Pluralism versus Homogeneity' sponsored by the Israel Academy of Science and Humanities. The invitees included Jeffrey Alexander, Bjorn Wittrock, W.G. Runciman, Ralf Dahrendorf, Alain Touraine, Edward A. Triyakian, Ulf Hannerz, Erik Allardt, Gerald Delanty, Piotr Sztompka, Stanley J. Tambiah, Raymond Budon and Donald Levine. I was the only scholar from India and I read a paper entitled 'Challenges of Modernity in an Age of Globalization' which appears in the volume that emerged from the seminar, published by Brill (Leiden) in 2005.

Jerusalem is the birthplace of the three Semitic religions–Judaism, Christianity and Islam–with the persisting conflicts between them. Synagogues, churches and mosques exist close to one another, but communal clashes erupt often. In contrast, the residential enclaves of these religious communities are exclusive with their own specific norms and practices. For example, when we asked the taxi driver to take us to the Jewish enclave on a Saturday, the Jewish Sabbath, he told us that people could throw stones at us. Similarly, it was a risky proposition to visit a Muslim enclave on a Friday. Israel had three weekly holidays–Friday, Saturday and Sunday–respecting the sentiments of Muslims, Jews and Christians respectively. Shops and establishments belonging to these religious communities remain closed during their sacred days.

We visited Bethlhem, the birthplace of Jesus, Gethsemane where he prayed before he was crucified and Calvary where he was crucified. We bought three bottles of wine manufactured by Franciscan Monks and gave them to the Jerusalem Mar Thoma Church in Delhi and to the church in my ancestral village.

One of the most enjoyable evenings during our visit was a supper with a couple, Shmuel and Shoola, at their home. I asked Shmuel, a sociologist, why the Mar Thoma Syrian Christians of Kerala did not have any church in Jerusalem in the compound wherein numerous Christian denominations have theirs. Shmuel asked me, 'T.K., is the Mar Thoma Church linked with the state in Kerala?' The answer was certainly not in the affirmative and that explained the absence of the church in Israel. When we were about to have our supper, Shmuel gave a cap each to me and Josephine and requested us to join him for the prayer. He said covering the head with a cap during prayers is a Jewish custom and added, 'To pray before supper is *not* an indication of religiosity.' To hear this from a sociologist was indeed amusing.

CHAPTER 11

On the Travails and Triumphs of Publishing

Having studied in a vernacular school in my native village, I shifted from the Malayalam medium to English only when my college education started after my matriculation. Therefore publishing in English was a nightmare for me. And yet, I can look back somewhat triumphantly on the story of my publishing. So far I have published thirty one books of which I am the sole author of seventeen, co-authored five, edited three and co-edited six. Seven of these books were published by Sage, four by Oxford, two each by Macmillan, Pearson Longman, Popular Prakashan, Orient Longman/BlackSwan, one each by Polity Press, Thomson, Vikas, Hindustan Publishing Corporation, and the Government of India among others. (See Appendix-5)

Perhaps publishing research papers in referred academic journals is more tortuous. I have published over 200 research papers but ninety of them were published in books edited by social scientists, mainly sociologists. These were invited papers that are generally accepted for publication. The remaining 110 research papers I have published appeared in sixty-three academic journals–thirty-three Indian and thirty foreign–including the *Commonwealth Journal of Political Studies, Comparative Studies in Society and History, Sociologia Ruralis, International Review of Sociology, International Sociology, International Social Science Journal, Asian Survey, Social Forces, Social Compass, International Migration, Current Sociology, Asian Journal of Social Sciences, Mobilization: An International Journal, Sociological Bulletin, Contributions to Indian Sociology, Indian Journal of Social Sciences, Contributions to Nepalese Studies, Economic Weekly, Economic and Political Weekly, Journal of Social and Economic Studies, Social Action.* Twenty nine of the journals were foreign: eighteen European, five North American, three South Asian, two South-east Asian and one African. And the process is continuing.

One of the frequent accusations hurled at academics is that they dwell in their ivory towers and do not publish for common readers. To steer clear of this I have published over a hundred articles in popular journals and magazines and little over fifty newspaper editorials, mainly in *The Times of India, Hindustan Times, The Hindu, Indian Express* and a few others. While most authors want their books to be reviewed, and hopefully favourably, they refrain from reviewing others' works. But even here I cannot be easily faulted; I have reviewed over sixty-five books in fifteen academic and popular journals and three newspapers. In spite of this enormous range of publishing, I have no evidence that others read what I write. In fact I frequently joke that only one person reads what I write–the proofreader!

The British saying 'publish or perish' emphasizes the inevitability of publishing by academics but its sequel 'publish and perish' points to the risk of being exposed if one gets published. I am afraid this applies to me but I know many clever academics do not publish but incessantly criticize those who do. P.C. Joshi, the economist and sociologist, once told me that a colleague criticized whatever he wrote, which prompted Joshi to retort, 'Please provide me with an opportunity to criticize you.' Since then his colleague's sharp tongue took a long break.

What I want to communicate to my readers is that the only way to survive in this world is constant and relentless struggle. Therefore, I propose to focus mainly on the obstacles and difficulties I encountered in the process of publishing. Please note that there were no computers and emails when I started publishing in the 1960s. The first 'research paper' I published appeared in the *Economic Weekly* in 1965. I had already published eight articles in journals such as the *AICC Economic Review*, *Kurukshetra*, *Seminar*, *Indian Journal of Social Work*, *Indian Co-operative Review*, *Indo Asian Culture* and *Quest*, but from the perspective of academic social science they could not be considered research papers.

When I was on the faculty of the Delhi School of Social Work (since 1964), one of my lunchmates was K.N. Vaid who used to teach labour welfare. One day in the course of our conversation, he observed, 'A sociologist cannot get published in the *Economic Weekly* unless his/her paper is forwarded by M.N. Srinivas.' I was curious to test the veracity of the statement and the only way out was to send a paper to the journal. I was in the process of writing my PhD thesis, so it was not difficult to compose a research paper. I despatched a paper entitled 'Sociology of Gramdan Villages: The Case of Rajasthan' to the *Weekly* and waited with bated breath. There was no acknowledgement whatsoever but after about six weeks I got fifty offprints and a cheque for Rs 50. The editor, Sachin

Chaudhari, wrote a note thanking me for sending the paper to the *Weekly*. I was overwhelmed and rushed to Vaid, who was shattered to learn that the influence he attributed to Srinivas was a figment of his imagination.

My first paper in the *Economic Weekly* appeared in June 1965 and the second paper exactly three years later in June 1968. By that time it had become the *Economic and Political Weekly* and the new editor was Krishna Raj. The data for the paper was drawn from fieldwork in seven villages in Rajasthan and its title was 'Strategy for Social Change: A study in Untouchability'. I argue in the paper that untouchability is practised in rural India in two broad contexts and designated them as 'ritually polluting behaviour' and 'secular status affecting behaviour'. The data revealed that the resistance to ritually polluting behaviour was much more intense as compared to behaviour eroding secular status. The theoretical-conceptual inspiration for writing the paper was drawn from Gunnar Myrdal's *An American Dilemma* in which he argued that to diminish discrimination against black people in the USA one should identify and attempt to change the 'soft spots' and gradually move towards the 'hard spots'. My paper started with a discussion of this framework and suggested that the soft spot in the Indian situation was the secular dimension and a change in this would release waves of repercussions through cumulative causation and would gradually change the ritual dimension also. The editor of the *Economic and Political Weekly (EPW)*, without any reference to me, scissored away this portion. Consequently, when the paper appeared in print it was conceptually naked. I was greatly embarrassed but could do nothing. To add insult to injury Suresh Shukla, the sociologist of education, who worked at the Central Institute of Education, Delhi University, wrote a rejoinder in the *EPW* rightly criticizing the conceptual inadequacy of my paper. This instance reveals how editorial arbitrariness can damage the academic standing of authors.

Between 1965 and 1975 five of my papers were published in the *EPW*. There were two distinct advantages in publishing in the journal, one being that it is a weekly unlike many academic journals that publish only two or three issues annually; two, the *EPW*'s circulation is much higher compared with journals of specialized disciplines.

Between 1976 and 2008, no paper of mine was published in the *EPW*, although I submitted a paper in 1982 entitled 'Health and Society in India: Towards a Sociological Understanding' for publication. After waiting for several weeks I wrote to the editor and Krishna Raj replied on 1 October 1982, informing me that it would be published soon. I waited for the promise to be kept for thirty-three years! However, my book *From Mobilization to Institutionalization: The Dynamics of Agrarian Movement in 20th Century Kerala,* published in 1985, was reviewed in the *EPW*. (Incidentally, this book won the G.S. Ghurye award for the best book published in 1985 in sociology and social anthropology). The reviewer was G.K. Leiten, a Belgian scholar doing his PhD at JNU. The book was widely perceived as an anti-left, particularly anti-CPM work, and the review was a long and devastating critique. I did reply, but what was published in the *EPW* (1988) was a short, garbled version.

After a thirty-three-year gap, I submitted a paper to *EPW* in 2009 after Krishna Raj left and a new editor, C.R. Reddy, took over. That paper was published in 2010. But I am still waiting to hear about the fate of a paper which I submitted in 2012. If a journal's editor does not find a paper publishable, the author should be informed or given the comments of the reviewer so the manuscript can be rewritten. But if the editor is silent, it poses an ethical dilemma to the author because the paper cannot be submitted to another journal according to the norms prescribed and prevalent in the world of publishing. A journal as widely read as the *EPW* should be following author-friendly principles and policies.

In the course of my fieldwork for my PhD spanning eighteen months, I lived both in peasant and adivasi villages and noticed some basic social structural differences. Following the tradition of dichotomous constructions of societal types, almost axiomatic in sociology and social anthropology those days, the rural–urban continuum was endorsed widely in Europe and also in India. But I was uncomfortable with this formulation and wrote a paper: 'The Rural Urban Continuum Re-examined in the Indian Context', and submitted it for publication to the *Sociological Bulletin,* the official organ of the Indian Sociological Society (ISS) in 1966. Editorial decisions were taken by the then president of the ISS, G.S. Ghurye and the secretary K.M. Kapadia, both from the department of sociology, Bombay University. I waited for more than six months but there was no communication. In the meantime I came across an announcement in *Sociologia Ruralis,* the official organ of the European Rural Sociological Society that the journal was planning a special number on the rural–urban continuum and research papers were welcome from all parts of the world. Since I had not heard from Ghurye or Kapadia, I duplicated the copy of the paper and despatched it to *Sociologia Ruralis* by surface mail. I could not afford to send it by airmail.

To my pleasant surprise, the editors of *Sociologia Ruralis* accepted the paper, informing me that it would appear in 1967. Almost one year had elapsed after my submission of the paper to *Sociological Bulletin* when I received a letter from K.M Kapadia, saying my paper was accepted for publication. I wrote to him, informing him that the article was going to appear in *Sociologia Ruralis* but I had no objection if the *Bulletin* reproduced the paper with due acknowledgement. I have not heard from Kapadia since then.

The publication of my paper entitled 'The Concept of Dominant Caste: Some Queries', published in *Contributions to Indian Sociology* in 1970 raised a storm, even if it was a storm in a teacup. T.N. Madan, the editor of *Contributions*, sent it to two referees, both social anthropologists, one from the UK and the other from the USA. Both recommended it for publication. However, they observed that the author of the paper was highly critical of Srinivas. In fact, one of them wrote, 'Your author does not stop by smashing MNS's head with a pickaxe, but he wants to chop off his head with a blade!' (I am quoting from memory, so these may not be the exact words). Having read this out to me, Madan asked me, 'T.K., do you want to publish this paper?' I could see that Madan was somewhat nervous about it so I told him, 'Madan, you are only the editor but I am the author and I am willing to face the consequences.' The paper was published and earned me the sobriquet of 'Snooty' in the Indian sociological world.

I was a lecturer those days and that too in the DSSW. For such a person to critically examine a conceptual formulation of the reigning deity of Indian sociology was an aberration and smacked of arrogance in the perception of professional colleagues. I feel this attitude is the biggest limitation in knowledge advancement because knowledge improves through interrogation. Suresh Shukla, who criticized my paper in the *EPW*, telephoned me and said, 'Oommen, if you want to become a reader you would have to leave Delhi,' to which I quipped back, 'One of us–me or Srinivas–would have to leave'. What I want to indicate is the tendency of academic colleagues that may be formulated as 'If one wants to prosper professionally one needs to keep in good humour those who matter in the profession'. But my naivety could not comprehend this.

In the same year, that is, 1970, I had another uncomfortable but dissimilar experience. Rajni Kothari was the shining star in Indian social science, presiding over the Centre for the Study of Developing Societies and CSDS was justly famous for electoral analyses, among other things. Kothari initiated the publishing of a series of papers about the fourth general election in the *EPW* (if my memory serves me right). I had never studied electoral behaviour and yet I was asked to write a paper. Given my inclination, or should I say disinclination, to study one Lok Sabha constituency, I decided to write a general paper about the general election. Its title was 'Transitional Anomie in Indian Politics'. Based on the available media reports on the election I argued that voting behaviour was neither 'traditional', that is determined by caste, religion and such other primordial factors, nor 'modern' in that voters do not always vote based on ideological orientations or party affiliations. Indeed, voting behaviour was undergoing a 'transitional anomie' suggesting that over a period of time it might turn 'modernist'. My argument did not fall in line with the 'paradigm' championed by the Kothari school and was not accepted for publication. However, it was published in the *Humanist Review.* I realized that one cannot easily take an independent position in the world of scholarship in India; it is more pragmatic to accept the patron–client relationship.

Sometimes a paper commissioned for a particular context and expected to be published in a volume may find its place elsewhere. In 1982, as Y.B. Damle was about to retire, the department of sociology at the university of Pune decided to hold a seminar on Indian sociology. D.N. Dhanagare who joined the department after leaving IIT Kanpur was the central figure in organizing the seminar and wrote to me on 2 March 1982:

> Perhaps you know that Professor Y.B. Damle will be retiring from service in March 1983. A felicitation committee is going to be constituted soon. As part of the felicitation for Prof. Damle we propose to hold a National Seminar on 'Theory and Concept in Indian Sociology' sometime in February–March 1983... In view of the sustained work you have done in Indian Sociology and also in view of your concern for theory and methodological rigour, I invite you to participate in this seminar...

However, Dhanagare wrote to me in his letter dated 12 December 1983 that the seminar had nothing to do with Damle and that there would be no Damle felicitation volume. And so I withdrew the paper I had written for the seminar and submitted it to the *Sociological Bulletin.*

Broadly speaking perspectives in envisioning the future of Indian sociology differ, some arguing for indigenization and the other for modernization. Damle was for modernization which in effect meant Westernization, particularly Americanization. His pet authors were Talcott Parsons and Robert Merton and I have seen a photograph framed and hung in his drawing room, titled 'The Parsonians'. (Mercifully, I am not in the photograph). Part of his academic mission was also to offset the undue importance given to British social anthropologists in Indian sociology. I had all along felt uncomfortable both with indigenizers and modernizers and wanted to mould concepts and theories of Western origin to comprehend Indian social reality. I had published several papers on this theme and brought them together in one volume entitled *Alien Concepts and South Asian Reality: Responses and Reformulations* in 1995. The paper on 'Contextualization of Indian Sociology' belongs to that mould.

The Indian Sociological Society (ISS) used to have one conference every two years, and it was customary to invite a few sociologists to write working papers for the plenary sessions. I was invited to write a working paper for the ISS conference held in 1976 at Chandigarh when S.C. Dube was the president and Yogendra Singh, the secretary. Commissioned to write a paper on social movements, I wrote, 'Sociological Issues in the Analysis of Social Movements in Independent India'. As is the norm the paper was published in *Sociological Bulletin*, the official organ of the ISS. I was again invited to write a working paper in 1984 when the conference was held at Surat. Y.B. Damle was the president and D.N. Dhanagare, the secretary of the ISS at that time. The theme on which I was invited to write was 'Ethnicity and Nation-Building in India', but the title of my paper was 'Insiders and Outsiders in India: Primordial Collectivism and Cultural Pluralism in Nation-Building'. I hoped that the paper would be published in *Sociological Bulletin*, as was the norm, but it was not, perhaps because it was perceived as 'anti-national'. I have had no communication from the decision-makers of the ISS about this paper to this day.

However, the paper did see the light of day. The International Sociological Association (ISA) was planning the launch of a new journal, *International Sociology*, coinciding with the XI World Congress of Sociology, to be held in New Delhi. As I was in touch with Martin Albrow, the founding editor of the journal, I showed it to him. He was immensely impressed by the paper and included it in Vol.1 (i) of *International Sociology*. Thus a paper rejected by *Sociological Bulletin* found its place in an international journal. I was delighted when I received a letter from R.A. Schermerhorn, the author of the fascinating book *Ethnic Plurality in India,* saying that my paper helped him understand the intersections between traditional Indian society and modern Indian polity, which he missed capturing in his book.

Schermerhorn wrote on 2 June 1986:

> This is to congratulate you on your highly perceptive article 'Insiders and Outsiders in India: Primordial Collectivism and Cultural Pluralism in Nation Building' which appeared in the fledgling journal *International Sociology* now published by the ISA. You have enlarged our thinking tremendously on issues of cultural pluralism as they apply to India by showing how really unique the situation is and how complicated. Furthermore, and this is equally significant, you have shown that the usual analyses of economists and political scientists when applied to the Indian scene are woefully inadequate... I must reiterate my indebtedness to you for the highly illuminating article you have given us. It has helped to clarify my thinking in many ways.

My exposure to *International Sociology* was a great academic boon for me and I have published several papers over the years in the journal, even after Martin Albrow left the editorship. My diffidence with regard to competence in the English language continues to haunt me. But the encouragement I received from persons like Martin was a great morale booster. In a letter dated 15 October 1990 and marked 'Personal', he wrote:

> You write and speak with a style which I appreciate greatly, no verbiage, no jargon, yet homing in on major issues. In my view there are not too many people writing in Sociology today with this talent–perhaps Daniel Bell is the most notable and I have not been able to persuade him to write for us. But we don't need him if you are with us!

The most controversial paper I published in the *Sociological Bulletin* was 'Disjunctions Between Field, Method and Concept: An Appraisal of M.N. Srinivas' which was the text of the seventh M.N. Srinivas Lecture. There were two responses to that lecture. For A.M. Shah, perhaps the most faithful student of Srinivas, it was a violation of the 'norms of academic discourse'. The text of my lecture extended to twenty-one printed pages and his condemnation of it was fourteen pages! Shah claimed that my lecture 'appalled' many sociologists, but he did not reveal the details of the survey he undertook to make this assertion. At least a dozen people told me, either face to face or telephonically that they greatly appreciated and fully enjoyed the lecture. According to Shah I was discourteous to Srinivas because I criticise him after his death. But I wrote a scathing critique of Srinivas's concept of 'Dominant Caste' in 1970 when he was very much alive. At any rate, if one goes by Shah's norms, no academic critique is possible after the death of an author. May I remind him that the 'doctrine of infallibility' is inapplicable in academics.

The other commentator was M.V. Nadkarni who confessed that he 'enjoyed reading' the printed version of my lecture but he averred that there was no necessary link between caste and Hinduism. I had not invented this link and in fact, found it in the writings of Srinivas. The then managing editor of the *Sociological Bulletin*, N. Jayaram asked me whether I would reply to Shah and Nadkarni but I declined and do not intend to do so even now. All the relevant documents are in the public realm and the readers should make their evaluations. The point of the matter is that if succeeding generations do not critically evaluate the work of their predecessors, disciplinary growth would be stunted. This seems to be one of the problems with Indian sociology.

I conclude my publishing experience in academic journals with special reference to the *Sociological Bulletin.* In the light of my initial unpleasant experience, I did not dare to submit any paper for publication to the *Bulletin.* But since I participated in the seminar on 'Dimensions of Social Change in India' held at the Institute of Social and Economic Change, Bangalore, organized by M.N. Srinivas, I was asked to write a report on it and it was published in 1973, my first publication in the journal although not a research paper. But N. Jayaram reported in his 'Sociological Bulletin at Sixty':

> The highest number of contributions by a single author is seventeen, and that record is held by T.K. Oommen... with his last article he overtook the founder president G.S. Ghuryes' long standing record of sixteen articles published during the first fourteen years... Oommen's record, it appears, will remain unbroken for many years to come.

Incidentally, I published two articles in *Sociological Bulletin* after Jayaram's report and the record now stood at nineteen. I am reporting this story to motivate young authors who are easily crestfallen when they face rejections.

The story of publishing books was both agonising and exciting for me. Let me recall a few of them. My first book, *Charisma, Stability and Change* is based on my PhD thesis. In the late 1960s when I finished my thesis, I submitted my manuscript to the University of California Press for its series on South Asia. On 18 September 1969, Philip E. Lilienthal, the then director of UCP wrote to me, 'The subject of your book is certainly a most interesting one, and we have a high regard for your professional competence.' I did not have any prior interaction with him and his opinion about my 'professional competence' could only be based on the manuscript submitted to UCP. I was very hopeful of getting a favourable response from Lilienthal.

In a letter dated 1 January 1970 from Lilienthal, I learnt that the manuscript was with a reviewer and he would report on developments in the matter soon. In the same letter he wrote: 'I was delighted to receive a telephone call from Srinivas over the weekend. He and his family have recently arrived in this area, and I look forward to a reunion with them before the week is over.' However, Lilienthal through his third letter dated 26 March 1970 informed me:

> There is, as you know, lively interest in Gramdan as a socio-political movement and as a significant aspect of the dynamics of change in rural India. Your treatment is excellent of its kind, but its kind is too particularistic for our purposes and on this account I fear that we are not in a position to offer you publication by the University of California Press.

What intrigued me most was the comment that my treatment of the subject was 'too particularistic', because the UCP had already published at least one single-village study. I had followed an experimental research design through which a comparative study of four Gramdan and three non-Gramdan villages selected from the three regions–irrigated plain area, arid zone and the hilly area of Rajasthan–was undertaken. It was not a simple ethnographic account of these villages but was an effort to interrogate Max Weber's postulation that charisma was a system-changing force. The core argument in the book was that the Gramdan movement, which I conceptualized as a charismatic movement, was a system-stabilizing force. Thus neither in terms of the vast empirical data nor in terms of the sophisticated theoretical argument, could the book have been described as 'particularistic'.

Having failed with the UCP, I submitted the manuscript to the Oxford University Press (OUP). Those were the days when one-village ethnographic studies were a staple in Indian sociology/social anthropology. My study was considered 'unfashionable' and OUP did not publish my manuscript.

I have come across seventeen reviews of *Charisma, Stability and Change*; ten in journals and seven in newspapers: a rare phenomenon these days. It seems that newspapers have largely abandoned their responsibility of informing the public about happenings in the academic world. Among the journals which reviewed the book were: *Sociologia Ruralis, Behavioural Sciences and Community Development*, *Political Science Review*, *Eastern Economist*, *Yojana, People's Action* and *The Century*. Akhilanand wrote in *The Century*: 'The book is a must for those who want to understand the genesis of the post-Gandhi non-violent movement in India and also for those who feel this movement is a failure and yet are not clear about the rationale behind it.' K.D. Gangrade, a professor of social work commented in his review in *Peoples' Action:* 'Oommen has made a unique contribution to the theory of change as well as charisma.'

What was most upsetting for me as a sociologist was that not a single journal on sociology and social anthropology in India reviewed the book. It was subjected to a cognitive blackout by fellow academics and I was rejected by them as a sociologist. Quite a few sociologists and social anthropologists who made it to the top in India got instant recognition when they published their PhD dissertations, three of them being M.N. Srinivas for his *Religion and Society Among the Coorgs of South India*, T.N. Madan for his *Family and Kinship: A Study of Pandits of Kashmir* and Andre Beteille for his *Caste, Class and Power*. My experience was diametrically opposite and the reason seems to be that I was a deviant; the theme of my PhD dissertation was unconventional. Innovate and perish was the dictum that prevailed in Indian sociology. But I did not give up.

I published a book on doctors and nurses in 1978 which, as far as I know, was the first book on 'modern professions' authored by an Indian sociologist. Given the inextricable intertwining between caste and occupation in traditional Indian society, analyses of caste also meant study of occupations. But European colonialism irreversibly transformed this and a few from all castes, particularly the so-called upper castes, abandoned their caste-linked occupations and took to 'modern' ones. My initial interest was to study nursing as a profession because in spite of being less prestigious and even stigmatized, many Syrian Christian families encouraged their daughters to take up nursing as a career. In the course of my investigation I discovered the basic differences between doctors and nurses as professionals and studied the former too. I submitted the manuscript to Macmillan and the editor agreed to publish it. Later I learnt that the expert who reviewed the manuscript, was M.S. Gore who did not restrict his approach to participant observation and qualitative data. I have mainly used the 'survey method' to collect data from 545 nurses, 140 house surgeons and 337 physicians although I did collect qualitative data too when observing the role behaviour of the three categories in the out-patient, in-patient and emergency wards. I was convinced through my study of Gramdan villages that to be eclectic in data collection is of great advantage and persisted with it.

The academic reception to *Doctors and Nurses* discerned in terms of reviews was very disappointing. I came across only four reviews in newspapers: *Tribune*, *Sunday Standard*, *The Times of India* and *Hindustan Times.* Among the journals only *Contributions to Indian Sociology* published a short review of fourteen lines but the anonymous reviewer acknowledged that 'This pioneering study constitutes the first detailed and systematic study of professions in India'. K.K. Kapila wrote in the *Tribune*:

> This unique book will be of great value to all those who are interested in the sociology of professions and of organizations besides being of direct use to those involved in the study of role theory and sociology of medicine. Sociologists and social scientists of all persuasions will indeed find Dr Oommen's methodological approach and theoretical framework of considerable value, providing new insights as they do.

And, Girija Kumar, the well-known librarian, wrote in the *Sunday Standard*, 'Though intended primarily for those interested in the sociology of professions, this pioneering study contains sufficient raw material for being made the subject of popular reading.' It was gratifying that the *American Journal of Sociology* reviewed the book although not very positively.

My agony again was that sociologists and social anthropologists of India were largely tardy in publicly acknowledging the arrival of the book. But a couple of positive responses which I came across are worth recounting. In a seminar organized by S.K. Lal of the department of sociology at Jodhpur University on 'Sociology of Professions' (in 1979) L.P. Vidyarthi reportedly referred to the book in glowing terms. Another participant in the seminar, Ram Ahuja of the department of sociology, Jaipur, wrote to me to communicate his own appreciation about the book.

My third book *From Mobilization to Institutionalization: The Dynamics of Agrarian Movement in 20th Century Kerala*, was reviewed in less than a dozen publications. It was perceived as an anti-Marxist analysis and G.K. Leiten reviewed it in *EPW* as noted above. The title of his review was 'Broadsides

From an Indian Behaviouralist', and it caricatures the author of the book not only as an anti-communist but also as anti-upper caste. I sent a detailed rebuttal with the title 'Travails of a Firangi Defender of Indian Communism', but Krishna Raj, the editor, published a short and truncated version, with the title: 'Kerala Agrarian Movement'. I wrote in my rejoinder thus:

> Scholarly writing is a risky proposition in that it can fall into anybody's hands, including... the prejudiced and the unlettered. And nobody can stop it from being subjected to fierce, even virulent criticism. Be that as it may, the critic is not expected to mutilate, misquote or misrepresent facts and arguments. Leiten does all these and much more...

Apart from writing monographs I have also brought together my published research papers belonging to the same theme; I have nine such collections. The first two of them were published in 1984: *Social Transformation in Rural India: Mobilization and State Intervention* by Vikas Publications and *Social Structure and Politics: Studies in Independent India,* by Hindustan Publishing Corporation (HPC). The first of these volumes was widely and favourably reviewed but the second volume was largely ignored by newspapers and journals. The HPC book contained my research papers published in outstanding journals such as *Journal of Commonwealth Political Studies, Social Forces, Asian Survey, Contributions to Indian Sociology, Sociological Bulletin, Comparative Studies in History and Society, Political Science Review, Humanist Review* among others. HPC's was a new venture which started a series: 'Studies in Sociology and Social Anthropology', under the editorship of M.N. Srinivas and its associate editor was A.M. Shah. I was one of the editorial advisers with Scarlet Epstein and Owen M. Lynch. This experience taught me that the reception of a book depends not on its content but who publishes it and how well it is marketed.

My second experience in this context, came in 1990 when Sage Publications brought out *Protest and Change: Studies in Social Movements* and *State and Society in India: Studies in Nation-Building*. From 1990 to 2005 I published seven books through Sage but breaking the ice was rather tough. I had submitted the proposal for the two volumes of collected papers sometime in 1988 to Tejeshwar Singh of Sage Publishers. Tejeshwar knew me as the author of *Doctors and Nurses* published by Macmillan as he was working with that company in the 1970s but I met him only in 1985 when I was organizing the World Congress of Sociology. The contract to print the Programme Book of the WCS was a massive task. After the printed copies finished, Sage had to produce some 200 copies of the Programme Book at very short notice–this created some unpleasantness between me and Tejeshwar, because of financial and organizational reasons. But when I submitted my proposals for the two volumes in 1988 he came to JNU to talk about it, saying that publishing collected works of single authors was not the policy of Sage. I argued that breaking old practices leads to creativity and innovation so by the end of our conversation, the thorough gentleman and the true professional that Tejeshwar was, agreed to process the manuscripts. Sage made history because these were the first collections by a single author published by Sage and I felt gratified.

Both these volumes were well received by the academic world. While only three newspapers reviewed *Protest and Change*, twelve journals including *Social Forces*, *Contemporary Sociology*, *Eastern Anthropologist*, *South Asia*, *South Asian Survey*, *Contributions to Indian Sociology*, *Sociological Bulletin and Indian Anthropologist* reviewed the book. Anjan Ghosh in *Hindustan Times* suggested that, 'with institutionalization of social movement studies in sociology curriculum this book should be an oft-used one'. M.S. Gore wrote in the *Sociological Bulletin*:

> Oommen's book is not meant to be week-end reading. It requires one to sit up and read carefully. Progress is necessarily slow and the chances are that individual scholars will read selectively from it. They are likely to find the reading variously supportive or provocative, but always stimulating and instructive.

But alas! Veena Das dismissed the book as 'trivial' in a review in *IIC Quarterly* and Aditi Kapur, probably studying sociology in Delhi University at that time found it 'confusing'. Alain Touraine, the French sociologist known for his outstanding contribution in the area of social movements, observed: 'Few sociologists in the world have been able to integrate so deeply studies on social movements and analyses on nation building.'

State and Society was equally well received; thirteen reviews in all, of which nine were in journals such as *The Book Review*, *Social Policy and Administration*, *Sociological Bulletin*, *Social Action*, *Journal of Contemporary Asia*, *Indian Anthropologist*, *Contributions to Indian Sociology*, *India Quarterly* and *Seminar*. Rajen Harshe wrote a long review in *India Quarterly* and Sujata Patel observed in *Sociological Bulletin*:

> This volume, though small and compact, packs in many issues and has some surprising new formulations which would be of interest to all those dealing with the dynamics of state and society in India... Not only does Professor Oommen move over from the predominant post-Independence sociological proclivity to understand all contemporary processes in terms of the caste system, but he accepts and affirms the need to evaluate the contemporary crisis in terms of other processes and forces.

The positive acceptance of these two books may have encouraged Tejeshwar to publish a third book of mine, again a collection of papers, *Alien Concepts and South Asian Reality,* in 1995. With these publications I started to feel that I was being noticed by the academic community in India and elsewhere. But a true breakthrough occurred in 1997 when I met Anthony Giddens at Rome at a seminar. As we were leaving for our respective destinations, Tony for London and I for Delhi, we spent some time together at the Rome airport. Impressed by my presentation at the seminar, he told me, 'T.K., your name should be on the Polity list.' And so it was that my book, *Citizenship, Nationality and Ethnicity: Reconciling Competing Identities*, published by Polity Press in 1997, was conceived at the Rome airport. This was the only book for which I received an advance payment while signing the contract.

Citizenship, Nationality and Ethnicity was reviewed only in four newspapers but in ten journals including *American Journal of Sociology*, *Kyklos*, *International Affirs*, *Economic and Political Weekly*, *The Book Review and Sociological Bulletin*. Sociologist T.N. Madan in his review published in the *Sociological Bulletin* certified: 'The book is a product of widespread reading (covering the first, second, and third worlds) and careful reflection'. Niraja Gopal Jayal, the political scientist, wrote in the *EPW*, 'An impressively vast historical and comparative canvas forms the background and basis of this attempt at sweeping away the dusty cobwebs of historical and sociological scholarship and disentangling the often confused discourse around these concepts'.

And another political scientist Shobhana Menon wrote in *The Hindu:*

> ...Oommen's sociological excursus affords a welcome relief in a scholarly milieu dominated by historians and political theorists. The situations he examines in their variegated

diversities span continents and historical epochs. Bolstered by his wide reading of empirical facts, he approaches current interpretive literature with a high degree of expertise.

I was happy that most of the reviews were positive but most reviewers were political scientists. Another instance of the limited thematic canvas within which Indian sociologists and social anthropologists traverse, those imprisoned in their ethnography found the book not very convincing. There was a sequel to *Citizenship, Nationality and Ethnicity,* a book entitled *Citizenship and National Identity: Between Colonialism and Globalism* edited by me and published by Sage publishers in 1997. And a third book jointly edited by S.L. Sharma and me, *Nation and National Identity on South Asia* published by Orient Longman in 2000 added and concluded my foray into this theme. After A.R. Desai's *Social Background of Indian Nationalism* published in 1948, nation and nationalism was a frozen theme in Indian sociology for three decades. I attempted to resurrect it but I am not sure whether I succeeded. Students of sociology in India are fed even to-day mainly on the staples of family and kinship, caste and religion, village and town. Of course, some side dishes are added but nation and nationalism are left out for political scientists and historians to nurture. However, I thought that it was too crucial a theme to be left out by sociologists.

The only monograph I published through Sage was *The Christian Clergy in India* (that too as a co-author). Unlike *Doctors and Nurses, The Christian Clergy* was rather well received, viewed in terms of the number of reviews in six newspapers and seven journals including *Biblio, South Asia, Sociological Bulletin, Man in India, The Journal of Religious Studies* and *The Book Review.* In Indian society, priesthood was hereditary and confined to Brahmins; although they had a high ritual status ordinary priests were not perceived as learned. In contrast, in the Christian West, the clergy was a prestigious profession and ranked high along with medical doctors, lawyers and university teachers. Generally speaking, the Christian clergy undergoes long training in theology after the required/prescribed secular education. For these reasons the study of Christian clergy was a rare effort in India and was an all-India study of priests from all denominations except the Catholics.

Having failed to publish my PhD thesis from the Oxford University Press and since I was successful in publishing through several other publishers I did not approach OUP with a proposal. Also, because I knew that the experts associated with OUP were pro-social anthropology, if not anti-sociology. At any rate, available evidence was that they were not well-disposed to me. Therefore, I was pleasantly surprised when Rasna Dhillon, who was trained in the department of sociology at Delhi University and working in the acquisition department of OUP, approached me for a manuscript sometime in 2000. I shared my apprehensions, but she brushed them aside and insisted that I should publish from OUP too. My first OUP book was published only in 2002, a collection of essays entitled: *Pluralism, Equality and Identity: Comparative Studies.*

While at a dinner at the India International Centre, Manzar Khan, the then head of OUP at Delhi, asked me, 'You are a prolific writer but why are you not writing for us?' I told him, 'OUP does not publish books ...only authors.' He was curious about my comment and requested me to elaborate. I told him that if he surveyed Indian authors published from OUP in sociology he would discover that an overwhelming majority would be from the Delhi University sociology department; in fact PhD theses submitted to the department. *Pluralism, Equality and Identity* was not reviewed widely, in fact, not a single journal in sociology or social anthropology found it worth noticing.

But the reviews it received were fulsome and the reviewers were mainly political scientists. For example, B. Vivekanandan wrote in *International Studies:*

> The depth of understanding Oommen has displayed regarding the texture, not just one or two societies, but of a number of societies across the world is salutary…Indeed it is a scholarly expression of a world mind, trying to judge various societies in the proper perspective and without prejudice.

Similarly, Philippe Tulkens in the *EPW*:

> This book is a very important contribution to the study and the understanding of social evolution at the world level… one of its strongest points is that the conclusion arrived at from the analysis of some particular contexts have a value as models and can consequently be fruitfully applied to other contexts.

The book brought together eight previously published research papers, each of which compared two or more societies across the world. Although a late beginner with OUP, I published three more books between 2007 and 2010. The 2007 book was also a collection of papers discussing the not-so-happy interface between the proximate disciplines of sociology and social anthropology entitled: *Knowledge and Society: Situating Sociology and Social Anthropology*. Given OUP's proclivity to publish social anthropological works I was apprehensive but an enlarged second edition of the book was published in 2013. I chanced to edit the two-volume book on social movements in Oxford in India *Readings in Sociology and Social Anthropology* thanks to the persuasions of its general editor, T.N. Madan. In fact Madan had asked me much earlier to edit a volume on ethnicity but I was reluctant partly because of the nebulousness of the concept and partly because my own conceptualization of ethnicity was radically differed from the existing ones. I consented to edit a volume on social movements but it grew into two, Vol. I focusing on identity and Vol. II on equity and security. The series edited by Madan are mainly aimed at students and I do not know whether these volumes are prescribed even in the limited number of universities which teach social movements.

The series edited by T.N. Madan started with a volume on social stratification by Dipankar Gupta. I thought that my paper on dominant caste should be included in the volume and I knew Dipankar thought it was the best critique on the notion of dominant caste. To omit it was an editorial decision and hence one cannot grumble about it. However, in two other volumes, the editors wanted to include my papers and sought my permission which I granted. One was 'The Legal Profession in India: Some Sociological Perspectives' published in the Silver Jubilee Special Issue on the legal profession in India, published in 1986 in the *Indian Bar Review* to be included in the volume on the sociology of law, edited by Indra Deva and the other was 'On the Craft of Studying Social Movements: Two Illustrations', published in *The Eastern Anthropologist* in 1987 to be included in the volume *Methodology and Field Work* edited by Vinay Kumar Srivastava. These two papers were excluded at the instance of the 'experts' of Oxford University Press which smacks of prejudice and arbitrariness, because the editors of these volumes found the papers of high quality.

I published two research papers both relating to 'research methodology' in 1987. In addition to the paper are mentioned above published in *Eastern Anthropologist*, 'Theoretical Framework and Empirical Research: Their Interaction in the Analyses of Two Social Movements', was published in the *Sociological Bulletin.* These papers were intended to fill the gaps left by the two volumes on research methodology with special reference to India: Andre Beteille and T.N. Madan, (eds), *Encounters and Experience, Personal Accounts of Field Work* in 1975 and M.N Srinivas and Others (eds), *The Fieldworker and the Field* in 1979. These books reported on fieldwork done in a variety of empirical situations but there was no study of social movements.

In 2010, I edited another book based on the papers presented in an Indo-German seminar held at Munich. In 2006, the organizers of the Frankfurt Book Fair invited India to be the guest of honour. As a part of it, the National Book Trust (NBT) sponsored three seminars one each on German language and literature, history and sociology. Bipin Chandra, the then chairperson of NBT, asked me to organize the seminar on sociology. My task was to identify Indian scholars who would contribute to the seminar and locate a German scholar who would identify the German contributors and host the seminar. Hermann Schwengal of the University of Freiburg readily agreed to undertake this task.

In preparation to the project four Indian scholars and four German scholars met at the University of Munich. The theme was inequality with special reference to the working class, peasantry, middle class and citizenship. Two scholars, one each from India and Germany made presentations on the four areas and formulated their papers in the light of their presentations and discussions in the seminar. The eight papers were edited and introduced by me and published with the title: *Classes, Citizenship and Inequality: Emerging Perspectives,* in 2010 by Pearson. Only a few reviews appeared in India but they were positive. I understand that the reception of the book was much better in Germany.

My last book, *Social Inclusion in Independent India* was published in 2014 by Orient BlackSwan. It was a matter of great gratification for me that Orient BlackSwan brought out a second edition (paperback) of the book on social inclusion within eighteen months. I first submitted the manuscript to OUP. Although I have published four books from OUP, two of these were collected essays and two were edited volumes. I thought I should publish one monograph from OUP, but that did not fructify. From this experience I came to the conclusion that whether or not one can publish through a given publisher depends on those who are associated with the decision-making process of the firm at a particular point of time. The publisher usually obtains manuscripts through its acquisition editor, gets it evaluated by specific readers/experts and arrives at decisions. The processes involved are by definition 'professional' and anonymous but the evaluators would invariably know whose work s/he is evaluating, particularly when the author is a widely published one, because self-referencing cannot be avoided. From the comments of the readers I received from OUP I could guess who they were. Most comments were trivial and one could write them even without reading the manuscript.

I have noted that the first manuscript I submitted to OUP in 1970 was not published. But between 2002 and 2010, that is during the span of eight years, four of my books were published by OUP. And the last manuscript I submitted to OUP in 2012 was also not published. The wavering fortunes of particular authors with specific publishers can only be understood in terms of the internal organizational milieu and power structure of publishing companies. The story may be similar everywhere. Thus between 1990 and 2005, Sage published seven of my books but it has come to an abrupt halt since then. After *Turning 50: Memories, Moments and Dreams*, I was subjected to a complete blackout by Sage.

I pointed out to OUP after reading the reports on *Social Inclusion* that the two readers either did not read my manuscript or did not understand the ideas I was formulating and communicating. One of them observed that the manuscript was not based on field data generated by the author; another opined that the manuscript was neither a monograph nor a textbook, as if there are only two genres in academic works. It seems to me that the crucial decision-maker makes up his/her mind to publish or reject the manuscript in advance and the exercise of processing it is 'adjusted' accordingly.

However, there is another way of going about the process of decision-making. I will illustrate this also with an example. The manuscript of my book *From Mobilization to Institutionalization*, widely perceived as an anti-left book was read by a Marxist, perhaps D.N. Dhanagare, who made several disapproving comments. The publisher gave me the option to revise the manuscript in the light of these comments or to write a preface defending the position. 'I had taken the latter suggestion and wrote a thirteen-page preface. Here, the intention of the publisher was to publish the book and not to reject it on flimsy grounds. The point to be noted is that the author who is a victim does not have easy escape routes.

Against this background it is interesting to note that Dhanagare observed in 2011 that I have pointed out how in applying 'class analysis' as a framework, a researcher has to face complications in an Indian setting. He commented:

> While there are several acclaimed books to Oommen's credit by now, his initial studies have proved to be pace-setters and pioneering works in the Sociology of social movements in India. Above all, in these studies Oommen has not only maintained analytical rigour but also has demonstrated how on a sound basis of grassroots level empirical data, theoretical

abstractions are possible, that was something uncommon in sociology in the 1960s and 1970s.

One of the accusations frequently levelled against academics is that they live in the isolation of their ivory towers. But this cannot be said about me; I have published some 120 articles in popular journals and over fifty articles in the editorial pages of newspapers. I have published in the *Times of India* mainly when Dilip Padagoankar was at its helm, in *Hindustan Times* when Amulya Ganguly prodded me. Both in *The Hindu* and *Indian Express* my articles stopped appearing when the higher-ups seemed to have intervened. To be a public intellectual in India, one needs the blessings of decision-makers who act very privately. Let me illustrate it with one example.

The press in India is equally arbitrary as the reputed publishing houses. Little over 50 per cent of my newspaper articles (twenty-seven) were published in *The Times of India* between 1970 and 2008. Usually one or two letters to the editor appeared after each of these articles was published. On 27 March 1999, *The Times of India* published an article of mine entitled: 'Conversion Debate: A Clash of World Views'. The context of this piece was that during the course of the first fifty years, independent India had only fifty cases of physical violence against Christians but within ten months after the first NDA government came to power there have been 110 cases of physical violence against them. The attributed reasons for these attacks were fraudulent conversions of Hindus to Christianity. I argued that whenever conversions occurred from Hinduism to non-Indic religions such as Baha'i Faith, Christianity and Islam violence followed. In contrast, if conversions take place to Indic religions such as Buddhism or Sikhism from Hinduism no violence occurred. I concluded that the conversion debate is a clash between 'static' and 'dynamic' religions. Here static referred to non-proselytizing and dynamic to proselytizing religions.

My colleague M.N. Panini wrote a rejoinder to my piece but the *Times of India* did not publish it. It seems that he then sent the piece to his illustrious uncle M.N. Srinivas who sent the piece to the paper after the required polishing and it was published on 22 April 1999 with the title 'Conversion and the Curse of Caste'. He accused me of making 'several misrepresentations regarding Hindu Society, Hinduism and the results of conversion'. The main thrust of his rejoinder was that the untouchable converts to Christianity are not treated equally within the church, a well-known and well-documented point. However, I did not refer to this point at all in my piece nor did I make any 'misrepresentations' about Hinduism or Hindu society. Therefore, I wrote a clarification to Srinivas' rejoinder which the *Times of India* refused to publish.

A letter to the editor stated that if inequality persists within the religions to which conversion took place the fault lies with 'the Hindu social order' which gives pride of place to caste. Several persons talked to me after reading Sriniva's rejoinder, among them P.C. Joshi who said 'Srinivas stand diminished by publishing this piece'. But the hapless author has no escape route in the world of newspaper publishing to defend himself/herself.

Although I have published widely and have met and/or corresponded with a large number of sociologists and political scientists from the USA, the UK and numerous other countries, it cannot be said that my works are widely read. Let me refer to one instance here. Dough McAdam wrote to me in August 1993, 'I am embarrassed to say that you were right in presuming that I had not previously read your work–yet another telling example of the provincialism of American Sociology…'

However, as and when foreign sociologists read the works of Indian sociologists they usually react positively. Robert D. Benford wrote to me in 1992 after reviewing my book *Protest and Change* for *Social Forces* rated as one of the four top journals in sociology in the USA, 'As you can tell from the review, I was quite impressed by your work. *Protest and Change* represents a remarkable achievement in synthesizing structural and interpretive approaches to the analysis of collective action.' Benford however, confessed, 'Unfortunately until *Social Forces* sent me your book to review I had not encountered your name in our literature. Obviously this is due in no small way to provincialism in our academy.'

Those area study specialists who work on India may be better acquainted with the works of Indian social scientists. But here the wedge between sociology and social anthropology surfaces and hardly any Western sociologists attempt the study of 'other cultures'. However, some area study specialists in social science tend to cross disciplinary barriers.

My experience is that political scientists who study India are better disposed to Indian sociologists than Western social anthropologists, probably because of the similarity in themes they study. When the Rudolphs (Susanne and Lloyd), who studied India for more than half a century were felicitated at the University of Chicago on their retirement, invitees from India included political scientists, historians and sociologists, including me; but not a single social anthropologist was invited from India. Morris-Jones, the famous British political scientist, who edited *Journal of Commonwealth Political Studies*, found my paper 'Myth and Reality in India's Communitarian Villages', eminently suitable for publication in his journal. In fact, Norman D. Palmer, the US political scientist, proposed my name to the East-West Centre at Honolulu for a fellowship based on this paper. My family circumstances at that time did not favour acceptance of the fellowship, which is another matter. I could publish in *Asian Survey* and *Social Forces,* journals on political science and sociology respectively, both published from the US but could not publish in *American Anthropologist.* I am making this point because I find some social anthropologists in India cribbing constantly against the distinction made between sociology and social anthropology, forgetting that this is a product of historical circumstances, even if not applicable to the specific Indian situation. I elaborate on this point in my book *Knowledge and Society: Situating Sociology and Social Anthropology.*

CHAPTER 12

National Fellowship of the Indian Council of Social Science Research

The Indian Council of Social Science Research (ICSSR), established by the Government of India to foster social science research, focuses mainly on training in research methodology and encouraging university and college teachers to do research. The most prestigious programme of ICSSR is to invite National Fellows from social science disciplines to conduct research on a topic of their choice and write a book/monograph within the duration of the fellowship, which is two years. ICSSR had offered over fifty fellowships till 2010 of which eleven were from sociology/social anthropology –M.N. Srinivas, S.C. Dube, Y.B. Damle, Victor D'Souza, L.K. Mahapatra, M.S. Gore, P.C. Joshi, Ramkrishna Mukherjee, Leela Dube, A.M. Shah and A.R. Desai. I became the twelfth National Fellow in sociology when I accepted it for the period 2010–12.

The ICSSR National Fellowship was earlier offered to me for the period 1994–96 but I could not accept it as I was still working at JNU. I was keen to take up the fellowship because I had been working on the theme of social inclusion for quite some time and was also critical of the general tendency of Indian sociologists to avoid addressing social policy issues. Most Indian sociologists think they should produce and disseminate knowledge, but application of knowledge is not their concern. However, ever since I came across Robert Lynd's question: 'Knowledge for what?', I was keen to generate usable knowledge. While Indian sociologists did produce valuable knowledge about basic social institutions and social structures of India, they did not produce or encourage usable knowledge. Let me illustrate.

The three most popular themes of research in Indian sociology were, and still are, family and kinship, caste and religion and the village social system. But rarely was there research on patriarchy and the oppression of women, which could help to transform the family as an institution, providing tranquillity to all family members. And, when women researchers embarked on this vital task, men came to be portrayed as enemies of women, creating and reinforcing conflict in the family. The enormous amount of research on caste did not address the ways and means of establishing harmonious inter-caste relations or creating consensual equilibrium in the village social system. In one word, the questions: 'What is it?' and 'Why is it?' were asked and answered to a large extent but the question 'What it ought to be?' was scarcely posed. With our adoption of a democratic constitution, the wedge between constitutional values and societal values needed to be filled. By and large Indian sociologists failed to do this because of their disenchantment with social policy.

This is paradoxical because sociology, along with economics and political science, is widely perceived as one of the policy sciences, particularly in North America and West Europe, from which Indian sociology borrows conceptual and theoretical frameworks. Further, Indian sociologists are accused by planners, administrators and even fellow social scientists of being unwilling to pursue research on themes relevant for social policy. The ICSSR National Fellowship afforded an opportunity to me to partially fill this long-pending gap in Indian sociology.

Although social exclusion is as old as humanity itself, social inclusion as an approach to the social welfare of the deprived gained wide currency only in the post-industrial, democratic, capitalist Western societies after the demise of welfare states. The socially excluded category consisted of the mentally and physically disabled, aged invalids, those who survived attempted suicides, children subjected to abuse, single parents and those who indulged in substance abuse, delinquent behaviour or prostitution. That is, those socially excluded were mainly the victims of urban industrial societies, particularly of the West. But in the less developed agrarian societies of the East, those who are subjected to chronic unemployment, livelihood insecurity, inadequate consumption levels and nutrients, poor housing and education too are socially excluded. That is, social exclusion is a phenomenon conditioned by the nature of society. In economically less developed countries the economic factor assumes great importance as the basis of social exclusion.

India's first Prime Minister, Jawaharlal Nehru, adopted planned economic development as the instrument to eradicate poverty from free India through Five Year Plans. However even after ten plans, spanning half a century, poverty persisted as a serious problem. Because of the magnitude of poverty and inadequate resources at the disposal of the state, it was not possible to eradicate poverty. This gave birth to the advocacy of the institution of market as an agent to eradicate poverty and through that, social inclusion. Thus the Eleventh Five Year Plan adopted 'inclusive growth' as its motto. But there is a basic contradiction in this motto because unless inclusion focuses on the poor, economic disparity between the rich and poor would increase. And this is precisely what has happened in India. At any rate, income poverty is only one aspect of social exclusion and it is here that the capital importance of sociology as a policy science surfaces.

The phenomenon of social exclusion is normal in the Durkheimian sense of the term in that one cannot visualize a society where there is no exclusion. Be that as it may, the contexts of exclusion vary between societies. In monocultural and monoracial, that is stratified societies, the bases of exclusion are class, gender, age, disability and sexual orientation. In contrast, in culturally and racially heterogeneous societies, factors such as religion, language, race, tribe, place of origin, ecological zones and the like also add on to the bases of exclusion. However, in those societies where theologically sanctioned exclusions exist, which manifest in institutionalized inequality as in South Asia's caste system, the quality of exclusion differs and hence the usual measures of social engineering are inadequate to establish an inclusive society. To cap it all, the phenomenon of intersectionality, that is, the conjoint functioning of two or more factors, say caste and patriarchy, would lead to cumulative exclusion. Since Indian society is at once stratified, heterogeneous and hierarchical, the approach required for social inclusion will have to be different. As a National Fellow of ICSSR I have worked on this proposition, which has tremendous implications for evolving an equitous and democratic society in which all the constituent elements can maintain their identity and uphold their dignity.

I have identified several socially excluded groups in India. The prominent among them are Scheduled Castes (Dalits), Scheduled Tribes (Adivasis), Other Backward Classes (OBCs), religious and linguistic minorities, migrants and refugees, regionally disadvantaged people, women, the poor and the disabled (including sexual minorities). While all these are socially excluded, the sources and intensity of their exclusions vastly vary. Therefore, I have argued for evolving a social morphology of the excluded based on the causes of exclusion (social aetiology). Also, the excluded categories differ because they are constituted differently; some are organic collectivities and others are aggregative collectivities. While groups should be target of inclusion in the case of organic collectivities, individuals ought to be the target in the case of aggregative collectives. Also, the possibility of internal differentiation of organic collectivities through the process of social inclusion is recognized. This calls for the elimination of the creamy layer from all social categories so that the benefits can seep down vertically, benefiting the truly disadvantaged. Thus the composition of social groups change as the process of social inclusion proceeds.

There were two discussions on the book I wrote as a National Fellow, one at the India International Centre (IIC) New Delhi on 15 January 2015 and another at Hyderabad Central University (HCU) on 2 January 2015. The IIC function was presided over by T.N. Madan, the social anthropologist, and the two discussants were sociologist Satish Deshpande and political scientist Valerian Rodrigues. The IIC meet was well attended and I had to autograph quite a few copies of the book bought by those who attended the function. At HCU I delivered a talk on the book to an impressive audience.

The new trend of the studied indifference of the print media to academic books is worrying and my book, published by Orient BlackSwan in 2014 was barely reviewed. The theme of the book–social inclusion–is of utmost importance in the ongoing journey of the Indian Republic to evolve an equitous, democratic and just society. As a sociologist, it is particularly worrisome for its author because it was a conscious attempt to provide a policy thrust. Is the indifference to the theme of the book an indicator of changing times from planned economic development with the thrust on distributive justice to crass competition ordained by the rapacity of the market?

Generally speaking, the Indian–print and electronic, including the newly emerged social media–seem to be opting for utterly sensational themes. This is true even of academic and intellectual themes. Thus if a publication is partisan and is capable of generating adequate sound and fury, it would be picked up by the media. This fast-growing trend is a worrisome omen for the thinking citizens of India. The demise of public intellectuals seems to be happening in India even before their birth.

Part 2
Beyond Sociology

CHAPTER 13

Sundry Assignments and Responsibilities

I have been engaged in a large number of assignments, in addition to teaching and research in sociology.

In 1970, when the Ford Foundation entrusted the task of analysing labour problems, industrial and agricultural, to the Shri Ram Centre for Industrial Relations and Human Resources (SRCIRHR) in 1970, C.P. Thakur, an economist and co-ordinator of the study, invited me to contribute a paper relating to agricultural labour. I wrote 'Agrarian Tension in a Kerala District: An Analysis', which was published in the *Indian Journal of Industrial Relations* in 1971, the official organ of SRCIRHR. This study reinforced my interest in rural Kerala resulting in my book on the agrarian movement in twentieth-century Kerala.

Given this background, it was not surprising that the National Commission on Agriculture, Government of India, invited me to be a member of the panel of sociologists and political scientists, in 1971. Other members of the panel included P.C. Joshi and Andre Beteille. The panel meetings were held at the residence of C. Subramanium, the Minister of Agriculture, who took a great deal of interest in the Green Revolution. The association with this panel further stirred my interest in agrarian issues.

My next foray into a new area was when sociologist M.S. Gore was the chairperson of the National Committee on Police Training in 1974 and commissioned three scholars–Yogendra Singh, Imtiaz Ahmed and me–to write a paper on 'Police and Society' analysing the reasons for the estranged and tense police–people relationship in the Indian context. The police is widely perceived as a negative force in India so much so that mothers often invoke them to frighten and discipline their young children. This initial perception about police as a brute force gets reinforced through subsequent interactions in the life of citizens. The paper suggested that unless the relationship between police and citizens becomes mutually supportive, the police could not function as an effective law and order agency.

The setting up of the National Planning Commission provided the required fillip to several provincial states to launch their own planning machineries. Thus the government of Orissa (now Odisha) constituted a planning machinery (1977–80) to establish a state planning committee which consisted of an interdisciplinary team with economist Nilkanth Rath as its chairperson. I was the sociologist member, although it was rare to include a sociologist in such committees.

I would like to recall a memorable incident in the context of my numerous travels between Delhi and Bhubaneswar. There was no direct air-link between Delhi and Bhubaneswar, the capital of Orissa those days so I used to take a flight from Delhi to Calcutta and stay overnight at the Utkal Bhawan, the government guest house of Orissa and fly to Bhubaneswar in the morning from Calcutta. Sometimes the flights got delayed and the passengers got stranded at the airport. On one such occasion, Rajiv Gandhi was the pilot and after the flight took off he came to apologize to each passenger, something which I had never experienced as a passenger, although delayed flights were common when the Indian Airlines Corporation (IAC) had a monopoly in this sector.

I was invited to write a research paper, 'The Legal Profession in India' in 1983 to be published in the *Indian Bar Review* and a textbook for law students which co-authored with C.N. Venugopal, my colleague at JNU, entitled *Sociology* in 1988, published by the Eastern Book Company, Lucknow. Both these projects were done at the initiative of N.R. Madhava Menon, who subsequently became a leading figure in law education in India. Menon, the first vice chancellor of the National Law School, Bangalore, persuaded me to become a member of its Governing Council (1989–94). As is well-known, the series of national law schools subsequently established in India provided the much required fillip for modernization and professionalization of law education in India. Subsequently, when the West Bengal National University of Juridical Sciences (WBNUJS) was set up, Menon as its first vice chancellor, invited me to be a member of its first Executive Council in 1999. I continued in this position till 2015, contributing to the moulding of this institution.

After Menon left WBNUJS, I was a member of the Search Committee to appoint VCs and was its chairperson in 2011 when the fourth VC, Ishwar Bhatt, was appointed. He was a professor of law in the university of Mysore and several eminent persons, including Madhava Menon, recommended his appointment. However, his term as vice chancellor became a tension-prone period resulting in several competent faculty members leaving the institution. The VC suspended the registrar for 'misconduct and financial irregularities'. The registrar resorted to legal remedy and a court case between him and WBNUJS was filed in the West Bengal High Court. Two Enquiry Committees were set up by the VC to inquire into the 'misconduct' of the registrar.

I was upset about the developments not only because of my long association with WBNUJS but also because I was chairperson of the Search Committee which selected Vice-Chancellor Bhatt. My assessment is that since the Search Committee did not meet the candidates for the position of VC it could not make a proper assessment; search committees should make it mandatory to meet candidates before an appointment is made.

I was a member of the first Executive Council, Central University of Gujarat (CUG) during 2010-13. It was a pleasant experience to work with the first Vice-Chancellor of CUG R.K. Kale, a former colleague from the School of Life Science of Jawaharlal Nehru University. Similarly, as visitor's nominee to the Central University of Sikkim during 2011-14, I enjoyed working with Mahendra Lama who was a colleague from the School International Studies of JNU. I was a member of the Courts of two central universities–Puducherry and Shatiniketan. But I did not attend a single meeting of the Courts of these Universities. I did not find it rewarding to attend such meetings in which one cannot make any creative contributions. Apart from these assignments in institutions of higher learning, I was also associated with the India International Centre (IIC) as a member of its Advisory Council and Convenor, Society and Social Development, during 2002–04. As the convenor, I had to identify appropriate themes and speakers which gave me an opportunity to interact with a social circle beyond the sociological world. Later, during 2010–12, I was a member of the Library Committee of the IIC when the chairperson was Soli Sorabjee, the legal luminary. His balanced views and attitudes provided me ample opportunities to contribute to the building of the IIC library.

There were opportunities and occasions when I was involved in programmes associated with foreign institutions. I was Programme Co-ordinator during 1970–71, the first year of the Wisconsin University College Year India Programme. The Delhi School of Social Work, Delhi University, hosted this programme for undergraduate students from the USA. This interdisciplinary group came to India for a period of one year and chose subjects of their interest from one or more departments and colleges of Delhi University. As the programme co-ordinator, my task was to guide them to select appropriate courses, keeping in mind their academic inclinations.

During May–June 1971 an opportunity to go to Japan as visiting lecturer, at the Asian Leadership Development Centre (ALDC) Tokyo came my way. ALDC hosted young leaders in the age-group of 20–30 from South-east Asian countries to train them in leadership skills and roles. My stay of six weeks in Japan was both pleasant and awe-inspiring. Although an Asian country Japan was already far ahead of India and the culture shocks I underwent were many.

I arrived at the Tokyo International Airport in an early morning. I took a taxi to the International House of Japan (IHJ), and when we arrived, the taxi-driver demanded a much higher amount (US $80) instead of US $35, the actual fare. This was shocking because I was expecting decent behaviour in country such as Japan. The driver was a bully but I settled the matter amicably by paying him US$ 40. Incidentally, this was a contrast to what happened in Singapore.

In 1990 when my wife and I were returning from California, we spent a few days at Singapore. We stayed in one of the two YMCAs in the city and once when we were returning from 'Little India', the famous shopping centre, the taxi driver took us to the other YMCA. I had kept the address written in Chinese and had shown it to him when we got into the taxi so I threatened to file a complaint to the local police. He instantly apologized and showed us the chart which shows the taxi fare from Little India to different destinations in the city, then charged only the stated fare in the chart. When I narrated this incident to the receptionist, he told me that had I complained the taxi driver's licence would have been withdrawn for six months. This showed a contrast between 'democratic' Japan and 'autocratic' Singapore.

At Tokyo's IHJ, I approached the man who was cleaning the floor and asked for the receptionist. He said, 'Please go to the reception desk.' When I reached there I saw the same person standing at the reception, without his apron. When I had first asked him 'Do you speak English?' he answered, 'little little', in a Japanese accent, but at the reception he was speaking flawless English! I later learnt that most people multi-task in Japan and those who work in the tourist sector are specifically trained in conversational English, something India should learn to follow.

What I observed during my first visit to Japan in 1971 (I visited the country several times since and the last visit was in 2014, forty-three years later, for the World Congress of Sociology of ISA at Yokohama) was the total absence of division of labour between manual and white collar workers as illustrated at IHJ where the cleaner was also the receptionist! While travelling by rail in Japan, I noticed that just one person mans a railway station, particularly small ones. Thus the station master who signals the arrival and departure of the trains even picks up the waste littered by passengers when the trains leave stations.

In contrast, the acute division of labour in India between those who work more or less at the same level adds to inefficiency. For example, we have typists, steno-typists and stenographers. The typists will only type the manuscript given to them, and stenographers will type only the dictations they take. The steno-typists, the middle category, are expected to do both. Thus even if stenographers sit idle they will not agree to type the written manuscripts given to them. The elaborate division of labour usually believed to be a mark of modernity adds to increased expenditure and added inefficiency in India. Do sophisticated economists take into account the impact of minute divisions of labour impacting India's economic development adversely?

My mother wanted me to be a priest when I was miraculously saved from a snake bite when I was fourteen years old. But I was not inclined to be one, although not averse to accept some short-term assignments of a scholarly nature from the Church. I have been invited to speak by several denominations, particularly the Catholic Church, Church of North India (CNI) and my own denomination, the Syrian Mar Thoma Church, the Catholic Church being in the forefront in imparting training in non-theological subjects to the clergy. In 1975, 1976 and 1977, the church launched a programme for sensitizing its bishops drawn from Asian countries about secular themes referred to as the Bishops Institute for Social Action (BISA) and I was a member of faculty at Kuala Lumpur and Manila. What I noticed was that as students/trainees, bishops are no different from young university students in absenteeism, late coming and other wayward behaviour although most of them were over fifty years of age. I found role-taking and role activities substantially mould the behaviour of persons irrespective of their age, education and ecclesiastical status.

An important church-related assignment was to work as a social science consultant to the National Commission on Theological Education (NCTE) during 1978–85, appointed by the senate of Serampore College which established and administered theological colleges of non-Catholic denominations. There were four members of NCTE including myself: John Augustine, an Indian sociologist, Reverend R.W. Taylor, an American theologian and Hunter P. Mabry, who was trained both in social ethics and sociology. The Commission was to 'study and recommend the priorities in theological education … in the light of the major issues in Christian ministry in India to-day'. Since the general impression was that Christian theological education in India remains an artificial transplant without indigenous roots in India, the Commission was to identify the ways and means through which Christian theological education can be contextualized, taking into account Indian social reality.

The project was an ambitious one and it, conceived a four-volume publication: (1) Social Structure, (2) Social Roles, (3) Theological Training and (4) Financial Structure and Policies. However, as one of the members passed away and another withdrew, it was decided to have only two volumes; one on social structure and social roles and another on theological training and financial policies. I was to write volume I and Hunter P. Mabry to write volume II. I co-authored Volume I, with Mabry which was published in 2000 by Sage Publications. Volume II has not been published yet.

My involvement in the clergy study unfolded that team work is an extremely tortuous task irrespective of the composition and background of the team members. The team for the clergy study consisted of two US citizens who lived in India and two Indian sociologists. I visited Bangalore every summer since three of them lived there, spending six to eight weeks working for the project. Initially the team visited twenty-five theological colleges in different parts of India, collected data through questionnaires distributed to students and faculty, apart from interviewing them in groups. Data from pastors, bishops and theologically trained women and wives of pastors were collected through mailed questionnaires. Apart from the data collected from over 2000 respondents, content analysis of selected theological journals and case studies of a few parishes were also undertaken. Unfortunately, although the study was massive in its conception, it could produce only one volume of 375 pages. Thus the product of team work is often much less than its potential.

I was also associated with the World Council of Churches (WCC), a global body of non-Catholic Christians, for a decade, 1979–89. My initial entry was facilitated by Ninan Koshy who was the Director of International Affairs of WCC and was my senior at S.B. College, Changanacherry. I participated in several seminars and consultations of the WCC not only at Geneva, its headquarters, but in several countries across the globe. However, my involvement with the Church and Society division of WCC occurred at the instance of David Gosling, a British citizen who was teaching physics at the St Stephens College, Delhi University. He was a trained priest also. We were co-participants in several seminars and consultations. Gosling left Delhi by mid-1970s and joined WCC as the Director of Church and Society division.

My association with Church and Society division of WCC took me far and wide and I was elected to its executive committee (1979–83). During 1984–89 I was elected as one of its two vice chairpersons, the other being a lady from Latin America. Most of the executive committee members were drawn from the laity–scientists, social scientists, activists and other public intellectuals. It was an enlightening experience as unlike in India where those associated with religion are often perceived as representatives of conservative forces, in the Christian world, an association with religion could often be 'progressive' and even 'radical'. This variation is critical in religion playing its roles as a change-promoting or change-retarding force in society.

The National Council for Teacher Education (NCTE) came into existence as a statutory body in pursuance of the NCTE Act, 1993 'to achieve planned and co-ordinated development of the teacher education system in India'. After eighteen years of its functioning, the Supreme Court of India appointed a high-powered commission on Teacher Education in 2011, under the chairpersonship of Hon'ble Justice (Retd) J.S. Verma, former Chief Justice of India. The Commission which submitted its report in August 2012 recommended the appointment of a Task Force to finalize the restructuring plan for the NCTE headquarters as well its four regional offices. The NCTE appointed the Task Force on 8 March 2013 and it submitted its report in July 2014. This was/is my last official assignment. I was the only sociologist in the Task Force.

The major recommendations of the Task Force were establishing two additional RCs at Kolkata to cater to the north-eastern states and another at Lucknow besides the present one at Jaipur; the NCTE Act must be suitably amended but in the interim the NCTE should notify appropriate regulations under the NCTE Act to make the Appeal Committee a statutory body;

an academic wing (AW) of the NCTE should be established at Delhi, to discharge its academic developmental functions and articulate the academic vision of the NCTE; empanel experts and propose the composition of expert committees; suggest areas of research relevant for the NCTE and collate and present data to the expert committees to facilitate decision-making.

My work as a member of the Task Force afforded me an opportunity to understand the deficits of the NCTE, which was concerned with school education in India.

CHAPTER 14

The Planning Commission Project on Poverty Among Religious Minorities

The Great Indian Poverty Debate emerged after the Structural Adjustment Programme (SAP) was ushered in. Although India became politically independent in 1947, the economic disparity between the richest and poorest segments in Indian society widened. Although the 'Hindu rate of growth' was abysmally low, the tendency was to analyse poverty in the general population, ignoring the variations of poverty which existed among social categories, such as gender, caste groups and religious communities. It is against this background that the Planning Commission, Government of India, commissioned a study on 'poverty among religious minorities'. This is a politically inflammable topic because if religious minorities are victims of a more intense level of poverty, the state could be accused of not taking appropriate measures and pursuing a patently discriminatory policy.

The credit for commissioning the study of poverty among religious minorities in India goes to D.T. Lakadawala, a former deputy chairperson of the Planning Commission, who was the chairperson of the Institute of Social Science (ISS) New Delhi during 1985–94. George Mathew, who completed his PhD with me, was the director of the ISS and the project was executed from the Institute and Anand Inbanathan who completed his PhD in 1986 under my supervision worked as the research officer. The study was for a period of two years and the report was submitted in 1990. I have no idea what action was taken by the Planning Commission based on the findings and recommendations of the report.

The recognized religious minorities of India are Muslims, Christians, Sikhs, Buddhists, Jains, and Zoroastrians. Two other religious minorities, Baha'is and Jews, were not yet recognized as minorities by the Government of India so were not included in the study. Data for the study was culled from official documents and research studies.

The geographical distribution of the minorities in India indicates a countrywide distribution of Muslims. Christians are concentrated mainly in the southern and north-eastern regions of India. Jains are located in the western region, Sikhs are found mainly in the Punjab, while the urban-based Zoroastrians (Parsis) are concentrated in Maharashtra. Buddhists are mainly in Maharashtra, Uttar Pradesh, Arunachal Pradesh, Sikkim and Mizoram.

At the state level, concentrations of minorities cluster in and around a specific locality implying firstly, that religious ties are strong, and secondly, living in enclaves provides some security, especially for minorities who have been victims of communal strife. This also helps in policy formulations, which can be both area- and religion-specific.

The demographic distribution of minorities has a bearing on their relative socio-economic and political standing in India.

In states where the non-Hindu religious groups were/are the majority of the population, they display less of the typical features of a minority. There are also other consequences, such as with the Christians of Mizoram, ST converts, who exhibit a high literacy rate of 60 per cent, among the highest in India. The religious groups are also likely to have better opportunities for employment in those states where they form a substantial proportion of the state's population.

Although discrimination in employment is faced by religious minorities (non–Hindus) in various states, it is not on a large scale, or of a systematic and sustained kind. Of a more subtle variety, it may take the form of delaying promotions to certain positions, or giving favoured positions to those of the majority religious group. Further, in a democratic country as India, where numerical strength has a direct relation to political power, the non-Hindu groups in states in which they are the majority, have the power to formulate policies beneficial to themselves, unlike in a state where they form only a small group.

The overall development of the states also has a bearing on the absolute poverty of the people, and consequently, on the minorities too. For example, in a poor state like Bihar, one can hardly expect a large proportion of the minorities to be prosperous. Neither does the absence of discrimination make a religious group affluent. For example, in Kerala, which has the highest literacy rates, Muslims have remained educationally backward indicating that they have not responded positively to the educational opportunities in the state, partly due to the greater importance given to religious learning rather than 'secular' education.

A factor responsible for the incidence of poverty to a large extent is the lack of education. Educational backwardness is very often influenced by religious beliefs. Muslims place a greater importance on religious education and thus, children find it difficult to cope with secular education at higher levels (university or professional) of education. This is in contrast to Christian institutions where secular education of a high standard is imparted to people of all religions.

Religious ideals also have a bearing on the type of occupations pursued by those of a particular faith. For example, Zoroastrians are influenced by two values enjoined by their religion, the desire to accumulate rather than to consume material goods, and to maximize one's 'material prosperity', so they tend to 'select financial vocations in favour of other possible pursuits'. Muslims are traditionally against modern banking and Jains generally do not take up agriculture. Though these attitudes are undergoing change (as in the case of Jains in Karnataka), religious and caste groups had in the past been identified by their occupations. On the other hand, certain religious beliefs have also hindered their progress. It is observed by a researcher that most Muslims have 'a stubborn resistance to the re-orientation of retrogressive attitudes and beliefs and any reform of outdated institutions'.

The employment position is an important index of the economic progress of religious minorities. Artisans and those engaged in traditional occupations are poorer than the others, unless they take to modern technology. Further, to remain close to the workplace, many people live in unhygienic surroundings that adversely affect general health and therefore, their level of income.

The literacy rate of women usually affects that of the whole community. Among the Muslims, the female literacy rate is so low that it has lowered the literacy figures for the Muslim population as a whole. The more serious and damaging part is that Muslim women do not play an important role in the intellectual development of their children (the lack of education among the mothers has a negative impact on the children's development), do not contribute to economic activities of their families and live in relative ignorance all their life. The fact of women remaining illiterate has an immediate effect on succeeding generations of female children particularly, who have to follow the purdah system like their mothers. However, some changes are occurring, especially in urban areas, where at least some Muslim families send their children to high school. Female illiteracy can be directly linked to the overall backwardness of any community, female illiteracy and economic backwardness mutually 'causing' and reinforcing each other.

A contrasting situation is seen among the Parsis, who display an unusually high female educational level. 'Literacy in the Bombay constituency reaches 90 per cent with the females leading the males by a fraction of 1 per cent', according to one study. Incidentally, among Parsis, the females outnumber males, but the reverse is true of all other communities–minority or otherwise.

Inter-community comparisons show that because of their relatively better education and occupational positions, the Christians are not as poor as the Muslims, but not affluent either. Muslims occupy a lower economic position to the other minority communities, but the Sikhs, the Jains and the Parsis are predominantly above the poverty level.

Despite affirming egalitarian values, all religious minorities do have caste-like sub-groups. Among Muslims, apart from the Shia and Sunni sects, there are several prominent groups like the Bohras, the Khojas and the Memons, but the income variations are primarily between Ashraf, Ajlafs and Arzals, converts from upper castes, OBCs and SCs, respectively. Divisions of this nature are also found among Sikhs and

Christians while many Christians do not identify with persons of their own religious group who are newly inducted, or those who have been converted from upper castes (Hindu). Thus conversion to Christianity does not automatically erase their erstwhile caste identity.

While the majority of converts were from the lower castes who sought to escape from their low social and ritual ranking in the caste hierarchy, it should also be noted that when castes from an area converted en masse, they invariably retained their customs and caste practices, which resulted in discriminatory treatment.

Communal strife, particularly between Hindus and Muslims, occurs regularly in various parts of the country. That economic prosperity inflames rivalry, jealousy and viciousness between communities is widely documented; therefore reducing poverty and inequality would at least partly lessen the social conflict which manifests itself in communal tensions or riots.

Muslim employees lose their peace of mind when there is communal violence, affecting their productivity and anxiety about their security adversely affects their work. At the workplace, latent animosity between communities exists due to factors such as imagined or perceived discrimination of the Hindus towards Muslims and Christians. Therefore, it is not poverty per se which needs to be addressed when dealing with religious minorities but also their perception (real or imagined) of being discriminated against.

Religious minorities over the whole country are not politically very active, that is, in contesting elections or being political leaders, in proportion to their numbers, their political participation usually confined to casting their votes, perhaps once every five years. Muslims vote en bloc, mainly on economic issues and for the party they think can protect them. Where demographic dispersal and concentration are taken into account, the minorities' political participation is likely to be much higher in states where they are in larger concentrations. In states where religious minorities in India are the majority community their involvement in politics is sure to be considerable and decisive (for example, Muslims in Kashmir, Sikhs in Punjab and Christians in certain north-east states).

The intensity of poverty and the associated handicaps and debilities do not occur uniformly in any religious group. Thus, any policy formulated to assist those who are below the poverty line has to take into consideration factors, such as the caste origins of converts, place of residence, economic development in that area and overall economic position of the group. Poverty studies being the forte of economists, the impact of non-economic factors is usually ignored, therefore the analysis of poverty among religious minorities by sociologists was an innovative endeavour.

In India, with its large population and extensive land area, the identification of 'Who is poor?' is the first major difficulty. The first step before any economic assistance is provided to minorities is to identify the persons who fall 'below the poverty line'. While the 'poverty line' may be variously defined, a large proportion of India's population suffers from 'absolute poverty' or even falls below the 'subsistence level' and the major consideration should be to meet the basic requirements of these persons. A large-scale survey to assess the economic condition of different groups has to be undertaken to cover the whole country and minimum support has to be provided to those on the verge of starvation.

Recently converted SCs have suffered from discrimination, 'untouchability' and economic deprivation for centuries, and their situation has only worsened. While the SCs who have remained Hindus (or are Sikhs and recently converted to Buddhism) receive government benefits in various fields, the converts to Christianity and Islam lose such benefits. Under the circumstances, SC converts to minority religious groups should also be eligible for the same benefits as SC Hindus. However, an indiscriminate reservation of benefits to all converts makes no sense. It is clearly seen that at least some of the converts (especially those and their families/descendants who had converted) about two generations ago or earlier, i.e. pre-Independence, are better off than those who converted after Independence. Thus, their present occupation and income should be considered before such benefits are provided to anyone

A systematic and concerted effort to encourage traditional arts and crafts would go a long way to eradicate poverty among Muslims. The government may consider providing special incentives to Muslims, to enrol their children in secular institutions. An important factor in the poorer condition of Muslims is their habitation in congested, unhygienic surroundings. A possible solution is to encourage Muslims (through more liberal credit facilities) to improve their habitation by building better amenities for themselves, or to give them a better land-layout to build their homes (or sell them land at less than commercial rates) and also provide some grants/credit. Admittedly, limited land and resources are available, but at least some financial resources could also be provided.

Since education is one of the most important avenues of economic and social mobility, the government may consider setting up primary schools in colonies where the poor of religious minorities live (colonies with SC converts, for instance). If the classes in these schools were also so organized that the children could spend some time assisting their parents in income-earning work, it would encourage attendance.

Ultimately, and in the long run, the economic condition of people will rise only when the whole economy grows at a much higher rate than at present. With over 800 million persons, and nearly half of them under the poverty line, it is that much more difficult for the government to provide any major benefits to the minorities alone. Problems of poverty among minorities are common to that of poor Hindus.

Jains and Zoroastrians are generally above the poverty line. As for Sikhs, although the component of SC converts (locally known as Mazbhis) is substantial (almost one-third), their concentration in Punjab with the attendant political advantages, reservation for SC converts to Sikhism since 1954 and the substantial agricultural developments in Punjab, have resulted in upward mobility, reducing numbers of people below the poverty line substantially. The converts from SCs to Buddhism (neo-Buddhists) are concentrated mainly in Maharashtra and Uttar Pradesh. Although the majority are below the poverty line, two factors favour them: one, the absence of communal riots targeting them and two, the benefits of reservation extended to them since 1990. In contrast, SC converts to Islam and Christianity are subjected to double discrimination as the benefits of reservation are denied to them. Since conversion does not lead to the diminution of caste discrimination, caste and not religion ought to be the basis of policy formulation by the state.

Poverty as a phenomenon afflicts a large proportion of the Indian population, and religions minorities in particular. The project sponsored by the National Planning Commission during 1988–90 helped to provide a comparative picture of poverty among religious minorities of India–and the fact that this was undertaken by sociologists and not by economists makes the study unique.

CHAPTER 15

The Global Studies Programme

Institutional innovations usually have modest beginnings in the inchoate ideas of a few individuals. The origin of the Global Studies Programme (GSP), indeed an institutional innovation, can be traced to the Teaching Network on 'European Social Structure and Cultural Globalization' launched by two faculty members, Frank Welz and Hermann Schwengel, at the Institute of Sociology of Albert Ludwigs University, Freiburg, Germany (ALU) in the late 1990s. While the programme was well received as a virtual university network in the German-speaking world, it was soon realized that to situate cultural globalization in its wider perspective, it was necessary to look beyond Europe. In this spirit, co-operation was sought from the CSSS, School of Social Science of JNU by Frank Welz through contacting me as I was a former president of ISA. The ALU–JNU collaboration came into being as a virtual university network which functioned during 1998–2001. Enthused by the success of this Europe–Asia collaboration, the prospects of incorporating another continent, preferably Africa, was explored. The University of Natal at Durban was adjudged to be conducive for two reasons: the social–racial composition of the student population of the University–one-third each of blacks, whites and Indians–and the presence of a faculty member known to the ALU–JNU network. (The university was renamed as Kwazulu Natal University hereafter KNU for certain local considerations). The three universities situated in three continents–Africa, Asia and Europe–became nodal institutions for operating the global studies programme.

The launch of the GSP was not a formal effort by three institutions, but based on the inter-personal familiarity between individuals and their interactions. It is widely recognized in sociology that primary groups play a pivotal role in the sustenance and progress of all civilizations. But with the onset of the global age, the mode of functioning of primary groups changed and their spatial reach expanded thanks to satellite communication and a 'network society'. This was reflected in the emergence of the GSP and the International Sociological Association (ISA), providing an interaction frame for the persons involved. Frank Welz, also an active member of the ISA wrote to me in May 1998 suggesting the idea of co-operation with JNU and I in turn, suggested the name of Ari Sitas, a former vice president of the ISA (1994–98), as the collaborator from Africa, who was teaching at KNU. The point here is that institutions have not only formal but also informal history which once recognized, helps a wholesome understanding of the institution.

It must also be underlined that those in the institutional network must have the required resources and pursue common goals. Selecting or opting for partners in a global programme is not a matter of random choice or personal preference but of mutual acceptance and compatibility of the sponsoring institutions.

Let me now indicate another resource which is crucial for launching a global project. The congruence between the goal of the project and stated objective of the financier is vital. This happened in the case of the GSP as a happy coincidence. The German Academic Exchange Service (DAAD) invited project proposals in January 2001 from those engaged or interested in 'internationalizing' education through collaborative teaching between at least three universities. The objectives of the DAAD and the GSP appeared to be made for each other. However, the GSP was still not out of woods because JNU could not sign the legal agreement to confer a joint degree to the students trained under the GSP. But KNU was ready to confer a joint degree along with ALU and the GSP and fortunately, the DAAD did not insist that all the three partners should conjointly confer the degree to the students trained. This points to the need for flexibility in launching and successfully operating global programmes.

Another pre-requisite for launching the GSP with three nodal campuses situated in three continents was information technology (IT) made functional through satellite communication. Although the faculty and students are involved in a great deal of face-to-face interaction when they are in particular campuses, they could sustain it only through virtual interaction when they moved to other campuses. Technology as the facilitator to communicate ideas is functional only when the prevailing or emerging thinking envisions programmes conducive to it. The container model of the nation-state and methodological nationalism implicated in it was already under interrogation by the last decades of the twentieth century. Transnational comparative studies were gradually crystallizing and the monopoly of northern countries in the production and dissemination of knowledge was becoming unacceptable.

Viewed with this background, the early twenty-first century was an opportune moment to launch an appropriate institutional vehicle in the context of globalization and the GSP may be perceived as a response to it. The two-year master's programme was launched in 2002.

In all, students from forty-five countries have been trained under the GSP, half from West Europe and North America and the remaining half from the rest of the world. This is a satisfactory situation given the traditional dominance of West Europe and North America. But viewed in terms of the proportion of their population, they are still dominant and others under-represented. However, the silver lining in this context seems to be that the GSP provided an excellent opportunity for the new generation from these traditionally dominant regions to moderate if not reject the stereotypes conventionally communicated by their elders about Asia, Africa and even Latin America. Also, the gender distribution of the GSP students has been very encouraging in that little over 50 per cent of the students were women.

In contrast to the diversity of the students, the faculty of the GSP was predominantly European, particularly German, although the participation of South Asian (read Indian) and South African faculty was not negligible. The inter-continental faculty of GSP is a breakthrough from the conventional academic hegemony of the First World during colonial times and the success of the GSP would ultimately depend upon the diversity of students and equality in representation of its student and faculty.

The cycle of the GSP starts after the application deadline date on 30 November. The GSP faculty located at Freiburg select approximately thirty-five students. To ensure diversity, each participating institution is guaranteed five seats to ensure the geographic spread of the students of the GSP. The other criteria for selection are grades, articulated motives, knowledge of English, exposure to foreign countries and value-orientations of students. Not only do students spend 50 per cent of their time in one location, that is Freiburg, but the core elements in the course, the theory-methodology set, is taught there. Apart from this, students do their thesis while located at Freiburg co-supervised by two faculty members of which one is from Freiburg. Both these aspects give primacy to Freiburg.

Students are expected to pay tuition fees at the different locations which range from 200 to 500 euros. In addition to this they have to meet travel and living costs. There are limited scholarships available at some locations for students from specified regions. For example, ALU (Freiburg) offers a few scholarships to students from Africa and JNU (New Delhi) to students from South Asia. Lack of funds for financial assistance is a major constraint of the GSP and nearly 3 per cent of students dropped out after joining the programme due to financial constraints. This is a problem usually faced by all global programmes.

Students complete the programme with 'good' to 'very good' academic grades. The high quality of courses offered and the inter-cultural exposure make GSP graduates well-received in the labour market. While the graduates prefer employment with international development organizations, they have also joined business firms, academic research centres, civil society organizations, media and even bureaucracy, showing that the GSP graduates' scope of employment straddles a wide variety of fields.

Every student of the GSP is expected to do an MA dissertation. The first four batches, who completed their studies between 2004 and 2007 submitted seventy-four dissertations.

More than 50 per cent of students wrote their dissertations on topics related to economic globalization, global politics and development. The rest chose topics like HIV, drug addiction, illicit trade or on social inequality, cultural globalization with reference to themes such as religion and categories such as youth. This indicates that student diversity often promotes a plurality of research themes.

Research by students and faculty too got a boost through the GSP. Of the students who graduated till 2007, a little over one-third joined PhD programmes, a few of them in prestigious universities such as Cambridge in the UK and Harvard in the USA. While quite a few have remained in the participating institutions, particularly at ALU and JNU, to pursue PhD, non-availability of fellowships is an obstacle. A Fellowship Programme was also initiated in 2008 to motivate GSP graduates to pursue research in the field of globalization.

An unanticipated but welcome development in research occasioned by GSP is collaborative research by the faculty of the participating institutions situated across continents. Several research papers have been co-authored by faculty of partner institutions and a joint publication series of books and an online journal of global studies are in the making. This is a quantum leap from the anthropologists of the 'advanced countries' during the colonial era studying 'primitives' to 'civilize' them and the social scientists of the Cold War era involved in area studies to 'modernize' Third World countries.

Let me conclude the GSP experiment by highlighting some of its intended features. One, the GSP is at once inter-continental, inter-disciplinary and inter-cultural. Two, it recognizes the cruciality of the partnership of participating institutions in devising course contents, pedagogical practices and field exposures of students. Three, the GSP facilitates autonomy as well as reciprocity in the learning process and evaluation modes respecting the differences of each location. Four, it jealously guards itself from falling an easy prey to the contemporary proclivity of commercializing higher education. Five, the GSP not only recognizes but also celebrates diversity of gender, race, religion, language and locality. Six, the GSP has recognized that scholarship is at once local, national, continental and global.

Finally, an unanticipated positive achievement of the GSP is that it triggered off research collaboration between faculties situated in different locations without involving the conventional patron-client structure, but promoting an egalitarian structure between the collaborators of knowledge production.

The GSP came to the CSSS at just about the time I retired, although I continue at JNU as Emeritus Professor. I persuaded the CSSS to pursue the programme and several colleagues–M.N. Panini, Anand Kumar, K.L. Sharma, Harish Naraindass, Maitrayee Chaudhari, V. Sujatha–actively participated in it. My own role was limited, delivering lectures when called upon and spending few weeks at ALU, at Freiburg, as a distinguished scholar. One of the highlights of my stay at Freiburg was an interview by Frank Welz and Anand Kumar on 'Approaching Culture Change in the Era of Globalization' which was published in *Social Identities* in 2003. However, I can legitimately claim that I was instrumental in bringing the GSP to the CSSS, via my association with ISA.

CHAPTER 16

Chairing the Gujarat Harmony Project

The Indian subcontinent, inhabited by one-fifth of the global population, existed for centuries with considerable internal harmony in spite of its cultural and racial heterogeneity. Although the pan-Indian unity was reinforced in the the anti-colonial struggle against British colonialism, the aspiration for establishing nation-states based on religious identity gradually surfaced both among the Hindus and Muslims. In spite of notions such as 'unity in diversity', 'composite culture' and 'composite nationalism' the subcontinent was divided into two countries based on religion in 1947 on the eve of British departure from India. India became a country predominantly populated by Hindus (82 per cent); Pakistan with 97 per cent Muslims and Bangladesh with 86 per cent Muslims. Notwithstanding the partition, Hindu–Muslim conflicts or 'communal riots' remained a recurring feature of Indian Republic. Between 1951 and 2002, the year in which the Gujarat communal riots occurred, the average annual count of communal riots stood at 300.

Gujarat was widely perceived as a riot-free Indian state until the first major riot broke out in 1969. It was then that the Sangh Parivar's aggressive stance towards Muslims began. The Hindu Sangram Samiti circulated a leaflet titled 'Awake Hindus, Awake Youths' which stated:

> Their (Muslims') main aim is not to destroy maximum possible Hindu Temples, but to destroy Hindu Religion and Hindu Culture and to rape Hindu ladies.... Hindu Youth, now it is time to test your courage and strengths. Prepare bombs, dharias, sticks, prepare bows to throw burning missiles. Leave defensive policy and attack now. Arise to avenge insult to our temples and ladies, and rush to Muslim areas with weapons and finish them.

The 1969 riots helped to strengthen the position of Bharatiya Janata Party (BJP) in Gujarat; from a mere 2 per cent vote share in 1967, the party polled about 10 per cent votes in the 1972 elections. Communal riots became a regular feature by the 1980s in Gujarat. The BJP floated a social coalition–the PAKH (Patel, Adivasi, Kshatriya and Harijan)–to counter the KHAM (Kshatriya, Harijan, Adivasi and Muslim), a social coalition of the Congress Party. The critical difference between the two coalitions was that the BJP excluded Muslims and gradually moved towards characterizing them, along with Christians, as the 'other'.

The campaign for the construction of the Ram Mandir in Ayodhya (Uttar Pradesh) had its reverberations in Gujarat too. Between 1987 and 1991 there were 106 instances of major and minor communal riots in Gujarat. The rath yatra led by L.K. Advani in 1990 from the Somnath temple in Gujarat to mobilize support for the construction of the Ram Mandir provoked violence all along its route; it left 116 dead across

India, twenty-six of them in Gujarat. When Advani was arrested, a strike was called in Ahmedabad by the BJP and the Vishwa Hindu Parishad (VHP) mobilized Hindus in large numbers, the SCs, Hinduized STs and OBCs joining the upper castes to attack Muslims. In the aftermath of the demolition of the Babri Mosque in Uttar Pradesh in 1992, the rioting that followed in Surat (Gujarat) resulted in the killing of 197 persons of which 175 were Muslims. In 1993, 14,094 persons were arrested in Gujarat under the Terrorist and Disruptive Activities (Prevention) Act (TADA), the majority of whom were Muslims. The Congress Party then in power in Gujarat was widely perceived to be pursuing a 'soft-Hindutva' agenda, alienating Muslims from the Congress, which increased the legitimacy of 'hard Hindutva' policy of BJP resulting in the electoral gains of the party. Thus in the 1991 Lok Sabha elections, the BJP polled 52 per cent of votes and captured twenty-one out of the twenty-two seats in Gujarat. The party repeated this performance in the 1995 Gujarat Assembly elections, winning 121 out of the 182 seats. Another Assembly election had to be conducted in 1998 thanks to the Kshatriya–OBC tension in which the BJP won the majority again.

The successive electoral successes of the BJP emboldened the Sangh Parivar, the cluster of associations that aim to establish a Hindu Rashtra in India, to take several steps. One, in June 1999, the government of Gujarat lifted the ban on its employees joining the RSS. Two, instructions were given to all schools in Gujarat to subscribe to the RSS magazine, *Sadhana*. However, the government of Gujarat withdrew the order following the public outcry all over India. Three, in the wake of the killing of Hindu pilgrims in Pahalgam in Kashmir on 1 August 2000 by Muslim militants, the VHP called for a Gujarat bandh which was supported by the state government.

Muslim business establishments in several towns in the state were attacked, burnt and destroyed during the bandh. Four, RSS and its affiliates started attacking Christians–there were at least forty such incidents between December 1998 and January 1999, an all-time high. The articulated reason for this flurry of attacks was proselytization by Christian missionaries. Five, the Gujarat Freedom of Religions Bill seeking to ban conversions of Hindus to other religions, read Christianity and Islam, was introduced in the Assembly. As the Bill contravened the provisions of Article 25 of the Indian constitution, it generated country-wide protests and had to be put on hold. Six, an effort was made by the police department to collect detailed information about Muslims and Christians living in Gujarat so as to readily identify 'trouble-makers' in the event of any communal conflicts. Seven, the RSS and its affiliates started indulging in cultural policing. For example in 1997, the Hussain-Doshi Gufa (later re-named as the Ahmedabad Gufa), an art museum, was raided and M.F. Hussain's paintings were burnt. In 1998, the sites of fashion parades and beauty contests were obstructed and the screening of the film *Fire* directed by Deepa Mehta was stopped for its depiction of lesbianism. Numerous pamphlets were in circulation invoking Hindus to be true patriots by boycotting Muslim labour and establishments. One of them exhorted: 'From needle to gold, do not buy anything from Muslims and never work in Muslim offices and do not employ Muslims'. The intended economic boycott of Muslims was to impoverish and demoralize them as a community.

The point of this short description is to emphasize the fact that the torching of the train compartment in Godhra that killed fifty-eight 'innocent' Hindu pilgrims returning from Ayodhya on 28 February 2002 happened in Gujarat, which was ready for retaliatory communalism. Whether the torching was a premeditated act or a mere accident is not yet unequivocally established. Be that as it may, the communal carnage that followed the Godhra incident exploded several myths about communal riots in India.

Generally speaking, communal riots in India are an urban phenomena because of the veil of anonymity which prevails in urban settlements. But Gujarat was gradually developing into a laboratory of Hindutva experiment and hence the 2002 post-Godhra riot engulfed rural Gujarat too. Traditionally, Muslims irrespective of their class and occupational backgrounds lived in walled areas in cities. Later, due to the increased perception of insecurity, a new pattern of ghettoization through co-operative housing societies based on religious identity emerged. This rendered communal targeting relatively easy and the Muslim co-operative house building societies could be easily targeted. Thus ghettoization as an avenue of physical security became a source of enhanced insecurity.

Although an attempt was made by the government of Gujarat to undertake an exclusive census of religious minorities–Muslims and Christians–it failed because of the public outcry. But the Sangh Parivar had done this quietly. Muslim business and trade establishments were systematically identified and the information was available to rioters so that they could selectively target Muslims. Thus both ghettoization and prior identification diluted the anonymity of urban Muslims which could have been a protective veil.

While upper caste-middle class Hindu men imbued by the RSS ideology provided the ideological justification for communal riots, the lower class from this social category undertook physical violence. But the Hindutva agenda of the Sangh Parivar to consolidate Hindus irrespective of their caste status, substantially added to the physical strength of rioters through OBCs, SCs and Hinduized STs. Further, in the 2002 Gujarat riots, both men and women of an upper caste-middle class background participated, leading to a consolidation of Hindutva forces cutting across caste, class and gender.

The lightning speed in the spread of violence was such that by the evening of 28 February 2002, the day the Godhra tragedy occurred, curfew had to be imposed in twenty-seven towns and cities of Gujarat. According to the submission of the additional director general of police to the Election Commission, 151 towns and 993 villages covering 154 out of 182 Assembly constituencies and 284 police stations (out of 464) were affected by the riots. The Gujarat government estimated that only 900 persons were killed although most enquiry committees put the figure at around 2000, which included Muslim politicians, intellectuals, judges, bureaucrats and professionals.

The media was sharply divided in presenting their 'versions of truth'; leading Gujarati newspapers justified and supported the riots, the all-India English media tried to present an 'objective' picture. In turn, this resulted in recriminations within the media. While the local Gujarat media branded the all-India English media as 'pseudo-secular', the latter labelled the former as 'communal'.

The intensity of hatred that was exhibited in the brutality of violence was abominable–even senior citizens, infants, physically and mentally challenged youth and pregnant women were not spared. Parents were murdered before their sons, daughters were raped in front of their parents. Women were special targets; their sexual and reproductive organs were attacked and mutilated. Children, born and unborn, were killed before their mothers. Apart from physical violence, an enormous amount of symbolic violence too was inflicted on the Muslim psyche. Mosques and tombs of Muslim saints were desecrated and destroyed; copies of the Holy Quran were torn, their pages strewn all over and defecated upon.*

As noted above communal riots have become a 'normal' phenomenon in independent India but the Gujarat 2002 riot attracted worldwide attention because of the widespread perception that the state government was involved. Narendra Modi, the then chief minister of Gujarat characterized the post-Godhra riot as a reaction to an action, namely torching of Hindu pilgrims, thereby providing a veneer of legitimacy. When a state government cannot control the situation the normal practice is to request for assistance of the central government and deploy the army expeditiously. This was not done in time.

The reports that appeared, particularly in the English media, both print and electronic, the conclusions reached by several fact-finding committees, the strictures passed by the Supreme Court of India and the unambiguous pronouncements by the National Human Rights Commission that there was 'miscarriage of justice' in Gujarat clearly point to the fact that the government in the state failed in its 'raj dharma', to re-call the words of the then Prime Minister, Atal Bihari Vajpayee.

These facts gave birth to a virulent controversy in India (and elsewhere) on whether the Gujarat riot of 2002 was one of those 'normal' riots which periodically erupt in India–or was it genocide? The state can be a party to genocide by inaction and/or by facilitating extermination of a people or nation by another people or nation within a state. Resolution 260 (111) of the United Nations passed on 9 December 1948 entitled, 'The Convention on the Prevention and Punishment of the Crime of Genocide', defines genocide as:

---

*as reported *in Communalism Combat*, 77-78, 2002, p.33.

> any of the acts committed with the intent to destroy, in whole or in part, a national, ethnic, racial or religious group as such: (a) killing members of the group; (b) causing bodily harm or mental harm to the members of the group; (c) deliberately inflicting on the group conditions of life calculated to bring about its physical destruction in whole or in part...

Understandably, it was the most widely reported incident in the media, both print and electronic. A large number reports by Enquiry Committees and books and articles by journalists, activists and academics have also been published. I documented all these in addition to the data collected directly from the field in my book: *Reconciliation in Post-Godhra Gujarat: The Role of Civil Society,* published by Pearson Longman in 2008. Therefore I need not repeat them here. And yet, it is necessary to provide the rationale for the Gujarat Harmony Project (GHP).

The central and provincial governments of India do take post-riot actions such as rehabilitation of the victims and appointments of judicial commissions to fix the responsibility. In appointing these commissions, care is taken to select 'appropriate' judges who would toe the official line and the inordinate delay in submitting the reports is the norm. For example, the Gujarat government did appoint a judicial commission, but the judges took twelve years to submit the report and as per information it is yet to be presented to the legislature. Therefore, the details of judicial reports regarding the Gujarat carnage of 2002 are not yet in the public realm.

In September 2002, when I was about to retire from JNU, Frederick Henring, assistant country director and N.M. Prusty, director, Emergency Responses and Rehabilitation of CARE India requested me to join what they designated as the Gujarat Harmony Project. After some initial hesitation, I agreed to join on the condition that I would have the liberty to mould the project so that its report would be of long-term value.

The Advisory Committee of the GHP, which I chaired, consisted of a political scientist, D.N. Pathak, Zubeida Desai, a physician, K. Srinivas IAS, a former district collector of Ahmedabad and Binoy Acharya, director, Unnati (an NGO located at Ahmedabad) in addition to ex-officio members of CARE India. There were twelve partners, two of them 'strategic partners'–Unnati and NIMHANS of Bangalore. The remaining partners were 'implementing partners', involved in the rehabilitation of victims of the 2002 riots in Gujarat. I was straying into unfamiliar territory and I knew that my academic peers would not endorse it as a scholastic endeavour. But since I believed that in the ultimate analysis production of knowledge should enhance human welfare, I decided to undertake the task.

Most of the reports, books and articles published on the Gujarat carnage of 2002 focus on the physical violence unleashed by the Hindutva forces and report that the violence happened with the complicity of the state. A couple of reports dwell upon the pitiable predicament of people in the camps set up mostly by Muslim organizations. According to one report, eighty-one relief camps were inhabited by 30,000 victims of post-Godhra violence. But the state government stoutly denied the very existence of the camps, thereby abdicating its responsibility to rehabilitate victims. The Committee sent to Gujarat by the National Commission for Minorities, reported that the state government returned Rs 19.1 crore of unutilized money from the grant of 150 crore granted by the central government. In fact, the grants by the central government were grossly inadequate, considering the magnitude of rehabilitation work required.

While there were numerous attempts to provide relief and economic rehabilitation, the healing of psychological wounds was largely overlooked. In addition to relief, rehabilitation and psychological care, the GHP attempted social reconciliation between the estranged communities which I designated as 'innovative intervention'. Generally speaking, if the hostile communities learn to establish harmonious relations, the benefits are durable and can prevent the recurrence of conflicts. However, the prevailing mood was that of taking revenge and wanting to punish those who indulged in violence. While the GHP was not against the due process of law in identifying and punishing the culprits, it held that reconciliation of the parties in conflict was essential, but this did not have much purchase.

There was also a tendency to advocate the widely acclaimed efforts of reconciliation attempted in South Africa. This was/is an utterly misguided attempt for several reasons. First, in the case of South Africa, the conflict was between a numerical minority of alien origin (the Whites) and a majority which constituted the native population (the Blacks). In the case of Gujarat, the minority (Muslims) was/is perceived as cultural outsiders to the society although they are insiders to the polity. Second, while there was no instance of political domination by the Blacks over the Whites in South Africa, in India domination alternated between the two religious communities; in the medieval period the Muslims were and in Independent India the Hindus are the dominant communities. Third, in the case of post-apartheid South Africa, the state led by President Nelson Mandela and the civil society represented through Bishop Tutu conjointly provided the leadership to bring about reconciliation. The only agency which attempted reconciliation in post-Godhra Gujarat was the GHP sponsored by CARE India. Even the Union government at the centre, which could have swiftly and effectively intervened, drawing its sanctions from the Constitution of India, remained tactfully non-committal. It may be re-called here that both in Delhi and in Ahmedabad the National Democratic Alliance (NDA) was the ruling coalition. In an interview, the then President of India, K.R. Narayanan revealed that he repeatedly reminded the prime minister of the need for effective intervention by the Central Government to quell the riot, which fell on deaf ears. Even the market forces which suffered huge economic losses remained silent. In such a milieu, the GHP could achieve precious little in bringing about social harmony, but the fact that it dared to do so was praiseworthy.

CHAPTER 17

Venturing into Security Analysis

'Security' was and still remains largely a theme analysed by political scientists, including those who specialize in international relations, military experts and strategists and occasionally, environmentalists. Even at the global level, only very few sociologists ventured into the analysis of security, the exceptions I know of being Barry Buzen and his associates, Ole Waever and Japa de Wilde, who co-authored a book on security. I had not even thought of an analysis of security till 2003. Therefore, I was surprised when I received a letter from Lieutenant General V.R. Raghavan (retired) who manned the Delhi Policy Group (DPG), 'an independent think tank committed to analyses of security policies in comprehensive terms', inviting me to be the first nominee to the chair on Non-Traditional Security. The chair was instituted with financial assistance from the Ford Foundation.

The DPG was established in 2003 and launched a project on Comprehensive Security with special reference to South Asia. Perhaps the DPG's aim to undertake a comprehensive analysis of security prompted the offer of its first chair to a sociologist, not a narrow specialist. Lieutenant General Raghavan wrote in his Foreward to my book *Understanding Security: A New Perspective*:

> The advisory group, which guides the work of the chair, made its choice on weighty considerations. It was felt that the subject of Non-Traditional Security was still in an exploratory stage and it would be helpful to identify its scope and content ... the subject lacks the coherence of an academic discipline. The challenges, or critique, that the subject has become an all-inclusive bag of separate issues also had to be faced. It was, therefore, felt that an overview of the notion of Non-Traditional Security from a completely new and innovative perspective should be undertaken. Clearly, the Chair had to be a person of not only high academic standard, but also one who was not tied to the perspective already in vogue.

Since Non-Traditional Security was a scarcely explored theme and the chair was a novice in the field, my tenure was only twelve months (it was extended for three months later) and the brief was to produce a monograph. My book of 174 pages was published by Macmillan India Ltd in 2006, reprinted in the same year and a Hindi translation was published in 2010. Available evidence suggests that the book was widely read but scarcely reviewed. I could locate only seven reviews–two in newspapers, *The Hindu* and *Tribune* and five in the journals *Front Line*, *IIC Quarterly*, *USI Journal*, *The Book Review* and *Mainstream*. Note that none of the journals are social science journals which indicates the narrow range within which social scientists in India function. And most of the reviewers, unsurprisingly, were persons associated with traditional security, not Non-Traditional Security!

R.K. Raghavan, a former director of the CBI, suggested that the book moves away from a state-centric approach to security in his review in *The Hindu.* K.S. Subramanian (IPS), a former director general of the state Institute of Public Administration, Tripura, concluded his review in *Mainstream* thus: 'The DPG must be grateful to him for opening up intellectual and conceptual challenges not dreamt of in conventional security analysis. P.S. Bawa, IPS (retired), in his review in the *India International Centre Quarterly* observed:

> ... the new paradigm propounded by Oommen is likely to give a new dimension to the strategies dealing with education, health, environment, gender issues, and security of the individual. Thus the book brings various aspects under the gaze of the international organizations, especially those sponsored by the United Nations and its millennium development goals.

In the *Book Review*, Rajesh M. Basrur, director of the Centre for Global Studies, Mumbai, noted that I had taken cognisance of not only physical and structural violences but also symbolic violence. And, the three cides–genocide, culturocide and ecocide–conjointly accounts for all varieties of insecurities, as I have argued in the book. Hamid Ansari, who retired from the Indian Foreign Service wrote in *Frontline* that he started reading the book with some 'diffidence' even 'apprehension', a new book on an old theme! But both reactions turned out to be unwarranted and he wrote: 'A sociologist of eminence has brought to the subject a refreshingly different perspective and has enriched the debate'. He went on to certify: 'Measured against the conceptual framework set out in the monograph, the shortcomings of all contemporary societies become evident.'

The purpose of this recollection of reviews is to show they were by non-social scientists, the social scientists subjecting the book to a cognitive black-out, exposing the resistance to innovation by most social scientists. In this context, Thorstein

Veblen's comment that social scientists are victims of 'trained incapacity' sounds convincing.

Going through available publications in the field of security, I found that there were two contending perspectives. The one-dimensional, 'realist', state-centric security analyses that are minimalist and the multi-dimensional, 'liberal', all-encompassing ones that are maximalist. Rejecting both, I have advocated an optimal view which avoids both individual idiosyncrasies and non-human elements. Thus the notion of 'psychic security' concerns the insecurity specific to particular individuals, although they are situated in shared socio-cultural milieux. Similarly, to include the insecurity caused by 'natural' calamities such as earthquakes, cyclones, tornadoes and tsunamis is to blur the distinction between manmade disasters such as famines, flood, pollution and drought, and the natural ones. This is not to deny the need to analyse insecurities arising from both psychological disorders and physical dislocations caused by natural calamities or disasters and the need to take appropriate preventive measures. The scope of security analyses should be delimited in terms of causal factors for which human groups and communities are responsible.

Capitalist liberal democracies stand on three pillars: a liberal democratic state, an open competitive market and a vibrant civil society. While these societies promise equality of opportunity (but rarely practise), liberty and dignity to all citizens, they rarely take responsibility for providing security to individuals and groups. This is the deep deficit of all contemporary societies.

The Advisory Group of the DPG identified Hamid Ansari, who was in the Observer Research Foundation those days after retiring from the Indian Foreign Service, as a potential successor to me. He told me, 'Professor I am going to be your unworthy successor at the DPG.' But destiny had a bigger design for him. Before joining the DPG, he was appointed as the chairperson of the National Minority Commission (NMC), and the rest is history. He was elected as the vice president of India, an office he occupied with distinction for two successive terms. I have often ruminated, 'If my "unworthy successor" at the DPG could be the vice president of India, what would have awaited a "worthy successor" of mine!' B.G.Varghese, the eminent journalist, joined the DPG as the second chair of Non-Traditional Security.

CHAPTER 18

Prime Minister's High Level Committee

On 9 March 2005, the Prime Minister's Office (PMO) issued a notification for constituting a High Level Committee (HLC) to prepare a report on the social, economic and educational status of the Muslim community of India. The HLC was to collate, consolidate and analyse information about Muslims and to identify areas of intervention by the government so as to improve the social, economic and educational status of the Muslim community in India.

Retired Chief Justice of the Delhi High Court, Justice Rajinder Sachar, was the chairperson and six others, including me as a retired JNU professor, constituted it: Saiyid Hamid, chancellor, Jamia Hamdard (New Delhi); M.A. Basith, senior director, Planning Department, Government of Karnataka (Bengaluru); Akhtar Majeed, dean, Faculty of Social Science, Jamia Hamdard (New Delhi); Rakesh Basant, professor of economics; Indian Institute of Management (Ahmedabad) and Abusaleh Sharif, member secretary, chief economist, Human Development Programme, National Council of Applied Economic Research (New Delhi).

This multi-disciplinary team consisted of a judge, an ex-ICS officer and educational administrator, two economists, one political scientist, one statistician and one sociologist, a rare instance in India. For example, when the State Reorganization Commission (SRC) was constituted in the mid-1950s, there was not a single sociologist or social anthropologist or linguist on the Commission. Similarly, the Mandal Commission, which was to identify the OBCs from caste groups in India, had no sociologists/social anthropologists as members (only as consultants) in spite of the fact that Indian sociologists and social anthropologists are widely recognized as analysts of caste system. Likewise, not a single sociologist occupied the position of a member, Planning Commission, during its existence for over six decades! All these point to the marginalization of sociologists in India in the context of policy formulations.

When the concerned joint secretary sought my consent I asked only one question, 'Who is the chairperson of the HLC?' And, when I learnt who it was I readily agreed because I had a nodding acquaintance with Justice Sachar, not as a judge but as a public figure, a social activist and I was favourably impressed by his style of functioning and value-orientation.

By March 2005, the HLC was set up at Sardar Patel Bhavan, Parliament Street, New Delhi and the first meeting of the committee was held on 12 April followed by a press conference. The responses to the committee as articulated in the media were polarized. The critics found it as an extreme and vivid expression of 'Muslim appeasement' and those who approved of the measure appreciated it as a long overdue step because Muslims, the biggest religious minority of India, counting some 140 million people, had also the most depressed segments of India's population. There was a third view that the committee's terms of reference should have included other religious minorities such as Buddhists, Christians and Sikhs.

The first meeting held on 12 April 2005 agreed on three crucial matters, that: the chairperson and committee members shall not receive any honorarium, only reimbursements of their travel expenses; the committee should submit its report within fifteen months, that is June 2006; and each member of the committee should contribute to the report, including drafting specific chapters. Yet it cannot be said that all members contributed in equal measure.

Given my background, the specific responsibility assigned to me was to draft three chapters out of the twelve to be revised based on the comments and criticisms made by other members of the HLC. The three chapters were: 'Context, Approach and Methodology' (Chapter 1), 'Public Perceptions and Perspectives' (Chapter 2) and 'The Muslim OBCs and Affirmative Action' (Chapter 10). Issues relating to demography, education, health, employment, credit, infrastructure and public policies were specifically analysed with reference to Muslims. But to situate deprivations of Muslims in a comparative perspective, the data were analysed with reference to other socio-religious communities, particularly other religious minorities and 'backward' groups in Indian society.

Issues relating to minorities are common to all polities and democratic states are expected to function in an impartial manner to ensure equity and justice for minorities also. It is possible that even if a state is impartial, particular minorities may perceive the state to be partial and unjust. Herein lies the crucial importance of collecting and analysing data so as to formulate robust social policies.

Muslims in India perceive that the Indian state's discrimination against them is because of their religious identity. Further, discriminations exist on the basis of other factors such as caste, regional-linguistic background and gender. This leads to intersectionality, which results in cumulative discrimination. Thus a poor Muslim woman with an SC background from Tamil Nadu may be subjected to multiple deprivations as compared with a rich Muslim male of an upper caste background who may only experience dispersed discrimination. That is, the internal differentiation of the Muslim community results in cumulative or dispersed discrimination. This fact was kept in view while drafting the report.

While the HLC was a tool exclusively meant for Muslims there were several programmes meant for the welfare of all religious minorities. But these efforts did not bring in any positive results in the Muslim perception, resulting in scepticism if not cynicism about the HLC too. Therefore, such efforts were of no avail unless the state was wholly committed and there was a change in the mindset of the section of the majority community which castigate minority welfare as minority appeasement. Additionally, thanks to historical factors, Muslims are also widely perceived as 'anti-national', creating a widespread sense of insecurity among the Muslim population, aggravated by the frequent Hindu–Muslim conflicts.

The constitutional protection extended to religious minorities to maintain their identity by preserving their mother tongue (Urdu in the case of Muslims) and the right to establish exclusive educational institutions (madrasas) had often diminished equality of opportunity for Muslims in the 'secular' contexts. Similarly, the proclivity of a section of Muslims to preserve their identity by their particular patterns of lifestyle (dress, hairstyle, dietary practices) often increase their visibility in public spaces, eroding their sense of security. The tendency to structure the curriculum content in educational institutions, particularly in schools, highlighting the value-orientation of the cultural mainstream alienates the minority communities, especially the Muslims. This often leads to Muslims retreating from public institutions deepening inequalities and alienation.

Measures expected to be taken by educational and employment institutions ensuring Muslim representation on selection boards and committees are not always observed. The provision of reservation for Muslims of lower caste origin for employment in public institutions does not exist. The forces unleashed by globalization adversely impact Muslims employed in traditional sectors and those who are self-employed. Muslims are predominantly self-employed and badly in need of loans, but quite a few banks do not extend help. The absence of civic amenities and infrastructure facilities in settlements populated mainly by Muslims is common.

The Census of India 1901 listed 133 social groups wholly or partially Muslim, based on the social stratification within the community. While the general population is divided into four categories, three Hindu and ST, the Muslim population is divided into two: Ashraf and non-Ashraf sections of Muslims, refusing to recognize the Arzals, 'unclean'/untouchables and the tribals who embraced Islam. The legal consequence of this is disastrous for Muslims of SC backgrounds. While the Presidential Order (1950) initially restricted the SC status only to Hindus, for giving the benefits of reservation, it was extended to the Mazbhi Sikhs in 1954 and to neo-Buddhists in 1990, leaving out Arzal Muslims which discriminates against citizens based on religion. Given this predicament of Muslims, the HLC argued that to bring about full participation of Muslims as citizens of India, the state and the populace at large should focus on the equity, identity, dignity and security of Muslims.

The Report by HLC argued for recognition of the internal differentiation of Muslims. It is widely recognized that the population of India is divided into four social categories:

Upper Castes, Other Backward Classes, Scheduled Castes and Scheduled Tribes. Similar categorization exist in the case of Muslims too: Ashrafs, Ajlafs, Arzals and those members of STs who converted to Islam. But this categorization is not accepted by the Government of India. Even the Muslim religious leaders are wary of this categorisation. In fact soon after the release of the Report a few Mullahs (priests) protested against it alleging that it is a devise to divide the Muslims, which adversely impacts their unity. Even those social scientists who researched on the social milieu of Muslims found only the Ashraf-Ajalaf dichotomy in existence. The HLC report brought out vividly for the first time the internal differentiation of Muslims based on the structure of their deprivations rooted in India's caste system.

Having squarely recognized the internal differentiation of Muslims based on caste, the HLC report advocated parity between the Hindu and Muslim populations, that is extending the benefits of SCs to Arzal Muslims, that of OBCs to Ajalaf Muslims and that of STs to Muslims of tribal origin. And yet the media misreported on this. For example, Rajdeep Sardesai, the vibrant editor of CNN-IBN those days waved a sheaf of papers saying they contained recommendations of the HLC for a Muslim quota. The fact was that Chapter 10 of the report which dealt with this issue was yet to be written by me and the HLC only recommended parity for Muslim Arzals and Ajlafs with Hindu SCs and OBCs respectively. Sensationalism and inaccuracy make a lethal combination, which undermines authenticity of the media.

The HLC made several recommendations which go beyond the welfare of Muslim community. A few seminal ones were: an Equal Opportunity Commission (EOC) should be established as a grievance prevention mechanism; creation of a National Data

Bank (NDB), where all relevant data for various socio-religious communities (SRCs) are maintained, also to situate institutions based on a diversity index; an autonomous Assessment and Monitoring Authority (AMA) is needed to undertake periodic evaluation of the development benefits which flow to different SRCs. Further, given the dismal representation of religious minorities in political bodies, two steps were recommended: to avoid declaring constituencies as reserved ones for SCs where religious minorities reside in a large proportion as this renders them ineligible to contest and to introduce a regime of nomination for minorities. The HLC also recommended the need for evaluating school textbooks so that they do not endanger the constitutionally guaranteed religious pluralism or secularism; given the constitutional mandate of providing education to all children through their mother tongues till the age of fourteen, schools in the Urdu medium and linking of madrasas with the general school system should be facilitated; provisioning of bank credits based on the size of the population and the occupations pursued to enable Muslims to avail of the benefits of globalization; the registration of trusts set up by the Muslim community such as wakf institutions and mosque committees should be made compulsory so that their resources can be channelized for the welfare of the community; and finally, the contents of the report should be freely and widely available so that the Muslim predicament is understood and evaluated objectively.

I would like to close this chapter by recalling HLC's experience in making its report. HLC collated data from the Census of India, National Sample Surveys, from banks and financial institutions, from government organizations and official commissions, public sector undertakings, universities and colleges. (However, the Ministry of Defence refused to provide data regarding the presence of religious minorities in the army, navy and air force). In addition to these secondary data, the HLC also directly collected data from numerous NGOs through public hearings. The HLC visited most states of India with a sizeable Muslim presence and met select members of the legislature, judiciary and executive. Almost all chief ministers interacted with the members of HLC. I vividly recall our pleasant interactions with three of them: Sheila Dikshit of Delhi, Buddhadeb Bhattacharjee of West Bengal and Vasundhara Raje of Rajasthan. However, the chief minister of Andhra Pradesh, Y.S.R. Reddy kept the Committee waiting for forty-five minutes, was imperious in his behaviour and did not even apologize for his late arrival. Narendra Modi, the then chief minister of Gujarat stated at the outset that he was against appeasement of minorities. At this point, I told Justice Sachar that there was no point in holding a meeting with the chief minister and got up to leave. When Modi explained that he had nothing against the HLC but was articulating a general principle, Justice Sachar intervened and persuaded me to attend the meeting–which I did.

My experience with HLC also taught that in any team work, contributions of the different members vary substantially and it is impossible to assign credit proportionate to their contributions of each member.

CHAPTER 19

Social Inclusion Research Fund, Nepal

With the dismantling of socialist states, welfare states diluted the content of their welfare programmes for the needy and poor. This aggravated the condition of the poor and by the mid-1960s, some economists referred to the exclusion of the poor from the market. By the mid-1970s, the term 'social inclusion' was invoked in West Europe to refer to the rehabilitation of a variety of socially stigmatized collectivities from different socio-economic backgrounds–the socially and physically handicapped, aged invalids, those who survived attempted suicides, children subjected to abuse, single parents, and those who indulged in substance abuse, delinquent behaviour or prostitution. In South Asia there are groups and communities which are excluded social categories–the organic collectivities–thus both excluded individuals drawn from aggregative collectivities and excluded organic collectivities were included in the process of social inclusion in South Asia.

The two Hindu-majority South Asian countries are particularly in need of social inclusion because of the firm grip of the caste system. Ever since it became a Republic in 1950, India initiated several measures to bring about equality, liberty, dignity and security for its citizens. In contrast, Nepal continued as a monarchy till 1990 and its 1856 Civil Code, which officially recognized the social status of caste groups based on their traditional status, came in the way of social transformation. The Social Inclusion Research Fund (SIRF) was conceived as an instrument of intervention to usher in an egalitarian society in Nepal. Communities which are excluded and discriminated based on gender, religion, caste, class, language and region had demanded their social inclusion and responding to this, the Norwegian government consented to finance the Social Inclusion Research Fund (SIRF) in 2004. SIRF received the approval of the Government of Nepal in 2005 and the idea was incorporated into the interim constitution of Nepal in 2006.

The first phase of the SIRF was for a period of three years (2006–09). The Fund was administered by a secretariat housed at the Netherlands Development Organization (SNV), functioning from Kathmandu. The three-fold objectives SIRF pursued were: to support critical and high quality social science research on causes of social exclusion and ways to accommodate and manage Nepal's diversity; to make social science research more relevant to excluded and disadvantaged communities and their aspirations; and to ensure that social research contributes more effectively to policy debate and participative democratic process.

Having satisfactorily completed the first phase, the Norwegian government had agreed to continue financial assistance for another term of three years (2009–12). I was invited to be a member of the SIRF Steering Committee at this juncture. Of the seven members of the committee, five were from Nepal and one each from Norway and India. The first task of the second phase of SIRF was to identity the deficits of the first phase so that its functioning could be improved upon. A two-person committee was charged with that responsibility–Om Gurung of the department of anthropology and I were given this task. The guiding questions posed were: what are the neglected themes in social inclusion research in Nepal and is it possible to construct a social atlas of excluded groups in Nepal based on the research already done?; was the procedure of selecting researchers fool-proof and what steps need to be taken to eliminate ghostwriting of research proposals and reports?; what are the appropriate prerequisites (educational qualification, experience, competence and motivation) which enable researchers to study the intricate and complex theme of social exclusion?; how can one ensure that the researchers are drawn from all relevant identity groups without sacrificing the critical minimum competence required for undertaking research?; how can one ensure that a researcher studying his/her identity group/s would maintain the required level of objectivity and what control mechanisms can be introduced to detect biases?; is adequate caution exercised in selecting reviewers of research proposals and research supervisors who are objective and competent?

While *all* societies are stratified based on class, gender, age, region and rural–urban differences, most contemporary societies are also heterogeneous based on race, religion, language and such factors. But a few societies are also plural with a polarization between those who are defined as insiders to the polity, the core members, and those who are perceived as outsiders. Additionally, societies in South Asia, particularly Nepal and India, are hierarchical thanks to the deeply entrenched caste system.

The plurality of Nepal is embedded in two dimensions–cultural and territorial. Cultural insiders in Nepal are the inhabitants of the hill territory where life is conditioned by Sanskritic Hinduism. In contrast, those who inhabit the plains (the Terai region) are cultural outsiders who follow the folk versions of Hinduism. Hill people are subjected to certain hostile ecological disabilities, such as harsh climatic conditions, inhospitable terrain for agriculture, scanty transport and communication, so if they are socially superior, they are economically disadvantaged. In contrast, if the plains people are socially inferior they have economic advantages.

Be that as it may, the inhabitants of both the hill region and plains region are subjected to caste hierarchy. Broadly speaking, there are three social clusters in Nepal: the upper castes (traditionally Bahun (Brahmins) and Chhetri, (Kshariyas); the middle/intermediate groups (Vaishya, Janjati, peasantry and artisanal groups); and the lower groups (those who practise occupations with low prestiage and are below the ritual pollution line) referred to as Dalits now. While there was congruence between social status (caste) and material condition (class) in the past, limited social mobility, both upward and downward, has brought about status incongruence between caste and class. Therefore, some argue that the combination of lower class-upper caste may justify inclusion, but upper class-lower caste should not. At any rate, the combination of upper caste-upper class result in cumulative domination and lower caste-lower class brings about cumulative oppression. Social inclusion research cannot ignore these unfolding social realities.

The three tasks of undertaking research, formulating relevant policy and pursuing advocacy are inextricably intertwined. However, while these tasks are closely linked, they should be analytically separated for maintaining high quality and objectivity in research. Further, while research is the responsibility of the SIRF, advocacy should be the task of civil society, and policy formulation and implementation should be the task of the State.

Nepal was a country where 85 per cent its populace was excluded for centuries. SIRF I initiated the process of social inclusion research when the traditionally excluded communities were gradually emerging from the psychological cage they were imprisoned in for centuries. The coincidence of drafting an inclusive constitution, conceiving a federal polity and the launching of SIFR I was indeed a happy one. This was reinforced by the National Planning Commission (NPC) by adopting social inclusion as a policy plank in its Third Five Year plan and by instituting the National Inclusion Commission (NIC) of Nepal. Relevant data relating to the myriad groups and communities was not yet available. Therefore SIRF II recognized the need for creating a Social Exclusion Atlas for Nepal. It was decided to draw upon the expertise of the Anthropological Survey of India which launched and successfully completed the People of India Project (PIP).

The idea of exclusion/inclusion was not adequately operationalized in SIRF I. The listed excluded groups were women, Madhesis, Janjatis, Dalits, the hill groups and Muslims. But intersectionality which leads to exclusion (such as upper caste women who are victims of patriarchy) or cumulative exclusion (as in the case of lower caste, lower class, inhabiting hilly region) or the differences between the same social category inhabiting different ecological zones (Janjatis of the hill community and Janjatis among Madhesis inhabiting plains region) were left out. SIRF II decided to resort to these nuanced categorizations based on a social aetiology of excluded groups.

The near absence of a dialogue between researchers, policymakers and social activists during SIRF I was noted and we attempted to rectify it during SIRF II. It was also noted that SIRF I followed a 'fast-food syndrome' in that untrained, non-academic and part-time 'researchers' were granted research grants, which often led to ghostwritten research reports. Finally, most studies were micro, at best meso, and relied on qualitative data so had not produced research usable for policymakers. At the level of execution, SIRF I remained by and large urban-centric.

In the light of these experiences, SIRF II took the following cautionary steps: first, applications for research grants were first short-listed based on the stated qualifications and interviews of short-listed candidates held at three different locations outside Kathmandu. Second, the experts associated with SIRF II interacted with researchers on an ongoing basis and appropriate material incentives were given to research supervisors. Third, the initial training of researchers were made focused and purposeful by dividing it into two streams: general orientation for all on methodological issues and specific training for separate groups based on the nature of their projects. Four, a clear conceptualization of exclusion/inclusion was done during SIRF II. Those who were excluded were identified, while the causes of exclusion–'secular', 'ritual' and a combination of both these–were analysed to evolve a morphology of exclusion in Nepal. Five, transcending the micro-orientation of SIRF I, SIRF II graduated to meso (rural–urban, hills–plains) as well as macro (all-Nepal) studies. This facilitated the preparation of a Nepal Social Exclusion Atlas (NSEA), on which a Social Inclusion Index for Nepal (SIIN) was worked out. Six, it was proposed that social inclusion research should be undertaken in a comparative mode–comparing two or more excluded groups/

communities and the same group/community being studied by at least two researchers drawn from two identity groups. Seven, dialogues between researchers, activists and policymakers were organized in the course of SIRF II which led to their mutual sensitization. Sequencing of research, advocacy and policy formulation as well as their mutuality was amply unfolded to help moderate the demand-making and grievance-articulating tenor of activists, the intellectual arrogance of researchers and the patronizing tendency of policymakers. Eight, since collective research projects generate an enormous quantity of data, often of poor quality, and published by sub-standard publishers, SIRF II recommended establishing an SIRF Documentation Centre as a repository of all the data; launching a SIRF monograph series based on the high quality data collected which could be published either by the Tribhuvan University Press or by an established publishing house in South Asia; and allowing access to competent scholars to the Documentation Centre so that they can publish research papers of high quality in professional journals in Nepal and elsewhere. Nine, SIRF I was largely empirical and field-oriented and SIRF II retained this orientation but expanded its scope by attempting some conceptualizations and theory-building. Given the importance of migration in Nepal, both nationally and internationally, it needed to be linked to exclusion/inclusion–if earlier migration was induced by exclusion (practice of untouchability for lower castes and patriarchy for women), at present migration is largely voluntary, motivated by social mobility. SIRF II resolved to capture the changing dynamics of migration; an analysis of the existing legislations and policies which reinforce/obstruct social exclusion/inclusion was attempted in the context of emerging democratization of Nepal; it was necessary to undertake a content analysis of textbooks in schools and colleges prescribed in Nepal, so as to examine their potentiality for social inclusion and/or proclivity for social exclusion; and study of the media, both print and electronic, on social inclusion/exclusion needed to be undertaken. Thus a shift from the field-driven micro empirical research of SIRF I to macro research was visualized in SIRF II. Lastly, while insisting on the primacy of research, SIRF II squarely answered the question: Knowledge for whom and for what? The knowledge generated was meant for the benefit of the excluded, to motivate them to participate in nation-building in which they did not have any stake so far.

It is hoped that widening the scope of participatory development will accelerate the process of institutionalizing democratic federalism in Nepal.

Although independent India took numerous policy measures some seven decades ago to uplift the disadvantaged–SCs, STs, OBCs, religious minorities and women–it cannot be said that India has a well thought-out social inclusion policy. India can and should learn from Nepal in this context although Nepal is only emerging now as a democratic polity. Since 2005, Nepal has been pursuing a social inclusion policy although it has not yet achieved much. However, the model it is pursuing is worth adopting.

CHAPTER 20

Mentoring the Schumacher Centre, Delhi

A word of introduction to E.F. Schumacher (1911–77) is appropriate before we see what the institution in his name was about. He was a German economist deeply committed to the welfare of the poor. His book *Small is Beautiful* (1973)–in which he proposed the idea of appropriate technology for human-centric development instead of the cult of high technology, the reckless application of which destroyed nature–propelled him to global fame. Schumacher pursued 'Buddhist Economics' and endorsed the path of development advocated by M.K. Gandhi. In spite of all this, it cannot be said that he is well known in India. When I told a gathering in Delhi I was addressing that I had to leave so as to reach on time for a meeting at the Schumacher Centre, a young man in the audience remarked, 'Sir, I did not know that you have such a great interest in motor racing!' He knew only the racing driver Michael Schumacher.

The Schumacher Centre, Delhi (SCD) was registered in 2002, under section 6 of the Societies Registration Act 1860 as applicable to the Union Territory of Delhi. The first Governing Board (GB) of the SCD consisted of seven persons–I was the chairperson (I hold the position to this day) and D.K. Giri was the secretary. At present, after one and a half decades of its existence, the GB consists of nine members. The SCD formulated its first three-year strategy in 2004 and started functioning in a systematic manner.

The registration of SCD in 2002 and my retirement from JNU coincided. Further, the guiding principles of the SCD coincided with my own value-orientation. The vision of the SCD is an India without chronic poverty where all its citizens have the opportunity to live with dignity, freedom from hunger and deprivation. Its central mission is tackling the roots of poverty in India through revitalizing rural communities, promoting inclusive, harmonious and sustainable development through the application of appropriate technology. The SCD's operational focus is on development issues that include the livelihood of rural people, sustainable development, forestry, local democracy, women's empowerment and environmental protection.

In implementing its livelihood projects, the SCD follows Schumacher's three-step approach: one, mapping existing skills and resources of the people; two, building on resources and skills through Appropriate Technology (AT); and three, helping people to generate disposable income beyond their consumption to use for other developmental needs like health, education and leisure.

The SCD focuses on the entire value chain when addressing livelihood projects so that the continuum of Production → Technology → Market is kept in view. Markets must work for the benefit of the poor and conversely, the poor must get involved in the market so that it is not perceived as an enemy of the poor and the environment. The tri-sector approach promoted by the SCD is a joint venture with appropriate division of labour: the state/government should provide legal, financial and institutional support; civil society should facilitate social mobilization so that citizens pursue rights-based approach for their development and welfare; and the private sector should help developing technology, provide financial support and evolve a competitive market. If any of these partners–state, civil society, market–is allowed to establish its hegemony, balanced development becomes impossibile.

The SCD imparts knowledge through training programmes for NGOs and development organizations, providing consultancies to the government, business organizations and civil society organizations. It undertakes action research with special reference to rural India to generate relevant knowledge for balanced development. Thus the SCD is both a communicator as well as a producer of knowledge.

SCD had also taken several initiatives in shaping and applying Schumacher's ideas to suit the Indian context. As the chairperson I took a keen interest in this sector of SCD's activity. But let me candidly confess that several activities could not be systematically pursued because of a lack of appropriate personnel and adequate funding. For example, our journal *Samwad*, intended to be published once in three months on development issues had to be discontinued. Similarly, the monthly lecture/seminar series 'Small is Beautiful' could not be sustained for long. On the other hand, a dozen booklets and pamphlets have been published on a wide variety of themes and our initiative to create a network of 500 small NGOs and OASIS (Orissa Association for Social Initiatives and Service) has been a success.

The SCD can legitimately be proud of making conceptual

contributions to two areas: the tri-sector approach to development and appropriate technology. Under the aegis of the structural adjustment programme (SAP), the rapacity of market institutions increased manifold. In the emerging scenario, a 'good society' is perceived as one standing on three pillars: the state, market/business and civil society. The tri-sector approach is an offspring of this emerging trend and is in consonance with our objective of bringing about authentic transformation in the lives of the rural poor which falls in line with Gandhiji's notion of 'antyodaya' focusing on the weakest in society. The increasing acceptance of the idea of Corporate Social Responsibility (CSR) by business houses is a happy omen for the tri-sector approach which SCD supports. In fact, much before the tri-sector approach came into vogue I published a paper: 'State, Civil Society and Market in India' in *Mobilization: An International Journal* in 1996.

E.F. Schumacher proposed the idea of intermediate technology to cope with the inefficiency of traditional technology and to counter the ill-effects of high technology, particularly on the environment. But this imparted the wrong impression that Schumacher was anti-high technology and that he wanted to displace traditional technology. In fact, in the SCD's conceptualization all technologies are appropriate. We advocate technological pluralism instead of high-tech driven development which prompts unthinking production and rash deployment of technology. Much before my association with the SCD, I published a research paper entitled: 'Restructuring Development through Technological Pluralism' in *International Sociology*, in 1992.

In the course of one and a half decades, SCD has emerged as a trainer in capacity-building, following Schumacher's advice: 'Gift of knowledge is better than any material gift; but before you give it you must acquire it.' Fortunately, the leadership at SCD is well-endowed; its founder director, D.K. Giri (2000–13) has two doctorates, one from the UK and another from India and Susan Cherian who became deputy director in 2006 and succeeded Giri as director in 2013 also holds a PhD from JNU. We work in unison and with mutual recognition. In fact Giri wrote a poem dedicated to me which is reproduced below.

An Ode to a Professor

I was influenced and inspired by a professor who,
On record, I was not taught by
He was a model to emulate
But it was not easy to try

His commitment to the profession
Was hard to compare
The competence in his subject
Was the best by far

His oratory and articulation
Was music to the ear
His repartee, wit and humour
Cooled any intellectual thunder

He was a wizard of concepts
Loved to use them afresh
Invented ideas and expressions
Those were not easy to trace

He put the principle before the person
Whether in academic or public life

He argued for social cohesion and harmony
Explained and advocated the exclusion of strife

Mapping the content and context of an issue
Was his tool ever so effective
He found no phenomenon universal
It was all contextual or relative

To him, monolithism, homogenization, majoritairianism
Were anathemas to any society
A confirmed pluralist in his approach
Spice of life is the variety

He carried his intellectual conviction
And an audacity of expression
Crafted, spoke with equal sincerity
No matter the occasion

Self-hood, integrity and credibility
Were parts of his personality
He was meticulous and a word-keeper
Never compromising liberty or honesty

A commitment of his presence in an event
Couldn't be changed by the high and mighty
He treated all his hosts equal
Recognized no ranks but parity

He was unique in
Combining pragmatism and principle
He was not to trade off either
But never sacrificed a scruple

His scholarship was nationally unchallenged
Internationally fairly prized
But his studied views were unheeded by powers that be
Despair he did hardly disguise

He seemed aloof and reticent
With a serious exterior
But as he spoke with his sonorous tone
He regaled you with his wit and humour
A good human being with compassion and concern
Be them his students, colleagues or people in general
He would stretch out and reach them
With sympathy and support moral and material

I salute you professor
An author, thinker, orator, critique and commentator
Your observations and advice to us
Are invaluable and indispensable problem-solvers

You are a gift of God
To the academic community, evolving polity and
wider society
We will remember you ever
An ideal professor, as good an intellectual deity…

CHAPTER 21

The Padma Bhushan Award

It was on 5 May 2008 that I received the Padma Bhushan, the prestigious national award, from the President of India. Some of my colleagues in the academic circle feel that since decision-making in conferring such awards are made by non-academic persons one should not accept them. In multi-party democracies, parties which come to occupy power vary across time so if the award is bestowed on persons or institutions for their contributions to the society/nation it does not matter who conferred the award provided that the decisions are impartial. But it is difficult to agree that decisions are always 'impartial'.

The first person who told me that I deserve a Padma Award was M.N. Srinivas, himself a Padma Bhushan. He made this remark in 1986 after observing how I functioned as the secretary general of the XI World Congress of Sociology as he was the chairperson of the Indian National Organizing Committee (INOC) of the Congress. Thus there is a veneer of academic legitimacy for the award although it happened twenty-two years after he articulated it. Sociology as a discipline rarely attracts the attention of the public and recognition by the state in India. As far as I know only five sociologists received the Padma Awards in India: Radhakamal Mukherjee, M.N. Srinivas, M.S. Gore, Andre Beteille and myself. Once Dhirendra Narain, University of Bombay, told me that G.S. Ghurye was offered the Padma Bhusan but he declined because he thought that he deserved nothing less than the Bharat Ratna.

The Padma Awards are announced annually on the eve of Republic Day and prominently reported by the media. Usually, the focus of attention would be on those in the entertainment industry. For example, when Josephine and I went to Rashtrapati Bhavan to receive the award, the focus of media attention was mainly on cricketer Sachin Tendulkar and singer Asha Bhosle although the then foreign minister, Pranab Mukherjee, founder of INFOSYS, N.R. Narayana Murthy, and the metro man E. Sreedharan and others too were present to receive the awards. Those who were accorded the least importance by the media were, of course, those from academia.

During February and March 2008, I was honoured with eleven receptions, two of them in my native village in Kerala. The village reception was presided over by P.J. Kurien the then local MP and the family reception was inaugurated by P.C. Vishnunath, the local MLA. Three receptions were organised by Kerala organizations/associations in Delhi–the Kerala Development Society, Uttara Guruvayurappan Temple and Senior Citizens of Mar Thoma Church, Safdarjung where I have membership. Two receptions were organized by NGOs–Institute of Social Science and Sphere India–which functioned from Delhi. I was one of the persons felicitated by EDGE (Emerging Directions in Global Education) from among the Padma awardees of 2008 who made 'significant contributions to Education, Science and Technology, Engineering and Management' on 5 March 2008, at the India Habitat Centre, New Delhi.

Two felicitation meetings were organized by the CSSS associates and the managing committee of the Indian Sociological Society (ISS). But the Jawaharlal Nehru University Teachers Association (JNUTA) seemed to be impervious to the national honour I received–despite the fact that I had taught in JNU for thirty-one years and I was an Emeritus Professor. The thunderous reception given to me by the people of my village, which I left when I was sixteen years old and the lukewarm attitude of JNU which I served for thirty-one years, are in stark contrast.

Between January and May 2008 I received 193 communications congratulating me, including C. Rangarajan, chairman, Economic Advisory Council to the Prime Minister, K.K. Venugopal, Senior Advocate, Supreme Court of India, Navin Chawla, chief election commissioner; Satish Chandra, former chairman, University Grants Commission; and Manzer Khan, managing director, Oxford University Press, New Delhi. But three letters were particularly striking. P.C. Mathur, a distinguished political scientist, wrote from Jaipur:

> I will like to convey my own and my family's congratulations for the conferment of Padma Bhushan upon your extraordinary academic achievements (as far as I know you have held no administrative posts which are the usual stepping stones for such awards nor I have ever known you as cosying up to political power-holders and/or power-brokers) which makes your award very, very unusual.

In the same vein Ronald deSouza, another political scientist, who was at that time Director of Indian Institute of Advanced Study, Shimla wrote:

> Congratulations: I was delighted to learn on your being awarded Padma Bhusan in this years' Republic Day honours

> list. It is very heartening to note that the Indian State is willing to recognize an intellectual who has lived a life of dispassionate criticism and high intellectual integrity.

The reasons why I am singling out these letters are because the general impression is that Padma Awards are given only to 'sarkari intellectuals', that unless one takes a pro-state/pro-government position one cannot aspire to get a Padma Award. However, here is what Bindeswar Pathak, the founder of the Sulabh International Social Service Organization, wrote.

> Hon'ble Dr Oommen
>
> May I congratulate you on being honoured with the Padma Award for your academic excellence which in part is a recompense for ignoring great sociologists like Dr Yogendra Singh, Dr S.C. Dube and Dr M.N. Srinivas. Although they needed no official recognition but symbolic national laurels would have been in order.
>
> Your commendable role in the drafting of the prejudice-free report of the Sachar Committee has been widely acclaimed which was hard for the govt. to ignore. Max Weber had also written many reports, political and social, in his lifetime; one such analysis being, if my memory is right, in his book *The Protestant Ethics and the Spirit of Capitalism.* The tumultuous years in Germany between 1871 (when the German state was born) and the later conflicts which led to World War I (1914–18) shaped his thinking, quite the way your report reflects the situation of a divided Indian society and suggests political intervention to stave off a social conflict. Your book *Protest and Change* also has these references. While writing to you, these thoughts randomly come to mind which is neither needed nor timely. But, they are very uplifting.

I replied thus:

> Dear Dr Pathak,
>
> Many thanks for your letter dated 29 January 2008 to congratulate me. I have received numerous routine congratulatory messages–oral and written–but none of them was as reflective as yours. First, a correction; Padma Bhushan was conferred on Dr M.N. Srinivas (not Srinivasan) in the mid-1970s. As for Dr S.C. Dube, he amply deserved it but unfortunately he left us little too early. I agree with you that Dr Yogendra Singh does deserve it and let us conjointly propose him for the Award.
>
> I am a little intrigued about your invoking the word 'recompense' in this context. As far as I know recompense means one of the following: (a) make amends to (someone) for loss or harm suffered; (b) atonement or satisfaction given for injury; (c) compensate etc. I do not quite understand as to how the Award announced for me becomes a recompense for others. At any rate your statement assumes that the Indian state is aware of the contributions by *all* sociologists and it consciously *avoids* some of them and deliberately *patronizes* some others. You could not have entertained this false assumption if you were adequately informed of the procedure involved in selecting Padma Awardees.
>
> I am happy that you are aware of my book *Protest and Change*, but it is only one of the twenty-four books authored and/or edited by me.

Social Scientists in general and sociologists in particular were parsimonious in extending felicitations to me. But names which come to my mind from the academic fraternity are my teacher Y.B. Damle, Victor D'Souza, T.N. Madan, S.K. Srivastava, P.C. Joshi, Partha Mukherjee, John Kattakayam, M.N. Panini, Sujata Patel and a few others. Indeed a large number of my former students did felicitate me.

Let me stop by mentioning the person who proposed my name for the award. I knew from reliable sources that Hamid Ansari Sahib was impressed with my academic credentials, but when he suggested my name for the Padma Bhushan, he was not sure whether his proposal would be favourably endorsed by the decision-making committees. So the vice president of India was one of the first to call and ask me: 'Did you make it'? And he was delighted that I had!

CHAPTER 22

The Turbulent Presidency at the National Media Centre

Founded by a handful of print media persons, led by Upendra Vajpeyi, a Hindi journalist, the National Media Centre Co-operative House Building Society Ltd (NMC) was registered in 1986 with the vision

> to develop and sustain a community of like-minded individuals on a residential-cum-institutional campus for harmonious habitation and free intellectual discourse in an environmentally friendly setting and through democratic process.

And yet the NMC membership was not eagerly sought after and many had to be persuaded to join the Society. While every effort was made to bring in as many media persons as possible, members were also drawn from a wide variety of occupational backgrounds–academics, corporate employees, engineers, physicians, artists, lawyers and bureaucrats.

My admission to the NMC was based on mistaken identity. When Vajpeyi telephoned me to find out if I was interested in joining the NMC, he thought that he was talking to Thomas K.

Oommen, a journalist associated with the Times Foundation. The situation was further confounded because I used to publish editorial pieces in English newspapers, such as *The Times of India*, *Hindustan Times*, *The Hindu* and *Indian Express*. Although Vajpeyi discovered that I was not one of his tribe he goaded me to join the NMC and I relented.

I was to retire in October 1997 at the age of sixty but thanks to the extension in the age of retirement, I retired only in 2002. It was in March 2003 when I shifted to the NMC campus with no idea of what I was in for. I learnt that there was quite a turbulent socio-political atmosphere at the NMC–P.R. Chari, a retired IAS official, whom I knew because of our shared interest in 'national security', alerted me about the murky politics on the campus. I deeply regret that I did not heed his advice and contested the election in 2003 caused by the resignation of the managing committee (MC) before completing its term of five years. According to the prescribed rules of registrar, Haryana Co-operative Societies, the members have to elect fifteen committee members, who in turn elect five office-bearers–the president, vice president, general secretary, secretary and treasurer. Sunanda Sen got the highest number of votes and I received the second highest number, but we were both retired professors of JNU. Instead of an open election of the office-bearers, a caucus of journalists went into a huddle and identified I. Rammohan Rao as the vice president, Mahabir Singh as general secretary, O.P. Tandon as secretary and T.N. Ninan as treasurer, all of whom were media persons. When a suggestion was made to elect me as president because of the number of votes, (by this criterion Sunanda Sen should have been the president) the uneasy divide between media and non-media members surfaced. I was told that Rammohan Rao insisted that if I was made the president he would refuse to become the vice president. Under the circumstances, the caucus decided to name Inderjit Badhwar, a journalist, who polled much fewer votes than most other candidates as the president.

The 2003–08 MC ran its full term and a new MC was elected in 2008 which was also dominated by media persons and presided over by Raj Chengappa, a journalist, who resigned after two years. Seen in terms of its composition, the 2010–15 MC witnessed a paradigm shift: one-third (five out of fifteen) of its members were women (for the first time in the MC) and all the five office-bearers were non-media persons. The election of office-bearers of the 2010–15 MC took place on 18 November and I was elected the president, Sunanda Sen as vice president, Kulwant Singh, a former member of the Indian Economic Service and a World Bank expert on water, was elected as the general secretary.

According to the latest bye-laws of the MNC approved by the registrar, Co-operative Societies, Haryana with effect from 17 September 2010, just before the 2010–15 MC took over in November 2010, it was stated that:

> The president will generally supervise all the activities of the Society. He will preside over the meetings of the Managing Committee, General Body and other Committees headed by him. He will sign the proceedings register, resolutions, audited accounts and other documents, as required by the Managing Committee.

While the vice president would assist the president, the general secretary was the chief executive officer, empowered to sign the papers on behalf of the Society and the treasurer was responsible for the orderly conduct of its financial affairs.

Upendra Vajpeyi was the general secretary of the first MC. His general acceptability and unquestioned authority resulted in the concentration of authority in the office of the general secretary. The 2010–15 MC of the NMC appointed a Bye-laws Revision Committee towards the end of its terms for the twin purposes of re-visiting the goals of the NMC: one, as the phase of the admission of members and construction of houses was over, routine maintenance was more relevant and two, to revise the powers and functions of the MC and its office-bearers. But the committee is yet to submit its recommendations, I am told.

As a member of the 2003–08 MC, I knew the extremely ad hoc manner in which its meetings were convened; the members were informed of the meetings usually by telephone, invariably on the previous day. Although MC meetings are to be held as and when necessary according to the bye-laws of NMC, it was decided by the 2010–15 committee to hold MC meetings every second Sunday of the month and that the MC members would be informed in writing one week in advance. However, in the course of five years when I was the president, only thirty-nine MC meetings were held.

Earlier, the practice was to draft the minutes after the MC meetings and circulate them along with the agenda of the following meeting. But the circulated draft minutes became very contentious and several valuable hours were lost in finalizing them. We decided to change this practice and agreed on a procedure in which every decision would be formulated and articulated by the chair (president) and the minutes written by the secretary. There would not be any discussion on the minutes as the approval of decisions would be done as the MC meeting proceeded.

In spite of the systematic procedure followed, the MC meetings were almost always turbulent and two members turned out to be professional dissenters, resorting to tactics like walking out of the meetings and complaining loudly. This behaviour affected the harmonious conduct of the MC meetings. What was galling was that these two members would also send complaints about the MC meetings regularly, to authorities of the Haryana Co-operative Society.

In addition to protests by the elected members of the MC, non-MC members would insist on attending meetings. Disruptions would occur when non-MC members would come to the MC meeting unannounced and insist on being present as observers. And as the chair, I ruled that I would not conduct the meeting if this happened because decisions taken in such meetings would be illegal. Or a group of members, usually ten to fifteen, would charge into the meeting and insist that it should be converted into an 'extended' MC meeting. While I often concurred with the principle of extended meetings because it facilitated wider participation, I insisted that that due notice was to be sent to all the 190 members of NMC so that anyone who wanted to could attend. Once, some non-MC members barged into a meeting and actually held me a captive, although they did not call it a gherao. When I wanted to go to the bathroom, a man assigned to the task of restricting my movements actually accompanied me to witness my call of nature. He assumed that I was running away from the meeting.

Sometimes, elected members of the MC took utterly irrational positions and persisted in justifying them. For example, in September 2014, the issue of a second gate for the NMC came up for consideration as the existing one-point entry to the colony at a low-lying area was prone to water-logging. The decision had to be taken on an urgent basis as the Haryana Urban Development Authority (HUDA) was rapidly proceeding with the construction of the front wall of the colony after demolishing the original wall. Of the ten members of the MC present, five agreed with the proposal to construct the second gate and five opposed. As the chair, I could have exercised my casting vote as a bye-law of the MNC laid down that 'Each member shall have one vote. In the case of votes being equal the chairman shall have a casting vote' and a decision could have been taken. Even though I refused to do so saying the decision should not be made through a casting vote, two members who opposed the construction argued that the president's casting vote would amount to his exercising two votes, which was legally unsustainable! This incident reminded me of Bertrand Russell's observation: 'The fundamental cause of trouble is that in the modern world the stupid are cocksure while the intelligent are full of doubt.'

When I was president, there were three crucial issues that had to be dealt with. The first related to the fact that the NMC was registered as an organization not only to establish a co-operative house-building society but to set up a training institution for media persons too. This 'double-edge' of the NMC was a matter of irritation for the overwhelming majority of members who only wanted a house in a co-operative society, while a handful of media persons were interested in the institution as well. After considerable conflict, two organizations emerged with differing objectives: The National Media Centre Co-operative House Building Society Ltd (NMC) and the Media India Centre for Research and Development (MICRD). Those who joined the NMC initially had also to be members of the MICRD and make some financial contributions.

This duality did not bother members of the NMC as much as the way the 'media agenda' was imposed on them did. Two vital dimensions which did affect them were that the members did not have ownership of the plot of land or their houses, but were only in possession of these, although this was not explicitly stated in the bye-laws, the second relating to the bar against alienation. Clause 52 of the MNC by-laws read: 'No member should alienate any house allotted to him without concurrence of the Society'.

The MC of 2010–15 held a meeting on 23 January 2011 to discuss the Draft Conveyance Deed which would confer ownership of their property on the NMC members. The meeting was attended by thirteen MC members. Although the NMC was legally obliged to transfer the ownership to members right at the beginning as in all co-operative societies, an embargo existed for fifteen years through a Memorandum of Understanding (MoU) between the first MC and the director of Town and Country Planning (DTCP) of Gurgaon to prevent alienation of property so nobody could sell property. Viewed retrospectively, this could be viewed as a positive measure to check members who sought profits by selling their plots/houses at the market rate, much higher than what they paid for. But the new MC took the position that as the fifteen-year embargo was over, the Conveyance Deed could be executed.

In the meeting, it seemed reasonable to follow the Haryana Co-operative Act, 1984 to transfer ownership to NMC members. In spite of all the efforts made to arrive at a consensus, two MC members dissented, saying there was no need to confer ownership of property on individual members and that the NMC should have collective ownership in its property. Only a small group of ten to twelve members endorsed this line of thinking out of the 190 members.

The second critical issue that the 2010–15 MC had to tackle related to the alienation of property. According to the MOU between the NMC and DTCP, every member had to wait for fifteen years to secure the legal ownership of property as noted above. But some had to dispose of their property earlier than this prescribed time limit. As far as I know, the first person to dispose of his property was Swaminathan Aiyer, a journalist, who was migrating to the USA. Since he did not have the ownership of his property it was necessary to resort to the instrument of Power of Attorney (POA). By the time the 2010–15 MC took over, there were about sixty-five POAs who bought property in the NMC but had no legal documents to claim it and hence could not be members of the NMC. Constant tension between the two groups–the members and the POAs–resulted, the latter being treated as institutional orphans who could not attend the general body meetings or vote in the NMC elections and were charged double of the maintenance fees. The MC received applications from sixty-two POAs by the time it held its meeting on 13 March 2011 and to resolve the problem, decided to transfer membership to them in the MC meetings held on 10 April 2011.

Members joined the MNC over a period of time starting from 1984 and had to pay 'equalization charges'. By law, co-operative societies could charge only up to Rs 10,000 from the POAs who sought membership of co-operatives. But there was a small section of MNC members who wanted to collect 10 to 15 lakhs each from the POAs, which was patently illegal. Their intention was not simply to use the POAs as milch cows for the MNC but also to discredit and dislodge the MC. While strictly adhering to the legal prescription, I announced in the MC meeting that the NMC would accept voluntary donations over and above the Rs 10,000 the POAs had to pay, but none of the POAs volunteered.

The third issue which the 2010–15 MC inherited related to the nearly two acres of land in front of the NMC which opened to National Highway No 8. The MoU between the Society and the local government authorities stated explicitly that the land in front of the NMC would be maintained as a Green Belt and the land would be surrendered free of cost if required. The document was signed by the then general secretary of the NMC. But as and when the Delhi Land Federation (DLF) mooted the idea of establishing the Rapid Metro Link between two stations of the Delhi–Gurgaon Metro, the concerned government departments argued that since the land in front of the NMC was required to construct the Rapid Metro, a public facility, they could acquire the land without giving any compensation. Understandably, there was considerable resentment in the colony against the arbitrary decision and action of the DTCP, which was not legally entitled to take over the land. The land was transferred to HUDA which in turn leased it out to the Rapid Metro for ninety-nine years on an agreed royalty. The DLF was willing to provide compensation to the NMC but those who were opposed to the MC informed the DLF that they should not negotiate with the MC as its fall was imminent.

In the meantime, the NMC approached the National Green Tribunal (NGT) for justice as the local government authorities had changed land-use, from the promised Green Belt to facilitate a commercial venture as the Rapid Metro was intended to promote quick and easy traffic to the DLF-owned and administrated Ambience Mall, billed as the biggest mall in Asia. The NMC MC also filed its petition to the Punjab and Haryana High Court at Chandigarh, but the High Court held that since the Rapid Metro was a public utility project, the NMC had to surrender the land to the government without any compensation. The verdict that the action taken by the DTCP was in public interest, clearly demonstarates how legal interpretations ignore substance and opt for form. The change in land-use as well as mistaking a private profit-making enterprise for a public welfare project points to this.

When we decided to pursue the case in the Supreme Court, the high cost involved was an obstacle. I talked to

K.K. Venugopal, senior advocate at the Supreme Court of India who had an impeccable reputation, whom I knew through our association with the West Bengal National University of Juridical Sciences (NUJS) for nearly a decade. He heard me out but said that since the case was already rejected by the High Court, it could only be pursued for the limited purpose of seeking compensation. About the cost involved, he said it would be 5 lakhs each for the first five appearances and 7.5 lakhs each for the last two, totalling 40 lakhs. I told Venugopal that should I agree to pay the expected fee for him, he was sure to hear the news that the 'president of the NMC had been lynched by its members.' We roared with laughter and then he very kindly told me that, 'I'll argue the case free of cost as I want you to live a few years more.' When I reported the matter to the MC, I was surprised by the lack of any positive response in spite of the fact that the Society had saved Rs 40 lakhs!

If the turbulence in the MC meetings were storms in a teacup, the Annual General Body Meetings were tsunamis. Mercifully, there was only one general body meeting a year. The first GBM was held on 26 September 2011 and the focus was on the three big issues: pursuing the Green Belt case, admission of POAs and the issue of Conveyance Deeds. Although P.P. Chowdhary, an eminent lawyer who was a member of the NMC and subsequently became the Minister of Law and Social Justice in 2016, explained the advantages of Apartment Ownership Act, 1983 to the members, they opted for the Haryana Co-operative Act, 1984. Although there were these contentious issues, the GBM was smooth. One prominent male member complimented the chair by referring to me as a ringmaster while a lady member joked that she'd fallen in love with me (to which I quipped, 'It's a little too late!') There was all around appreciation about how the GBM was conducted.

The second GBM was held on 7 August 2012. It started with a member raising a point of order, generally invitations to disorder, regarding the admission of POAs to NMC. After a long and heated discussion a dissent note submitted by six members was received and appended to the minutes, which recorded:

> On the issue of transfer of membership of thirty members, the president stated in most unequivocal terms that the due process of law and prescribed procedure was followed by the MC while transferring membership to them. The fact that the competent authority in the Department of Cooperative Societies, Haryana has endorsed and approved the same was testimony to this, the president observed.

The matter relating to the admission of POAs to the MNC was raised yet again in the third GBM held on 5 August 2012. At the outset, a member, Rahul Dev, asked the president whether he had had received a letter dated 1 August 2012 from the assistant registrar proscribing the POAs from attending the GBM. I replied that I had not. Similarly, Pushpa Grimaji asked whether the transfer of membership to POAs was approved by the GBM and I answered that the issue was settled in the last GBM, the minutes of which were approved by the assistant registrar, Co-operatives. Therefore even if the assistant registrar wrote a letter as claimed by Rahul Dev, the official was guilty of self-contradiction and creating disaffection among the members of the NMC. The 'games' played by officials coupled with factionalism among members of grassroots institutions such as co-operatives and panchayats drains them of their efficiency and harmony.

The inter-factional tensions in NMC reached such a point that I constituted a ten-member Peace and Reconciliation

Committee (PRC) with L.L. Mehrotra, a retired Indian Foreign Service officer, as its convenor. The terms of reference of the PRC was 'to propose a solution for the smooth conduct of the third GBM slated to be held on 5 August 2012'. However, since the report of the PRC went far beyond its frame of reference, it was shelved and recommendations dropped. Thus my effort to bring about harmony between the warring factions met with failure.

The third GBM also witnessed an effort to undermine the legitimacy of the MC and usurp its authority. An Empowered Legal Committee (ELC) was proposed by one of the members of the MC, Narayan Parwani. Of the seven persons in the proposed ELC, none had financial authority. Since the proposed ELC was to take '… day to day legal and financial decisions to ensure that Society's interest in all legal matters are taken care of', I suggested that the general secretary and the treasurer too should be members of the ELC as they had financial powers. Members agreed to this but nobody suggested the inclusion of the third signatory of cheques–the president, in the ELC. When the general secretary recorded that the president shall be an ex-officio member of the ELC, there was a hue and cry in the Society.

The person who led this mobilization was Inderjit Badhwar who was the president of the NMC during 2003–08. His argument was that the president's presence in the ELC would create a 'clash of interest', a delightfully ambiguous phrase and questioned by no one. That the exclusion of the president from the ELC was actually inimical to the interest of the NMC unfolded soon when a cheque had to be issued to one of the lawyers engaged by the ELC. As the treasurer was away, I was asked to sign the cheque, but I retorted that since the presence of the president in the ELC was perceived as a clash of interest, it was improper for me to sign. A vilification campaign was then unleashed against me by the two convenors of the ELC prompting me to write a letter dated 7 September 2013:

> Dear all, particularly those who requested/advised/instructed/ordered me to sign the cheque,
>
> On 6 September when I was away to New Delhi, the office secretary, Ms Mariamma Raju, telephoned and told me that a lot of emails addressed to me (indeed a rare phenomenon) are coming to the office and whether she should take printouts and send them. I answered in the affirmative and got a bunch of communications by 3 p.m. when I realized to my dismay, that a campaign 'please sign the cheque', in which twenty persons were involved, was going on for the past one week! Because of my computer illiteracy, I was completely oblivious to what was happening. Now that I know of it I have both the legal and moral responsibility to respond.
>
> As you are aware, the Empowered Legal Committee (ELC) was constituted in the last General Body held on 23 June and the proposer of the resolution listed seven persons as members of the committee. Since the proposed committee is to have legal and financial autonomy, it is imperative that the three authorized signatories for the NMC cheques–treasurer, general secretary and president–should have been on the Committee. But none of them were included ... I suggested the inclusion of the first two and nobody at that point in time thought of including the third signatory. However, the general secretary suggested this subsequently in the GBM minutes which was rejected by the ELC members. Further, in a subsequent combined meeting of the MC and ELC the suggestion surfaced again and Inderjit Badhwar, one of the convenors of the ELC stated that there was 'conflict of interest' in including the president in the ELC.

But Sunil Mehta, the other convenor of the ELC is attributing the 'clash of interest' doctrine to me! Now you can discern how facts are misunderstood, mutilated and misrepresented. The question that I am asking myself is: if the president's presence in the ELC creates conflict of interest, how can he sign cheques for the ELC? Please enlighten me.

Secondly, the fact is that nobody ever asked me to sign the cheque meant for the lawyer arguing our case before the Green Tribunal. The office does not send cheques for signatures to me unless specifically instructed because the usual signatories are the general secretary and the treasurer. On 2 September, in the course of my morning walk, Sunil Mehta asked me while I passed the front of his house (it should be around 6.45 a.m.): 'Why don't you sign? It took a moment for me to capture the context of his question and I told him that since one of the convenors of the ELC pronounced that there is a conflict of interest in my being a member of ELC, it is inappropriate for me to sign the cheque. He then asked me, 'Why don't you resign?' When I was trying to respond, he made his third snipe, 'You are shameless.' At this point I walked away. (One of the members of the ELC, Mahabir Singh, was a witness to this vilification and aggression by Sunil Mehta).

There are three aspects to the issue:

1. If one wants to communicate to a person it should be done to that person instead of broadcasting it through email;
2. We should not de-legitimize an office (denying membership in a committee based on an imagined conflict of interests) and then ask that office-holder to be a party to the legal activity (for example, signing a cheque) of that committee;
3. We should not fancy that by intimidating, bullying, shouting and abusing we can get things done as is evident from the letters by the two convenors of the ELC circulated to the NMC members.

Dear Friends, please be a little more cautious and reflective before you come to an unequivocal and abrupt judgement. Thanks for your patience in reading this letter.

Your President in Agony,
T.K. Oommen

The most amusing thing to be noted here is that Inderjit Badhwar who became the president of the NMC subsequently (beginning 2015) included himself in the ELC, throwing to winds his own principle of 'clash of interest'.

The last GBM of the 2010–15 MC was held on 11 October 2015 and was relatively peaceful as the MC's term was almost over and the election for the next MC was fast approaching. As I look back at my tenure as the president of the NMC, especially at the tumultuous GBMs it was obvious that there was very little co-operation between the members of the National Media 'Co-operative' Society, I could pinpoint two basic sources of conflict. Firstly, the mismatch between the self-appointed elite of the Society (the media persons) and the background of elected leaders, particularly the president, vice president and general secretary, who were academics. Secondly, the MC of 2010–15 addressed basic and challenging issues, namely, providing ownership to members of their property (most members obtained their Conveyance Deeds), admitting almost all the POAs as members of the NMC and maintaining the two acres of land in front of the NMC as a Green Belt. The issues became vexatious not only because of the government and the private sector (DLF), colluded but also because some members of the NMC, worked against the interest of the Society.

Given the big challenges to be tackled, often on an emergency basis, some of the routine welfare measures could not be attended to expeditiously, be it the stray dog issue, the car-parking problem or the maintenance of roads. Also, the expected organic unity of the MC was imperilled because nearly 50 per cent of the members were opponents, a couple of them constantly and virulently, another group being slippery and unreliable. Even the five office-bearers were not on the same wavelength. To preside over the NMC for five years was the most turbulent assignment I have had in my life. But the fact that I survived it gives me some satisfaction.

CHAPTER 23

An Epilogue: Indian Sociologists, Professionals Without Professionalism?*

Of the four great professions which emerged initially in the West, university teaching and research was one, law, medicine and the Christian clergy being the others. Over time most occupations aspire to become professions, so much so that Harold Wilensky wondered in the mid-1960s whether all occupations were becoming professions! In defining professions, a three-set criteria is often invoked: a set of objective attributes; a set of subjective perceptions by professionals or the lay public; and a set of factors which influence the actual functioning of professions including individual motivation, group interest, the system of stratification, and so on.

---

* This chapter is an edited shorter version my article published in November 2000 in *Seminar* (495: 24–28) in the special number entitled 'Situating Sociology'.
Reprinted here with permission.

The general reckoning is that while workers have 'unions', professionals have 'associations', and professional association defines and characterizes professions. Indeed, professionals are expected to demonstrate a commitment to their chosen field of activity by being active participants in their professional associations. The most important function of these associations is facilitating peer-group interaction, which in turn enhances professional knowledge, reinforces professional identity, augments social standing and increases collective bargaining power. The Indian Sociological Society (ISS) as a professional association should be viewed in this context.

While the ISS had a nomadic past from 1967 to 1988, its office moving with the secretary, since 1989 it has been located at the Institute of Social Science, a non-governmental organization (NGO) situated in south Delhi thanks to its director, George Mathew, my former student. (In 2017 the ISS office shifted to its own building in South Delhi).

The ISS is a fusion of two associations, a trend contrary to the fission that prevails in other disciplines. Several reasons could be adduced for this. First, sociology is a smaller and relatively new discipline in India. Second, ideological polarization is not as marked in sociology as in some other disciplines (such as history). Third, the degree of specialization is not as sharp in sociology as in say, economics, which has separate associations of agricultural and industrial economists. Finally, the 'split' in sociology manifests in terms of different associations for anthropology and sociology in spite of the ambiguous disciplinary boundaries between the two disciplines in India.

The membership of a professional association is necessarily regulated through certain relevant prescribed qualifications. In the case of the ISS it is training in sociology and a commitment to the goals of the association. There are about 15,000 practising sociologists in India and of these, only 1700 or 9 per cent were members of the ISS in the year 2000. If membership in a professional association is taken as an important indicator of professionalism, evidently only a small minority of Indian sociologists are professionally committed.

As in other democratic voluntary associations, professional associations too recruit their leaders through periodic elections, but while any adult with a sound body and mind can aspire to the position of leadership in the former, in professional associations only scholars of high academic standing are expected to be elected to positions of leadership.

Generally speaking the elected presidents, the secretaries and managing committee members of ISS were of high professional standing. However, there have been some aberrations. In the fifty-year history of the ISS, the presidency was contested only thrice–in 1985, 1998 and 2000. In 1985 and in 2000, the contestants were scholars of high professional standing, but in 1998, as mentioned earlier, one of the two contestants was an unemployed young man. Although equipped with a PhD degree in sociology, he had not yet started his career. The fact that two of his teachers sponsored his candidature for presidency and ninety members voted for him was a clear demonstration of the lack of professionalism among Indian sociologists.

A lack of professionalism is visible in other contexts too. The two main activities of the ISS are publication of the *Sociological Bulletin* and organizing all-India conferences. One must note with satisfaction that the *Sociological Bulletin* has been published with notable regularity in the past half-century, a rare feat when compared with the publication record of other professional associations in India, particularly in the social sciences. But when one explores the 'inner life' of the *Bulletin*, the picture is somewhat bleak. The *Bulletin* is a biannual publication (later it became a tri-annual) and on an average publishes only a dozen research papers and two dozen book reviews a year. As for book reviews, it is difficult to persuade most sociologists to review books.

There are a few points to be noted here. First, the English language is a limiting factor for a majority of sociologists in India. The possibility of publishing in Indian languages should be seriously explored. Hindi, the widely used Indian language, is spoken by more then 350 million people. Even Assamese and Malayalam, the smaller of India's 'big' languages, are spoken by 20 million and 30 million people respectively.

Second, Indian sociologists, particularly senior and established ones, are not comfortable about submitting their research papers for peer-review in India. (Although they willingly submit to this process by foreign scholars.) Often they want an invitation to write with an assurance that whatever they submit will be published, which editors find unprofessional. Note that those who undertake peer-reviews are not always impartial as often, the 'background' of the author, rather than the quality of the research work, assumes primacy.

Third, the tradition of research is not strong in Indian higher education, even in university departments. I suspect that many of our academics rest content with their PhD dissertations and even those dissertations are not always published. If and when they do get published, it is often through quite unprofessional and low standard firms, mere printers rather than publishers. Understandably, research papers based on PhD work rarely find their place in high standard professional journals. And, the handful of competent and committed scholars still look towards the West for recognition and hence attempt to publish in western journals.

Finally, and most important, the greatest bottleneck professional journals, such as the *Sociological Bulletin* face is the inadequate supply of professionally competent sociologists willing to accept editorial responsibility. Editorship of professional journals is often voluntary work and the recognition accorded to editors is certainly not commensurate to their competence and hard work.

Let me now turn to the other major activity of ISS, organizing of all-India sociological conferences; it is the 'inner dynamics' of the conference which reveals the level of professionalism. To begin, it is extremely difficult to get invitations to hold conferences. There is no healthy professional competition among prospective hosts and the office-bearers of ISS have to often solicit invitations. Not only that, the hosts expect the ISS to assume the financial burden of the conference, at least partly. For the ISS, conferences have become fund-depleting projects, particularly in the recent past. To add to its woes, there have been instances, though rare, when ISS funds have been lavishly utilized by office-bearers.

It is important to recall that till 1986 the office-bearers and managing committee members attended ISS meetings, usually one or two in a year, by spending their own funds or through their employing agencies. However, thanks to the financial surplus created by the World Congress of Sociology held in 1986 in New Delhi, it became possible to reimburse the travel expenses to those who attend ISS meetings. Earlier the reimbursement was limited to ordinary second class rail fare. Gradually it was raised to second class AC and finally by mid-1990s the practice of giving air fare to office bearers and those seniors who were invited to conferences became common, resulting in the depletion of ISS funds. The point I want to make is that sacrifice and parsimony were replaced by lavishness, an indication of eroding professionalism.

Academic heavyweights seldom attend conferences unless they are specially invited to perform specific functions and paid for doing it. This may be in tune with what is happening in other professional associations in India but presents a contrast to the sociological associations in Western countries. For example, I have attended annual conferences of the American Sociological Association twice and seen nearly all top sociologists of the US interacting with fellow sociologists, unencumbered by their 'professional weight'. For academic seniors in India to attend professional conferences is not a demonstration of their commitment to the profession but a manifestation of their attributed professional prestige.

Then a junior colleague of mine wrote a report on the World Congress, which was subsequently published in the *Sociological Bulletin*. But he did not even mention me, the secretary general, the lynchpin of the Congress, by name or by designation. The rationale of this blackout was that the report was about the 'academic aspect' of the Congress, but I thought it was like writing the Ramayana without mentioning Rama! Finally, allegations about financial embezzlement were hurled at me. A 'friend' told me that it was rumoured that the secretary general had pocketed at least Rs 5 lakh. The point I want to make is that when one spends valuable time and works hard for the profession, instead of being rewarded and recognized one is held in contempt, vilified and punished. Such a social milieu cannot produce professionalism.

One more point before concluding. Two critical resources needed to nurture professionalism are time and money. Both should come as voluntary donations from the professionals. It is difficult to find competent professionals in India who are willing to convert part of their scholastic time into associational time.

The unwillingness to contribute financially is equally common. When the ISS started in 1951 the life membership fee was Rs 100, which worked out to be 25 per cent of the monthly salary of a lecturer. The life membership was subsequently raised to Rs 250 and then to Rs 500. Recently it was raised to Rs 1000, which works out to be about ten per cent of the present monthly salary of a lecturer. Yet, there is considerable resistance to the increase in membership fees at every occasion.

An attempt was made in 1999 to constitute an Endowment Fund. The target was to raise Rs 15 lakh which could be placed in fixed deposits, so that the interest could be used to run the ISS in a modest way. Of the 1700 members of ISS, it was hoped that at least 1100 would make donations, 100 members paying Rs 5000 each and 1000 members, Rs 1000 each. But only 130 members contributed: one member Rs 10,000 and eighteen members Rs 5000 each. But most members did not contribute. Admittedly, the fund-raising project turned out to be a dismal failure. Professional associations which insist on autonomy should learn to become financially self-reliant. The behaviour of the vast majority of ISS members does not augur well from the perspective of professionalism.

Viewed from several angles, be it the willingness and competence to publish and review books in *Sociological Bulletin*, the proclivity to attend all-India conferences, the attitude towards those who spend considerable time for the ISS, or the readiness to make financial contributions to the association, one cannot claim high professionalism among Indian sociologists. Yet it is true that the ISS is among the well-run professional associations, particularly in the social sciences. But there is a need for and the possibility of making tremendous improvements. This comment is not to castigate fellow professionals but to hold a mirror unto them. Maybe the image they see will help change the reality!

T.K. Oommen receiving Padma Bhushan Award from the President of India, 5 May 2008

Indian Sociological Society Diamond Jubilee Celebrations XXXVII, All India Sociological Conference, 11-13 December 2011

T.K. Oommen receiving the Lifetime Achievement Award of Indian Sociological Society from the Chief Minister of Orissa, 27 December 2010 at Cuttack

Presentation of Report of the Prime Minister's High Level Committee on the Status of Indian Muslims PM's House, New Delhi, 17 November 2006.

From left: T.K.A. Nair, Principal Secretary to PM; Manmohan Singh, Prime Minister; Rajindar Sachar, Chairperson, PM's HLC; A.R. Antulay, Minister of Minority Affairs; Saiyid Hamid, Member, PM's HLC; T.K. Oommen, Member, PM's HLC

Author receiving V.K.R.V. award from K.N. Raj

At the XI World Congress of Sociology, 1986

President of ISA, 1990

APPENDICES

APPENDIX 1

Farewell Speech at JNU, 22 October 2002

President K.R. Narayanan, Vice Chancellor Chadha, Dean Patnaik, Chairperson Haq, colleagues, friends, students and members of my family.

Broadly speaking, I have nothing to speak. In fact I am so overwhelmed by the affection showered on me through this Felicitation Seminar that I am not in a position to speak, at any rate, at length.

As I stand here and look around I see most of my colleagues, quite a few of my students and a handful of my friends with whom I have interacted in the past thirty years. Some of my students have been well-known scholars for several years and the youngest lot among them are being initiated into sociology through the MA course now. As I reminiscence I am reminded of the concluding sentences of a book entitled *In Defence of Democracy*, written by Bernard Crick, a British writer. Those sentences run something like this. Sir Winston Churchill left 10 Downing Street. Anthony Edens is its new occupant. But Thomas continues with his lifelong occupation, namely, breaking the stone. In the last thirty years of my life and work in JNU, many things have happened in the world, in India and indeed in JNU. Beginning with G. Parthasarathi the first vice chancellor and now with Professor G.K. Chadha the latest, I have been with all of them. I was privileged to work with K.R. Narayanan very closely, the most distinguished of all our VCs, who became the President of India. I am absolutely sure that historians will adjudge him as one of India's most distinguished Presidents. Incidentally, when Narayanan joined JNU as VC, I was the dean of student's welfare, endearingly referred to as the dean of student's warfare, those days. I resigned but the new VC asked me to continue in that position and hence the context of close interaction with him.

In spite of all the changes in JNU, for me there was no change. Symbolically speaking, I have been breaking the heads of my students and cracking some of the conventional ideas, so that they can think, re-think and even un-think: I regale in the durability of my life-long assignment and I have no regrets. Forty students who have completed their PhD thesis, one hundred students who have written their MPhil dissertations, thirty batches of MA students numbering over 2000 interacted with me academically in the last three decades. It is their patience which made my life worth living. On the other end of the continuum, my teacher, Professor Y.B. Damle of Pune University under whom I did my PhD, who will turn eighty soon, wanted to be here in spite of his recent bereavement (Damle passed away on the 9 October). He could not come also because the Pune airport remained closed for a few days. I am touched by the message he has sent; it is embarrassingly generous. He compares me with G.S. Ghurye in prodigious productivity and designates me as the Charavak of Indian Sociology. I am indeed overwhelmed. I have had the pleasure of working with Professor Victor D'souza, when he was the president of the Indian Sociological Society, in my capacity as the secretary general of the XI World Congress of Sociology in 1986. I am lucky to have a senior colleague in Professor Yogendra Singh during my tenure at JNU. All my junior colleagues, quite a few of whom have been my former students, were kind to me throughout my career. This event organized by a team of my colleagues and students under the leadership of Professor M.N. Panini is a standing testimony to their affection, indeed a finale. I am acutely aware of my proclivity to be abrasive in behaviour, causing momentary displeasure to my colleagues and students. But may I assure you all, that my abiding interest was and will continue to be, your long-term well-being and welfare.

The theme of the seminar is 'Rethinking Sociology: The Indian Context'. The concept note states that '...Oommen's contributions have strongly influenced other disciplines; his interests have extended far beyond India.' Referring to me as a pioneer in the study of said social movements in India, one of the areas chosen for the seminar is 'Social Movements: Protest and Change'. Given the fact that I have initiated the study of modern professions in India, another sub-theme of the seminars is 'Professions, Professionalization and Modernization'. Recognizing my shifting interest, the third theme selected is: 'Nation-State, Cultural Pluralism in Globalization'. Finally, given my proclivity to chisel concepts and formulate theoretical propositions based on empirical research, the theme 'Theory, Concepts and Social Facts: Situating Indian Society' was chosen. This is indeed a handsome academic tribute to me. I am fond of describing myself as an academic amphibian. Indeed the seminar has captured this spirit.

I believe that the two decades after the launching of the JNU enterprise in 1971 was the best period of Indian academia in independent India. JNU in general and the School of Social Science in particular, occupied a place of pride in that context. Speaking on the occasion of the first and so far the only Convocation of JNU (I am excluding special convocations) G.P. said, 'JNU is established to contain the crisis of growing irrelevance in Indian higher education'. I was privileged to be a participant in that experiment. Even if the outgoing generation has not achieved the goal, we are proud that we could launch the experiment. Those who remain with JNU now and those who will join the university in future should continue to pursue the initial mission, because obsolescence in knowledge is high, particularly these days. Interrogating the existing fund of knowledge and continuously replenishing it for societal well-being can be the only justification for a university to exist. I am sure that JNU will continue to respond to this challenge.

Ladies and gentlemen, I promised to be brief... please permit me to keep my promise. I am closing my response with an announcement. I propose to donate a small amount of Rs 1 lakh to the Centre for the Study of Social Systems to create an endowment. The interest accrued from that amount may be utilized for instituting an annual prize/medal for the best MA student of the year. Some of you may think that I am rich; still others may think that I am generous. I am neither. Therefore, I need to tell you the story behind this donation. I have been given three awards during my three-decade old career at JNU. These are the V.K.R.V. Rao Prize in Sociology in 1981, the G.S. Ghurye Award in Sociology and Social Anthropology in 1985 and the Swami Pranavananda Award in Sociology in 1997. The monetary value of these awards is measly, even as their symbolic significance is substantial. I have kept the award monies in fixed deposits and added a little to round them off, to 1 lakh. Through this gesture I want to sustain my connection with JNU, the School of Social Science and the Centre for the Study of Social Systems. I hope you will consider this as a token of my appreciation for the institution which nurtured me so long.

Finally, I am retiring tomorrow. But let me assure you that I will not retard. I promise to be active.

Thank you.

T.K. Oommen

APPENDIX 2

Vote of Thanks at the Inaugural Session of the XI World Congress of Sociology, New Delhi, 18th August 1986

Professor Fernando Henrique Cardoso, President, International Sociological Association; Professor Mysore Narasimhachar Srinivas, Chairman, Indian National Organizing Committee; Professor Victor Selvadore D'Souza, President, Indian Sociological Society; distinguished guests and dear delegates:

Let me begin by narrating to you an incident which occurred nearly a century ago. The year was 1893. The place: Sorbonne University in France. The event: Defence of doctoral thesis by a young student. His name: Emile Durkheim. The young examinee indicated to the learned committee of examiners that his dissertation was a treatise in sociology. On hearing this, one of the examiners observed, 'The man Comte who invented the term sociology was a mad man, and anyone who presents a thesis entitled "Sociology" is a madman too.' I am afraid most of us who are assembled here today have presented dissertations on sociology. But I firmly believe that sociology does not stand stigmatized any more as a discipline pursued by mad persons and this assembly is an attestation to that.

Almost all important events are rare; the World Congress of Sociology is a quadrennial event and hence its significance. The importance of an event is also enhanced by where it takes place. The fact that the XI World Congress of Sociology is the first in Asia invests it with an added importance. But the hallmark of a human event should be discerned in terms of who participates in it and under what conditions. We, seated in this hall now, hail from over sixty countries, our mother tongues are numerous, we were born of parents with distinct religious persuasions, we are different in our physical types, we represent many regions of the world, our lifestyles enormously vary, and, of course, our ideological preferences fall into a wide spectrum. And, more often than not these are divisive factors in the contemporary world. Notwithstanding this multiplicity, our discipline and profession provide us with the possibility of demonstrating our unity. Through the World Congress of Sociology, our collective identity is periodically affirmed; our capacity to recognize and respect mutual differences is reinforced. For providing us with this invaluable forum let us express our gratitude to those who conceived the idea of the World Congress of Sociology, the founding fathers of the International Sociological Association.

Any human enterprise needs to be continuously nurtured for its sustenance and in this the role of leadership is of vital importance. While the International Sociological Association has had a continuous supply of able leadership, we are particularly fortunate at the present juncture, in having a dynamic executive committee ably counselled and constructively guided by Professor Cardoso. This is evident in taking the decision to hold the XI Congress in an Asian country, despite persisting stereotypes and even prejudices. Through this decision the ISA has taken a firm step forward towards its authentic internationalization by providing a rare opportunity to the sociologists of this region. In extending sincere thanks to the ISA Executive Committee for this welcome decision, I am only endorsing the widespread sentiment prevalent among the sociological community in India.

While the whole is not the sum of its parts, the concreteness of the whole is to be located in the constituent elements. The International Sociological Association is an apex body consisting of its affiliates, the national sociological associations. ISA can successfully function only with the active co-operation of its constituting units. The Indian Sociological Society has amply demonstrated its national responsibility and professional responsiveness by hosting the XI Congress in India. I am tempted to thank three past presidents of the ISS–Professors M.S. Gore, S.C. Dube and Y.B. Damle–for laying the foundation and paving the way to hold this Congress in India.

Initiatives taken by professional associations such as the Indian Sociological Society is a necessary but not a sufficient condition for holding a mammoth event such as this in a country like India. Private foundations or commercial agencies do not readily finance such ventures. Fortunately, professional associations in India can draw upon governmental resources without necessarily sacrificing their academic freedom and autonomy. It is with pride, ladies and gentlemen, that the Indian National Organizing Committee would want to inform you that this Congress has been made possible due to the very generous financial assistance provided by the Government of India. It gives me great satisfaction to record with pleasure our sense of gratitude to the Government of India.

Governments in contemporary nation-states are too elaborate and even impersonal. When we think of an entity like this we have in mind specific departments and particular individuals. The Ministry of Human Resource Development, the Indian Council of Social Science Research, the Planning Commission and the Ministry of External Affairs extended financial assistance to us. The Reserve Bank of India as well as the State Rank of India readily responded to our requests. Apart from these, a large number of commercial organizations and a few educational institutions helped us either through modest donations or by advertising in the Congress publications. I thank all of them for their help.

I must specially mention the co-operation extended by UNESCO for this Congress. A large number of participants from Third World countries have been facilitated through its financial assistance. The administration of the funds has been rendered smooth due to the co-operation of the Indian National Commission of UNESCO. Let me thank all concerned for their help.

A large number of organizations and agencies have contributed to the making of this Congress in different ways. It is not possible to mention all of them here. But let me mention a few: the Jawaharlal Nehru University, Delhi University, the India International Centre, the Indian Statistical Institute, the American Express International Banking Corporation, the State Bank of India, the Indian Social Institute, the Vishwa Yuvak Kendra, Indian Tourist Development Corporation, Aurobindo Ashram, National Institute of Educational Administration, Indian Institute of Public Administration, our official carriers, Air India and Indian Airlines; our travel agents, Travel Corporation of India and Sita Travels, and the managements of our two major venues: Hotel Ashok and Taj Palace. Let me record our thanks to all these agencies.

We live in a world of growing specialization and continuous professionalization. Organizing conventions and congresses, I realize, is no more a layman's job but a professional task. We have been ably assisted by two professional organizers–QLT of Amsterdam and TCI, of New Delhi. If you find the organization of this Congress orderly, please remember that their expertise and effort contributed to it.

This is a congregation of academics and the Congress is geared to intellectual activity. But to sustain cerebration humans need physical, spiritual and aesthetic replenishment. You will have, ladies and gentlemen, a short but rich exposure to selected Indian cultural cuisine on Wednesday, in this very hall. I am happy to inform you that the event is made possible due to the support and co-operation extended to us by the Indian Council of Cultural Relations and the management of Hotel Ashok. Financial support is important but not enough in matters artistic. Several artists and organizations have graciously co-operated with us. It gives me great pleasure to thank all of them especially, Madhavi Mudgal, Anant Lal and Triveni Kala Sangam.

This morning we began with an invocation song organized by Professor Debu Chaudhuri, Dean, Faculty of Music and Fine Arts of Delhi University. We are thankful to the team for adding grace to this occasion.

The only occasion that we would all be together transacting academic business is this morning. Our communication is facilitated by the simultaneous interpretation provided by the faculty members drawn from the Centres of French and Spanish Studies of the School of Languages of the Jawaharlal Nehru University. We are certainly indebted to them.

In addition to the routine medical facilities available in all hotels, the Indian National Organizing Committee has commissioned a special team of health personnel to look after your medical problems. The team is working under the leadership of N. P. Singh of the National Association of Critical Care Medicine (India). We thank the team for its dedicated service to us.

As you are aware, we have organized a book exhibition coinciding with this Congress. We do believe that this exhibition would provide you with an adequate exposure to sociology in India. We are thankful to all the publishers and book-sellers who have co-operated with us to make this exhibition possible.

Some of you present here this morning are not delegates but guests. Please remember you are here because you are important for us. We know you are very busy persons and yet you made it a point to be with us, which is indicative of your affection for us. We appreciate your kind gesture and thank you for the same.

Numerous individuals contribute in a variety of ways for an event such as this. It is not possible to reel out a long list here but I will have an uneasy feeling if I do not publicly acknowledge the help extended by a few of them. G. Parthasarathi, Chairman, Indian

Council of Social Science Research has been the fountain of our strength. P.V. Narasimha Rao, the Minister for Human Resource Development and K. R. Narayanan, formerly Minister of State for Planning and currently Minister of State for External Affairs have been kind and considerate to us. Professors Manmohan Singh and Sukhumoy Chakravarty of the Planning Commission, both eminent economists, were sensitive to the needs of a sister discipline. Professor P.N. Srivastava, Vice Chancellor, Jawaharlal Nehru University, the institution from which the Indian National Organizing Committee has been operating for the past one year, helped us in a variety of ways. We are indebted to all these individuals and let me thank them profusely.

Aspirations are often elusive and their objectification invariably onerous. To translate the idea of holding the XI World Congress of Sociology into a concrete event was no small task. Financial resources and professional skills were essential pre-requisites. But another crucial input needed was voluntary work by professionally committed persons. The two committees constituted by the Indian Sociological Society conjointly provided this critical resource. The National Committee, chaired by Professor M.N. Srinivas, the senior-most living ex-President of the Indian Sociological Society and the Working Committee, guided by Professor Victor S. D'Souza, the energetic and young-looking present President of the Indian Sociological Society worked in perfect co-ordination to launch this Congress. It gives me great pleasure to thank the members of these committees, particularly the office-bearers and convenors of sub-committees, for their unstinting cooperation and devoted work.

It is not possible to thank every member of the Indian National Organizing Committee individually. But I must mention and we should remember the names of three of our late colleagues–Professor M.S.A. Rao was a member of our National Committee and the Vice Chairman of our Working Committee. Professor L.P. Vidyarthi and J.F. Bulsara were members of our National Committee and Working

Committee respectively. While thanking them posthumously for their help and co-operation, let us pray that their souls rest in peace.

You will soon realize, if not already experienced, dear delegates, that we have a band of dedicated staff and committed volunteers who hold themselves in readiness to make your participation in this Congress a pleasant experience. Permit me to thank them on your behalf.

Every institution has its core; every event has its special flavour. Dear fellow professionals, you constitute the core of and your enthusiastic response provides the special flavour to, this Congress. I know that you have arrived here wading through varieties of difficulties and in spite of numerous irritants. In your act lie the success of this Congress and the hope of the future ones. I am convinced that so intense is your professional commitment to and personal involvement with this Congress that you will readily ignore infrastructural inadequacies you may have to face during this week, in the course of the Congress. Let me thank you in advance for your co-operation.

I ought to have concluded by thanking myself. Bu t then, it is not polite, not even conventional for the person who proposes the vote of thanks to thank himself or herself. While I prefer to be a conformist in this respect, let me hazard an explanation for this somewhat comic situation. He who proposes the vote of thanks usually does most of the thankless jobs! Let me, therefore, conclude by thanking you all for providing me an opportunity to serve you.

T.K Oommen
Secretary General, XI World Congress of Sociology

APPENDIX 3

Welcome Speech at the XIII World Congress of Sociology, at Bielefeld, Germany on 18 July 1994

It gives me great pleasure to greet and welcome you all for the XIII World Congress of Sociology, the quadrennial event of the International Sociological Association. Perhaps, I should also wish you ample quantities of luck, as thirteen is believed to be an unlucky number in some cultures and civilizations.

As I started thinking about greeting you, I was reminded of the first sentence in the book *Human Types* by Raymond Firth, the well-known British social anthropologist, which reads as follows, 'In greeting each other Englishmen shake hands; Frenchmen in exalted moments embrace and kiss on both cheeks; a polite Austrian salutes a lady's hand with his lips; and Polynesians press noses.' But I learn that even in matters as simple as greetings, the boundaries have been shifting and often contested. A British journalist wrote in *Financial Times* in June 1993: 'We in Britain are suffering a crisis of uncertainty over how to greet each other: A hand shake? A kiss? Two kisses? Which cheek first? Should you make a smacking noise with your lips? Should your lips touch their cheek, or should you just lump jawbones?'

Indeed, we live in difficult and uncertain times: If I follow the saying, 'Do in Rome as the Romans do', I have to shake hands with you because Germans are said to be compulsive hand-shakers. But that poses the problem of physical accessibility since I am standing on the dais. If I am to follow the greeting styles of the multi-cultural United States of America, I have to choose between a hand-shake, a hug or the famous Manhattan air kiss. Once again the first and the second pose the problem of accessibility and I have no practice to perform the third. Therefore, I have opted for the Indian style of greeting, not because I am a cultural chauvinist but because it is eminently practical, avoids all complications, poses no boundary problems and yet is adequately intimate. We greet like this: Namaste.

Let me now turn to answering a question which numerous people all over the world, including, some Germans have asked me in the last four years. The question is: Why Bielefeld? Of course I told them the following: The decision regarding the Congress site is the privilege of the host, in the present case the German Sociological Association. The University of Bielefeld has a grand physical structure, carefully planned and well executed, to hold a mammoth world congress. Further, the university is celebrating its silver jubilee this year. The department of sociology of this university is not only one of the biggest in Europe but also one of the finest and is staffed by devoted and committed colleagues. But I have not told them two other reasons why Bielefeld is a place of crucial importance. Perhaps, many may not even easily recall them. Permit me to do it for you.

First, the historical importance of the Rhine–Westphalia region to which Bielefeld belongs. The treaty of Westphalia concluded in 1648 not only ended the Thirty Years War in Europe but laid the firm foundation of the concept of nation-state which incessantly informed, moulded and conditioned world history, diplomacy and international relations for three centuries. However, 'beyond the nation-state' is the refrain which rends the air of the world today.

Given this historical background and contemporary impulse I cannot think in terms of a more appropriate place than Bielefeld to discuss our theme: Contested Boundaries and Shifting Solidarities. Perhaps the fall of Berlin Wall adds spice to it.

Second, if you take a drive for fifteen to twenty minutes from here you will reach a neighbourhood called Oerlinghausen, the ancestral home of Max Weber. One cannot conceive of the discipline of sociology without Max Weber. Friends, we are in the land solemnized by the physical presence of Max Weber once. Indeed, it is a place of pilgrimage for sociologists. I am happy that you have not missed this opportunity.

Events of this kind cannot be organized without the unstinting co-operation and support, both material and moral, of governments. I am delighted to inform you that the German national government, the government of the Rhine–Westphalia region, the city government of Bielefeld and their agencies have helped the International Sociological Association, through our hosts, the German Sociological Association and the Society for International Sociology of Bielefeld. We are very fortunate that Rita Sussmuth, president of the German Parliament and a distinguished social scientist has taken keen interest in our Congress and consented to be the honorary president of the XIII World Congress of Sociology. Let me greet and welcome all those who have contributed to the organization of this Congress, particularly Professor Sussmuth.

In 1990 we received two firm invitations to hold this Congress. One was from Yugoslavia and the other from the Federal Republic of Germany. Neither of these entities exists today; the former has undergone a process of fission and the latter one of fusion. Such is the ephemerality of boundaries that they are constantly redrawn and contested and the solidarities anchored to them are consequently enlarged or contracted. The ISA programmes committee chaired by Professor Neil Smelser has aptly captured this mood which is amply reflected in the theme of this Congress.

The construction and sustenance of collective identities have been one of the greatest preoccupations of humankind particularly in the last few centuries. And nation-states and civilizations were and continue to be serious contenders in this endeavour. But globalization, pluralization and decentralization are all prescribed today with alacrity. I am sure advocates and opponents, of all shades of opinion, are present here and would articulate their ideas with vigour, wit and wisdom. I am certain that you are going to enjoy a great intellectual feast in this week.

Friends, we are witnessing and experiencing an exciting phase of human history which bestows on us a special responsibility. We are indeed shaped by contemporary events, we need to be responsive to them but above all we need to mould them. That is a challenge and a responsibility. True, we cannot ignore the rapidly emerging process of globalization but we should not allow ourselves to be swept away by the cultural hurricanes it produces. Pluralization is essential to provide the requisite anchorage to our specificities but we should not unwittingly fall into the trap of relativism. Decentring is indeed a process of empowering individuals and local communities but that should not degenerate into local chauvinism. How do we evolve an equipoise between these processes? That is the real challenge. I hope that our deliberations during this week will contribute towards a less uncertain future for humankind.

Thank you for your attention.

T.K. Oommen,
President, International Sociological Association

APPENDIX 4

Presidential Address to the ISA Council Meeting Held in Gavle, Sweden During 10 August, 1993

Friends, let me warmly welcome you all to this first ever ISA Council meeting held between the two World Congresses. To me it is a dream come true in that right from the beginning of my presidency I was determined to hold it in spite of several difficulties and mishaps. Permit me to thank Professor Goran Therborn of the University of Gottenberg, the present president of the Nordic Sociological Association, for inviting the Council to hold this meeting in Sweden.

The major item on our agenda is to discuss and approve, if found acceptable, the proposed amendments to our statutes. Several attempts were made to change the statutes in the past, but they were piecemeal efforts. The present task is to look at the statutes as a whole and to amend them to suit ISA's needs and aspirations in the light of our accumulated experience in the last forty-five years. The statutes of an association is like the constitution of a sovereign state, it is a blueprint of goals and guide for action. Goals and the strategies to achieve them change over time, and hence the need for periodic amendments of the statutes. In our case, the goals remain more or less the same but the milieu in which they are to be pursued has changed.

Keeping the above considerations in mind the ISA Executive Committee has appointed a Statutes Revision Committee with Professor Henry Teune of the Pennsylvania University in the USA as its chair. Let me thank Henry and his team for their hard work and hope that their efforts will not be wasted.

The rationale behind amending the ISA statutes, according to some, is provided by the disappearance of the Cold War, the demise of the bi-polar world and the emergence of a uni-polar world with market and democracy as its major pillars. But this is a matter of perception and one may have honest differences on this count. For example, some seem to think that the emerging world is a multi-polar one. While democracy is universally accepted, lurking suspicions still persist in regard to the functioning of an unbridled market. At any rate, to situate the rationale in amending the statutes of an academic association in the vortex of political transformation is simply to accept that professions are mere appendages to politics. While academics and academies often may not have a firm political voice, one should not accept instant marginality as our eternal predicament. Therefore, our effort ought to be to maintain and resist resolutely any encroachment on our autonomy as an academic body. To abandon one's autonomy is to abdicate one's responsibility.

As a logical corollary to the argument, it is proposed by some that concomitant to the transformation in the balance of power in the world, ISA should change from an association of associations, that is, a supra-national association, to an individual membership association. The argument seems to be that in a world increasingly governed by market forces, everything ought to be left to the logic of market. But let us remind ourselves that markets operate in various contexts and levels. In a community market the principles of economics and procedures of commerce are often moderated, even intimidated, by primordial ties. In the international context, the market operations are guided both by economics and politics. That is, the principles of markets can and do operate untainted only in the domestic situations of state-societies. Similarly, individual membership academic associations can and should thrive either within state-societies or regions placed more or less at the same level of economic development and/or political orientation. Thus the European Sociological Association, the Association of Latin American Sociologists, the South Asian Sociological Association etc., can function as individual membership associations. To extend the principle and practice to the global level is to invite disaster.

I want to list two reasons, one theoretical and another practical, why an individual membership ISA might mean its very demise. Individual membership associations are feasible only when two conditions are met: homogeneity and equity, if not equality. The world today is so heterogeneous, notwithstanding the ongoing process of globalization, and the prevailing economic disparities are so steep that an individual membership ISA would mean establishing, in fact reinforcing, the dominance of certain regions and countries through the overwhelming number of individual members they would have. This would further aggravate the present sense of alienation that our colleagues from less developed countries already have, leading, perhaps, to their total withdrawal from ISA.

To counter this argument, a graduated system of individual membership fees is suggested. In fact, this is already reflected in the existing and the proposed individual membership fee structure. And yet, a perusal of ISA's individual membership structure unfolds that individual members are mainly drawn from OECD countries. Why is this so? A graduated system of individual membership fee can be realistic only if it is charged in proportion to the wage-level of the members. If we do that, given the prevalent levels of wages in most countries and the present rate of bank charges, it would be a liability for the ISA. Let me invoke an example to clinch the argument.

Of the three categories of individual membership the comparable ones are 'regular' members and members from non-convertible currency countries (which incidentally is a vanishing category) as the supporting members get additional benefits, namely the two ISA journals. The fee of a regular member for a period of four years is US$80 (without journals) and the fee of a member from non-convertible currency countires is US$40. If we reckon the average salary of a US sociologist even as low as US$30,000 a year, US$80 is less than a day's salary. In contrast, a middle level sociologist in India (sorry, this is no national chauvinism but only familianity with data) gets only a salary of US$2000 a year, which means s/he is paying more than five days salary. That is, in wage terms our individual member from India is paying five times more as compared with our members from the US. If we follow the parity principle we ought to be collecting only US$6 from our Indian colleague, which is not worth collecting because of the banking charges! I hope I am communicating to you. Let me conclude this observation by repeating the theoretical point. Given the prevailing disparities in incomes, international associations based on individual membership are untenable.

The second point is a practical one. Consider the trials and tribulations involved in electing the president, vice presidents and executive committee members through postal ballots by our individual members distributed into some sixty countries now, but bound to increase in future. Anybody who is familiar with the international postal system would testify that (a) ballot papers will never reach their destinations in some cases (I am not talking about individuals in particular countries, but countries as such), (b) in some other cases they would reach after several weeks, even months after elections! Which means the effective electorate would be constituted by members drawn from countries with efficient postal systems. Somebody may come out with the brilliant suggestion to use telex, fax and/or e-mail without bothering about the postal systems. Apart from the untenability of maintaining the basic condition of secrecy in the voting system, there are two other obstacles in this context: the cost involved and the non-availability of these facilities in many countries. Thus, large individual membership international associations electing their office-bearers and managing committees through postal ballot is not in the realm of practicality at present.

There is however a genuine problem to be recognized and tackled in an international association such as the ISA. This problem has to do with the relative weight of representation and distribution of power in terms of the size of the constituent units and their financial contributions. In a way, the imbalance stems from the differing sizes of the building blocks of the world society, namely the state societies, usually referred to as nation-states. Nearly 26 per cent of the state-societies have a population of 1 million or less and 55 per cent have 5 million or less. On the other end of the continuum, there are only seven mega states with a population of one hundred million or more. Even within regional associations the size factor is often an irritant. Thus among the European Community countries, the giant Germany has nearly 80 million people. In contrast, Luxembourg has only a handful. One way of tackling the problem is resorting to proportional representation in terms of size of financial contribution. This would render international associations an arena of competition for power and domination among the affluent few. The other route is to provide for proportional representation based on the relevant category of population, in ISA's case the size of the sociological community and/or the size of membership in national associations. This would endanger the UN principle 'one-country one-vote'.

What is the way out of this impasse? As Alexis de Tocqueville taught us long back, authentic democracy and continuous participation are not sustained by casting votes in rare periodic elections but through involvement at different levels and contexts on a regular basis: the voluntary associations which are intermediary structures between the central state authority and the individuals-in-the-mass. While we do not have an exact parallel in the case of ISA, our Research Committees (RCs) are crucial intermediary structures which provide for sustained participation, enriching the democratic ethos of the ISA. The number of ISA RCs is approximately fifty and each one of them has its president, who constitutes the Research Council, a body comparable to that of the ISA Council. The preset proposal is to strengthen the Research Council so that it really becomes a parallel body to the ISA council. If anybody spends a few minutes of his or her valuable time, it would be easy to find that those who occupy offices, particularly presidents and secretaries of RCs, are precisely from those countries from which our individual members are mainly drawn. Thus although the principle of individual membership is not in full play, it is met more than halfway, through the proposed amendments which give substantial power to the Research Council consisting of RC representatives. This, I submit, would largely ameliorate the inadequate representation perceived to be in existence both for big and for affluent national associations affiliated to the ISA.

However, there is an important criticism voiced against RCs, which needs to be recalled and answered here. Which is that some of the RCs function as little republics, indeed as oligarchies. They do not, it is alleged, perhaps rightly, have statutes, or even when they have them, do not follow the prescribed norms in the statutes. True, these praxis-lags exist in some of the RCs and remedial steps are being taken. It is hoped that by the time we meet at Bielefeld in 1994, all the RCs would have the required statutes and would follow them both in letter and spirit. The threat of disenfranchisement from the ISA elections is already held out to them by the ISA vice president of the Research Council. In the proposed statutes, an organic linkage is worked out between ISA individual membership, RC membership, fee structure and its collection. These measures, I am reasonably certain, would go a long way to meet effectively the criticism currently levelled against some of the RCs.

Domination in an international association comes through various shapes, grades and different routes. I have already alluded to the domination by some sets of countries which already exists and which will be aggravated if the ISA becomes an individual membership association. But there are other sources of domination. One such is the language that we use for our deliberations. If we detach emotions from this discussion, we can easily see that a pluri-lingual association will attract more members to our fold. On the other hand, the prohibitive costs of simultaneous translations and the precarious financial condition of the ISA do not hinge together well. As of now the ISA has two official languages and the proposal to make Spanish the third official language has been pending with us for long, having endorsed in principle by the ISA EC. As sociologists, I hope, we are all committed to celebration of diversity and endorse the value of pluralism. It should be in this context that the case of Spanish as the third official language of ISA should be viewed and welcomed. But pluri-linguism should not lead us to the Tower of Babel, blocking communication itself. Therefore, even as we recognize pluri-linguism as a principle and a policy, we should be pragmatic enough to have a *link-language*. Therefore, in my view there can be several official languages for an international association but it should have *one* link language for effective and efficient communication.

I understand that there are certain misgivings about the proposed interim ISA council meetings as a regular feature. The objections essentially are based on two counts. First, paucity of resources, and second, the bureaucratic nature of the meeting and hence its repelling quality for the academically oriented. During my rather short association with the ISA, spanning only eight years, I have heard the frequently articulated 'complaint' that the ISA council is an inactive body which holds too much power. I suspect the argument has some force precisely because the ISA council is not an active body. Power which is not exercised is not power at all. The ISA council meets only once in four years and that too during the hustle and bustle of the World Congresses. The council members are involved in presenting their scholarly papers and/or meeting colleagues from different parts of the world. The only task they perform in their capacity as council members is to elect the ISA officers and leave to them the task of running the association on their behalf. While this delegation of responsibility is a fundamental principle of all representative democracies, the electorate should not be impervious to what the elected are doing. The ISA Council should receive a report of the activities of the ISA EC once in two years when the council meets.

The council members are presidents of national associations who hold office usually for two to three years. Most of the council members remain members on paper, in that they do not have the opportunity to attend even one meeting as the council meets only once in four years. The suggested periodicity would provide the opportunity to most members to attend at least one meeting of the council.

There are some new roles the council members can perform as representatives of the national associations. I have often come across the complaint that those who occupy positions in the ISA EC are persons with hardly any standing in their national associations, have contributed precious little towards its development etc. This criticism can be ignored only at the cost of the ISA losing its credibility. But the criticism itself has something to do with how the ISA Nomination Committee selects and presents candidates for various positions. It is quite conceivable that the national associations recommend one or two suitable persons to the Nomination Committee which goes to make a pool of candidates. Perhaps, there are other ways of doing this, but the purpose ought to be to have an ISA EC which consists of persons rooted in their respective national associations.

The point I want to make is this. The council should exercise the power and authority vested in it by the statues. To exercise power, the members of the council should interact. Interaction calls for resources–time and money. But the mobilization of the required resources and its effective utilization is a necessary prerequisite for the exercise of power. Therefore, I consider interim meetings of ISA Council as a historic step towards rendering the council visible and to re-appropriate its centrality in the context of the ISA.

The presidents of national associations who constitute the ISA council are not a bunch of bureaucrats, but scientists and leaders of the profession. Therefore, the council meetings could be serious academic enterprises too. I cannot think of a more appropriate forum which can take stock of the state of the art in the discipline in different countries. Therefore, I suggest that the interim meetings of the ISA council should be planned as exciting academic events in which the leaders of the discipline authoritatively articulate the state of sociology in their countries/regions. Incidentally, this has an additional pragmatic dimension, namely obtaining travel funds for the council meetings. As you know, those who provide funds are extremely reluctant to do so unless the meetings are scientific ones.

The tension between those who pursue theory and those who apply it to concrete problems is found in all disciplines but sociologists' predilection in this context is particularly acute, given its conventional orientation to shy away from meeting the demands of the current needs of society. However, today our discipline has to face squarely the challenge of its marketability, its usefulness. Confronted with the impending fear of the very 'end of sociology' the 1992 meeting of the Research Council held at Onati, discussed the market situation of sociological research. The participants, the presidents and/or the secretaries of the RCs, seem to have left with the feeling that we need to break the prevailing antinomy between the pure and the applied, the academic and professional orientations of sociology. If this is the general mood in the discipline, we need to take several steps to forge ahead. One of these steps is to bring into the fold of the ISA our colleagues who are practising professional sociology. The idea of bestowing 'A' category status to professional associations ought to be viewed in this context. Needless to say, this new initiative can only be pursued with the full concurrence and co-operation of the academic associations in particular countries affiliated to the ISA at present.

One of the problems an association like the ISA faces is the mode of its management. There are two basic issues here. First, the location of the secretariat and second, the background of the Executive Secretary (ES) we employ. Until recently, the practice was to shift the secretariat from place to place every four or six years if we found a combination of two things, namely a sociologist who is willing to accept the assignment of ES and a certain level of infrastructural facilities and limited financial help from one or another government or university. Latterly, we have professionalized the secretariat without perhaps fully realizing the financial implications involved. Thanks to a substantial financial subvention received from the Spanish government for the past six years, that is, 1986–92, we could manage without much difficulty. But the withdrawal of the financial support by the Spanish government has put the ISA in dire financial straits. The periodic shifting of the secretariat and the services of a sociologist Executive Secretary go together, in that we cannot find the services of a colleague for this purpose for a long period of time. On the other hand, professionalization of the secretariat and its location at one site on a long-term basis sit well together. Both have their advantages and disadvantages. The critical issue in the case of the first model is to find appropriate and willing sociologists to work for the ISA and in the case of the second model is to generate adequate funds. I suggest that we deliberate on this issue and provide guidelines to the ISA EC.

This brings me to my last point, namely the financial situation of the ISA. Those who argue for change of the ISA into an individual membership association see that as the solution to the financial problem also. The argument being, provide the individual members the possibility of participation through franchise and they will gladly pay the money required for running the association. I am afraid the postulated connection is weak; all that can be given to the individual member in the form of power is the right to vote once in four years in the election of the ISA officers. This in itself, is, I suspect, unlikely to be an adequate motivation to pay high membership fees. At any rate, colleagues from OECD countries cannot be compensated for their higher economic contribution in political terms as every member of the ISA would have only one vote each. On the other hand, national associations can and should be paying in proportion to their membership size and/or the size of their budget. This is the rationale behind the proposed collective membership dues.

However, even the proposed structure of fees–individual and collective–in itself is not capable of solving the financial difficulties of ISA, although it would contribute to a certain extent. It was my fond hope when I took over as president in 1990 to create a Corpus Fund which could be invested appropriately to ensure the generation of a critical minimum amount to meet the routine expenses of running the ISA secretariat. But as you all know I have failed miserably in this endeavour, for no fault of mine. None the less, I am convinced that unless this is done, the ISA will be permanently perching on the precarious financial edge and the president and his team will find hardly any time to attend to the more creative and constructive academic tasks. Let me close this address with the fervent hope that my successor will succeed where I have failed.

Thank you for your attention.

T.K. Oommen,
President, International Sociological Association

APPENDIX 5

Books, Monographs and Reports by T.K. Oommen

1. *Charisma, Stability and Change: An Analysis of Bhoodan Gramdan Movement in India,* Thompson Press, New Delhi, 1972.
2. *Field Studies in the Sociology of Education: The Report on the Punjab* (Co-author), National Council of Educational Research and Training, New Delhi, 1974.
3. *Doctors and Nurses: A Study in Occupational Role structures,* The Macmillan Company of India, New Delhi, 1978
4. *Social Structure and Politics: Studies in Independent India,* Hindustan Publishing Corporation, New Delhi, 1984 (a).
5. *Social Transformation in Rural India: Mobilization and State Intervention,* Vikas Publishing House, New Delhi, 1984 (b).
6. *From Mobilization to Institutionalization: The Dynamics of Agrarian Movement in 20th Century Kerala,* Popular Prakashan, Bombay, 1985.
7. *Indian Sociology: Reflections and Introspections* (Co-editor and Contributor), Popular Prakashan, Bombay, 1986.

8. *Sociology* (co-author). (A text book for Indian undergraduate students), Eastern Book Company, Lucknow, 1988.
9. *State and Society in India: Studies in Nation-Building*, Sage Publications, New Delhi, London, Beverly Hills, 1990 (a).
10. *Protest and Change: Studies in Social Movements*, Sage Publications, New Delhi, London, Beverly Hills, 1990 (b).
11. *Sociological Literature: South Asia (Chief Editor), New Delhi: SLSA Publications, 1992*
12. *Sociological Literature: South Asia (Chief Editor), New Delhi: Manak Publications Ltd., 1993.*
13. *Alien Concepts and South Asian Reality: Responses and Reformulations*, Sage Publications, New Delhi/London/ Thousand Oaks 1995.
14. Promotion of Social and Economic Democracy through Employment Intensive Policies (Co-author), International Labour Organization, Geneva, 1996.
15. *Citizenship, Nationality and Ethnicity: Reconciling Competing Identities,* Polity Press, Cambridge, 1997 (a).
16. *Citizenship and National Identity: Between Colonialism and Globalism* (editor and contributor), Sage publications, New Delhi/London/Thousand Oaks, 1997 (b).
17. *Political Action Outside Political Parties: Case Studies* (in Italian), (co-editor and contributor) Franco Angeli, Torino (Italy), 1997 (c).
18. *The Christian Clergy in India: Social Structure and Social Roles*, Vol. I, (Co-author), Sage Publications, New Delhi/London/ Thousand Oaks, 2000 (a).
19. *Nation and National Identity in South Asia* (Co-editor and Contributor), Orient Longman, New Delhi, 2000 (b).
20. *Pluralism, Equality and Identity: Comparative Studies*, Oxford University Press, New Delhi, 2002.

21. *Nation, Civil Society and Social Movements: Essays in Political Sociology* Sage Publications, New Delhi, London, Thousand Oaks, 2004 (a).

22. *Development Discourse: Issues and Concerns, Regency Publications, New Delhi 2004 (b).*

23. *Crisis and Contention in Indian Society, Sage Publications, New Delhi, London, Thousand Oaks, 2005.*

24. *Understanding Security: A New Perspective, Macmillan, New Delhi 2006/2008.*

25. *Social, Economic and Educational Status of Muslim Community of India, Prime Minister's High Level Committee, Cabinet Secretariat, Government of India, New Delhi, 2006 (co-author).*

26. *Knowledge and Society: Situating Sociology and Social Anthropology, Oxford University Press, New Delhi 2007/2013.*

27. *Reconciliation in Post-Godhra Gujarat: The Role of Civil Society*, Pearson Education, New Delhi 2008.

28. *Social Movements: Issues of Identity*, (ed) Oxford University Press, New Delhi 2009 (a).

29. *Social Movements: Concerns of Equity and Security*, (ed) Oxford University Press, New Delhi 2009 (b).

30. *Classes, Citizenship and Inequality: Emerging Perspective (ed), Pearson Longman, New Delhi, 2010.*

31. *Social Inclusion in Independent India*: Dimensions and Approaches, Hyderabad: Orient BlackSwan Private Ltd., 2014/2016

Name Index